D0354420

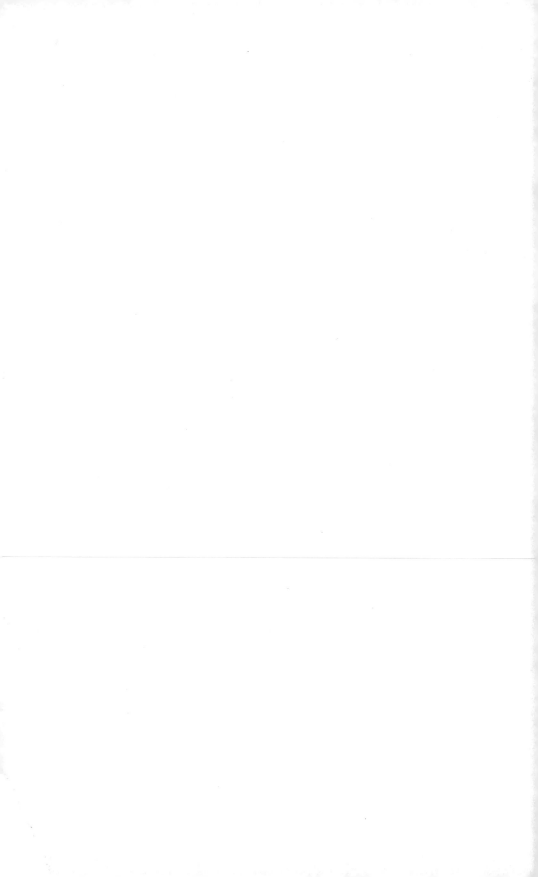

The Fear Within

The Fear Within

Spies, Commies, and American Democracy on Trial

Scott Martelle

RUTGERS UNIVERSITY PRESS
NEW BRUNSWICK, NEW JERSEY, AND LONDON

Library of Congress Cataloging-in-Publication Data

Martelle, Scott, 1958–
The fear within : spies, commies, and American democracy on trial / Scott Martelle.
p. cm.
Includes bibliographical references and index.
ISBN 978-0-8135-4938-5 (hardcover : alk. paper)
1. Communist Trial, New York, N.Y., 1949. I. Title.
KF221.C55M37 2011
345.73'0231—dc22

2010021010

A British Cataloging-in-Publication record for this book is available from the British Library.

Visit our Web site: http://rutgerspress.rutgers.edu

Manufactured in the United States of America

For
Margaret, Michael, and Andrew,
and in thanks to all those whose lives
are guided by the desire
to make this a
better world

CONTENTS

PREFACE

It's hard to write about the experiences of communists in the United States without running aground on partisan rhetoric and passions. For decades, no harsher invective could be hurled on American soil than to call someone a "communist," an insult that seems quaintly dated now despite its revival in the contemporary debate over health care reform. But half a century ago, political passions and divisions ran much deeper than the current left-right divide. Americans lost careers, families, freedom, and, in some cases, their lives in the showdown between communism and capitalism. It was not, to steal a famous line from Winston Churchill, America's finest hour.

The elements of anti-communist fervor in the middle of the twentieth century might have been specific to that era, but the template seems to be part of the national psyche. The United States has a habit of convulsing in fear during times of stress, and in the process undercutting the very freedoms of speech, political belief, and religious expression that Americans profess to hold dear. It cropped up anew after the terror attacks of September 11, 2001, in the adoption of the USA Patriot Act, a rushed law that gives government officials a disturbing amount of freedom to rummage secretly in the lives of ordinary Americans.[1]

That push against radicals and perceived enemies has a long history, beginning with the 1798 Alien and Sedition Acts from the nation's infancy. In more recent times, the U.S. government persecuted the foreign born over fears of anarchy and Bolshevism during and after World War I. The perceived threat gained credence with a skittish nation when a May Day 1919 plot to mail bombs to thirty-six public figures succumbed, fortunately, to incompetence. The plotters didn't put enough postage on the packages, and most of the bombs, without return addresses, were held up at the Main Post Office in New York City. But a couple of packages made it to their destinations and exploded, severely injuring the people opening them. A sharp-eyed postal worker, reading a newspaper account of those crimes, made the connection with sixteen under-stamped packages he had set aside in Manhattan, and the extent of the plot was uncovered.[2]

Another coordinated attack emerged a month later, with bombs exploding nearly simultaneously in eight cities around the country, including one outside the home of U.S. Attorney General A. Mitchell Palmer. That one killed the bomber, who apparently stumbled as he tried to place the delicate device. Palmer responded with an order for a national roundup of foreign-born radicals, and the infamous Palmer Raids, led by a young J. Edgar Hoover, were under way, leading to the jailing of several thousand people and the expulsion of several hundred, the vast majority targeted because of their beliefs and their birth certificates.

Two decades later, with another world war raging, President Franklin D. Roosevelt ordered the detention of 120,000 people of Japanese heritage—nearly two thirds of them American citizens—in remote concentration camps. Their crimes had nothing to do with radicalism. They simply shared an ancestry with an enemy. The incarcerated men, women, and children were finally released in January 1945, though many emerged to derailed careers, lost homes, and massive challenges in rebuilding lives and in regaining a sense of faith in their own citizenship.

Similarly, fear of communism mushroomed with the end of World War II and the onset of the cold war. The Soviet Union's co-option of Eastern Europe and Mao Zedong's rise to power in China merged with the atomic arms race and some spying scandals to create a general American hysteria about the "red menace." The fears were sparked by real events and real concerns—there *were* spies working for the Soviet Union—but the hysteria took on a life of its own.

This book focuses on one pivotal moment of that era, the indictment and prosecution of a dozen men who held top leadership positions in the Communist Party–USA (CPUSA). The charges were conspiracy to advocate the necessity of overthrowing the U.S. government, which was made illegal under the 1940 Smith Act, whose larger purpose was to force resident aliens to register with federal authorities (see chapter 1). Well known among scholars of the era (who still argue its details), the Smith Act cases—which began with the subject of this book, *Dennis v. U.S.*—have been largely forgotten by most Americans.

They shouldn't be. The use of the Smith Act against Communist Party leaders was an effective attempt by the U.S. government to criminalize political belief, flouting both the U.S. Constitution and a national tradition of political freedom and openness. The Smith Act was spawned by rising fear of fascism, and in some ways it is the sire of the USA Patriot Act. Both grew out of legitimate concerns, but the effects of the laws undercut the very thing they were supposed to protect: the American way of life. As the rallying cry went in the days after the 9/11 terror attacks, "The terrorists hate us for our freedoms." But the USA Patriot Act trumped many of those freedoms, giving the government the authority to, among other things, conduct warrantless searches, track personal reading habits, and muzzle those forced to cooperate with the secret investigations. Thus in the name of anti-terrorism authorities can enter private homes without the resident's knowledge, or demand details of the books that have been bought at stores or checked out from the library, all under a blanket of secrecy and, in many cases, without judicial review. In its name, and in search of radicalism, police have infiltrated peace groups and religious organizations. These are not the conditions of a free society. These are the acts of a police state, and they stand the nation's basic principles of freedom of belief and political association—not to mention the right to "life, liberty, and the pursuit of happiness"—on their head.

The Smith Act achieved similar ends, though it wasn't as draconian and didn't carry the "secret police" overtones. As interpreted by the U.S. Department of Justice and upheld, for a time, by the U.S. Supreme Court, the Smith Act equated active membership in the Communist Party with being a conspirator in seeking the violent overthrow of the U.S. government. In effect, the government outlawed a specific political belief, communism. And it was driven by the same fear that has forever shifted the balance of power in Washington to the president, who, as the American nuclear weapons program evolved, ended up as the sole person with the power to launch a nuclear attack while overseeing a vast national security apparatus that has toppled foreign regimes for no other reason than fears they were "soft on communism."[3]

The past repeats itself in other ways as well. As the Smith Act cases worked their way through the court system, conservatives, anti-communist lawyers, and even the U.S. attorney general urged local bar associations to investigate defense attorneys who worked with accused communists. That, naturally, made it hard for the accused to access legal advice, as lawyers turned down cases for fear of being tainted with the "communist" brush. At the time of this writing, Liz Cheney, daughter of the former vice president, stands in the middle of a similar storm over a campaign questioning the loyalty of lawyers who have taken cases representing detained terrorism suspects. Once again, fear eats away at some of the very things that Americans profess to hold dear: the legal traditions of the presumption of innocence and affording the accused access to legal representation.[4]

I'm not a communist myself, though, in truth, had I lived in the 1930s I likely would have been at some of the same meetings of political progressives that caused so much trouble for the attendees in the 1950s. But this work isn't about politics. Like my first book, *Blood Passion: The Ludlow Massacre and Class War in the American West* (Rutgers University Press, 2007), this is a journalistic look at a moment in history, and an effort to pull it from the ashbin, as it were, for a new examination. The goal is to bring a fresh set of eyes to the events that unfolded in 1949 in and around Judge Harold R. Medina's federal courtroom, just across the street from Manhattan's Foley Square, and how those events resonated across a fear-wracked nation. In the process, this story tells us about our national culture today—a parable, perhaps, about the costs of giving in to our fears.

A project such as this lives and dies on the knowledge, patience, and good graces of librarians and archivists, and I am indebted from coast to coast. Peter Filardo and his colleagues at New York University's Tamiment Library are the devoted keepers of what has to be the best collection of radical history in the nation, and I'm thankful for their time and guidance as I sorted through uncatalogued boxes of papers from the CPUSA archive, which the Tamiment received in 2006. And a special thanks to fellow writer Barbara J. Falk of the Centre for European, Russian, and Eurasian Studies at the University of Toronto's Munk Centre for International Studies, who generously shared her discovery at Tamiment of the CPUSA's newspaper clippings file—an invaluable road map to the nine months of courtroom testimony. In Independence, Missouri, the staff of the Harry S. Truman Library and Museum was similarly collegial and helpful, as were the folks in the Interlibrary Loan Department at the Leatherby Library at Chapman University in Orange, California, where I'm a journalism instructor. Director Gina Wilkinson and, principally, Maria Yanez made my life easier in ways immeasurable—including the hours I didn't have to spend on Southern California freeways trying to consult material at other libraries. The environment can thank Maria, particularly, for the reduced carbon footprint of this book. Angela Wilkerson, a project manager for WPA Film Library in Orland Park, Illinois, and Rukshana Singh, librarian for the Southern California Library for Social Studies and Research in Los Angeles, were instrumental and gracious in helping me run photos to ground.

I also was helped by the generosity of historians John Earl Haynes, Maurice Isserman (whose uncle, Abraham Isserman, providentially was one of the defense attorneys), and Stanley I. Kutler, who through e-mails collectively shared thoughts, confirmations, interpretations, and, in Isserman's case, personal files. Their generosity, though, does not equal culpability. Any misinterpretations or errors of fact are mine, and mine alone. Similarly, Daniel Green, defendant Gil Green's son, graciously helped nail down some elusive facts about his family history, as did Michele Artt, daughter of defendant Carl Winter, and to both I am grateful. Longtime friend and activist David Elsila provided guidance, and the occasional cold beer, as our paths crossed when my research coincided with his. Another longtime friend and fellow author, Robin Mather, gave a welcome reading of the first few chapters, and my parents, Walter and Dorothy Martelle, helped make sure I crossed my t's and dotted my i's. Thanks, too, to the sharp-eyed India Cooper, who copy-edited the manuscript, as she did for *Blood Passion*. Here's to more work together in the future. My wife, Margaret Mercier-Martelle, was as always my first reader, my cheerleader, and, when you get right down to it, my sustenance. Which is just more evidence that I am a lucky man to have found her, and to be sharing my life with her.

And finally, thanks to Jane Dystel—a writer couldn't ask for a better agent or champion—and her partner Miriam Goderich at Dystel & Goderich, and to Leslie Mitchner at Rutgers University Press, who all saw the same compelling lessons of *Dennis v. U.S.* that drew me into this obsessive venture.

CAST OF CHARACTERS

THE DEFENDANTS

Benjamin J. Davis Jr.
Eugene Dennis (Frances X. Waldron Jr.)
William Z. Foster
John Gates (Israel Regenstreif)
Gilbert Green (Gilbert Greenberg)
Gus Hall (Arno Gust Halberg)
Irving Potash
Jacob Stachel
Robert G. Thompson
John B. Williamson
Henry Winston
Carl Winter

THE DEFENSE TEAM

George W. Crockett Jr. (for Stachel and Winter)
Richard Gladstein (for Hall and Thompson)
Abraham J. Isserman (for Green and Williamson)
Louis F. McCabe (for Foster, Dennis, and Winston)
Harry Sacher (for Potash, Davis, and Gates)
Aided by David M. Freedman, Mary M. Kaufman (for Hall and Thompson),
    and Abraham Unger

THE JUDGE

Harold R. Medina

THE PROSECUTION

John F. X. McGohey, *U.S. Attorney*
Frank H. Gordon, *special assistant to the U.S. Attorney*
Irving S. Shapiro, *special assistant to the U.S. Attorney*
Edward C. Wallace, *special assistant to the Attorney General*
Lawrence K. Bailey, *attorney, Department of Justice*

THE SPIES

Elizabeth Bentley
Jacob Golos
Igor Gouzenko

MAJOR PROSECUTION WITNESSES

Louis F. Budenz
Angela Calomiris
Herbert A. Philbrick

TIMELINE

1935 Elizabeth Bentley joins Communist Party

1938 Bentley begins spying

1940 Smith Act adopted
Bentley meets Jacob Golos

1941 United States enters World War II

1943 Golos dies; Bentley takes over spy rings

1944 Communist Political Association (CPA) formed

1945 Bentley goes to FBI
Igor Gouzenko defects
World War II ends
CPA dissolved; Communist Party–USA (CPUSA) formed, beginning alleged conspiracy, with William Z. Foster replacing Earl Browder as chairman

1946 Frederick Vinson named to Supreme Court
Earl Browder expelled from CPUSA

1947 Bentley testifies before grand jury

1948 Presidential election year
CPUSA leaders indicted in July

1949 The Foley Square trial—eleven men convicted

1950 Alger Hiss convicted of perjury; Korean War begins

1951 Supreme Court upholds *Dennis* convictions; seven defendants go to prison, but Hall, Thompson, Green, and Winston flee; Hall is captured in Mexico four months later

1953 Vinson dies; Earl Warren named to Supreme Court
Korean War armistice
Stalin dies

1955 Davis, Dennis, Gates, Potash, Stachel, and Williamson released from prison

1956 Khrushchev reveals Stalin purges
Green and Winston surrender

1957 *Yates* decision guts Smith Act
Hall leaves prison

1958 Thompson leaves prison

1959 Hall elected CPUSA general secretary

The Fear Within

"Public opinion being what it now is, few will protest the conviction of these Communist petitioners. There is hope, however, that in calmer times, when present pressures, passions, and fears subside, this or some later Court will restore the First Amendment liberties to the high preferred place where they belong in a free society."

Justice Hugo Black, June 4, 1951,
DISSENTING FROM THE UNITED STATES SUPREME COURT DECISION
UPHOLDING *DENNIS V. UNITED STATES*

ONE

Fear, and Howard Smith's Law

DECEMBER 1940

It had not been a white Christmas in New York City, nor anywhere else along the eastern seaboard for that matter. A high-pressure system moving slowly from the southwest carried unseasonably warm air with it, and by midafternoon on Christmas Day the temperature in Manhattan was fifty-eight degrees—a balmy gift of summer in the heart of winter. Walkers coursed through Central Park under an enticing blue sky, and children played with new toys on stoops and sidewalks. Farther north in the Berkshires, and into the Green and the White mountains, bare slopes ruined New England ski holidays, while out on Long Island people basked on Long Beach's wooden boardwalk.

But the gift didn't last long. The day after Christmas, a cold-dragging low-pressure system eased in from the Canadian Plains and the Great Lakes and pushed the warmth out over the North Atlantic. Thickening gray clouds cooled the air over Manhattan, and by 3:00 P.M. a thick drizzle began falling, enveloping the city's skyscrapers in a murky shroud. It wasn't quite a wintry blast, but it was cold and raw and miserable

1

all the same, the kind of weather that left throats scratchy and noses runny, and turned people's thoughts to avoiding colds and the flu.[1]

As the weather worsened, several hundred people stood in a line snaking out the front door of Midtown Manhattan's General Post Office Building. It was—and is—a massive structure, filling two city blocks between Thirty-first and Thirty-third streets and stretching from Eighth Avenue to Ninth Avenue. To the east people hurried in and out of busy Penn Station, and a couple of blocks away holiday decorations splashed color on the austere grayness of Macy's department store. While the city bustled, the line outside the post office shuffled along slowly, at its longest stretching from the Thirty-third Street door west toward the Hudson River, then left at the corner and south along Ninth Avenue.[2] Over the course of the day more than ten thousand people would huddle there against the damp and the chill while they waited to talk to clerks inside the post office, answer fifteen specific questions drafted by the U.S. government, and have their fingerprints taken. None of the people in line were American citizens, which was, in fact, the sole reason they were there.

The federal government's registration of immigrants had begun in late August, and by the time it ended December 26, more than 3.6 million foreign-born people age fourteen and older had signed their names to cards swearing that they had never been convicted of a crime, nor in the last five years had they worked on behalf of a foreign government. The Immigration Service kept the completed forms. The fingerprint cards were forwarded to J. Edgar Hoover's Federal Bureau of Investigation in Washington, D.C. It was a massive undertaking that involved nearly every post office in the country. The FBI alone added some five hundred workers to handle the increased load, and the government's bill for the project ran to $3.1 million.[3] A few civil libertarians decried the program, but its defenders deemed the money well spent, a minor investment against growing international totalitarianism.

Fear drove the registrations. With war raging in Europe—Hitler's Luftwaffe was in the midst of near-daily bombing raids over England—Americans' ever-percolating suspicions of foreigners were running high. Nazi Germany and the Soviet Union had signed the Molotov-Ribbentrop Pact on August 23, 1939, vowing not to attack each other (and secretly dividing Europe into eastern and western spheres of dominance). Nine days later Hitler sent his army into Poland unencumbered, and Great Britain declared war to try to stop the Nazi march. Yet the fall of France in May 1940 was more troublesome for some Americans, who blamed it in part on a "fifth column of Nazi and communist sympathizers within France" aiding the attacking Nazis.[4] If the United States was dragged into the war, the thinking went, it would be good to know what fifth columnists might be on American soil waiting for just the right moment to strike out in the name of fascism, Nazism, or communism. The fear was not abstract—Hitler's Abwehr and Stalin's NKVD were actively trying to plant spies in the United States, and pro-Nazi and pro-Soviet agitation by American supporters was common.[5]

However real the threat, foreigners and "outside agitators" have long been bogeymen for those fearing political radicalism, and for U.S. Rep. Howard W. Smith, the Virginia-bred son of a successful farmer and businessman, no threat in 1940 was more trenchant than new-generation aliens arriving in America with dreams of organizing the working class into trade unions or, God forbid, the Communist Party.[6] And it was Smith, a slightly built but powerful member of the House Democratic majority, who was most responsible for that long, snaking line outside Manhattan's General Post Office.

Smith was born in 1883 at Cedar Hill in Broad Run, a rural crossroads deep in Virginia's Fauquier County some forty miles west of the U.S. Capitol Building. On his mother's side, Smith came from a long line of Virginians. Although his ancestral home was undamaged by the bloody Civil War, Yankee raiders had regularly swept through the farm and made off with food, supplies, and whatever valuables they felt like taking—indignities that entered into the family fabric. His mother, born in 1849, came of age in the midst of the war, and Smith was raised in a culture that believed the Lincoln-inspired Republicans were engaged in a conspiracy to rob the South of its riches and its legacy.

Smith's father, Will, was a farmer and a government man who divided his time between running a federal experimental farm in Arlington and managing his own fields and business interests at Cedar Hill. Monday mornings would find Will, a "stern-faced redhead with large ears, thick eyebrows and a long forehead," on the train to Alexandria, not to return until Saturday afternoon, which made him a stranger to his own children.[7] To bring in more money—and maybe just to feel engaged with the world—Smith's mother, Lucinda, known to most as "Lutie" or "Tee," rented out space in the family's thirteen-room farmhouse to Washington politicians and businessmen seeking a sanctuary outside the capital. It was a rural salon, the days filled with political talk and debate and the evenings devoted to sing-alongs around Lutie's piano. The Smith children absorbed it all, including the pomp and ceremony of the presidential inaugurations to which Lutie dragged them, beginning with Grover Cleveland's second term in March 1893, a month after Howard's tenth birthday.

The close contact with politics set the hook. Three of Will and Lutie Smith's four children entered politics, but young Howard went the furthest. He attended the nearby Bethel Military Academy, then studied law at the University of Virginia under Raleigh C. Minor, an ardent believer in states' rights over federal rights.[8] After graduating, Smith opened practice in Alexandria and immersed himself in local politics, eventually working his way into a judge's seat, and then Congress in 1930. Despite his time on the bench, Smith had no trouble ignoring some of the U.S. Constitution's protected freedoms for what he saw as the sake of the greater national good. That invariably meant an economy in which business owners—his peers—could act under their own free will, while their workers had no right to organize. Xenophobic and virulently anti-communist, Smith believed in "fighting the devil with fire." A key leader among the southern Dixiecrats, he repeatedly used his powerful chairmanship of the House Rules Committee to thwart civil rights reforms.[9] Smith finally lost his House seat to a primary challenger in 1966, two years after the Civil Rights Act was approved over his opposition.

But in the late 1930s, communism weighed heaviest on Smith's mind, as well as the minds of many others who wanted the government to track foreigners on American soil. It was not a new idea. The government had grappled with various forms of alien registration for decades. Some states had adopted their own laws—later thrown out by federal courts—denying certain benefits to foreigners.

But the tenor of the times added even more pressure. Fascists had won the Spanish Civil War, and Hitler and Mussolini were firmly in control of Germany and Italy. In the United States, the German American Bund, which styled itself as Nazism in America, organized a rally at Madison Square Garden on George Washington's birthday in February 1939. Some twenty thousand people cheered anti-Semitic and anti-government speeches while on the streets outside "storm troopers" and protesters—including Jewish veterans of World War I—clashed violently. The group earned a special mention in a spring report by U.S Rep. Martin Dies's House Un-American Activities Committee (HUAC); in response, the Roosevelt administration tightened rules governing registration of foreign agents and began sharing intelligence across departments.[10] In August, Congress passed the original Hatch Act, the first step in what would eventually lead to the "Loyalty Oaths," as "an explicit recognition by the Congress of the necessity for barring from government employment those whose interests were directed to the destruction of the traditional American way of life."[11]

Those governmental moves fed the public fear. At President Franklin D. Roosevelt's urging, that September the government embarked on a national campaign to ferret out saboteurs, leading to widespread dismissals of workers in sensitive industries such as shipyards.[12] The paranoia seeped down to the neighborhood level, producing more than three thousand tips a day to federal authorities by citizens who sensed spies in their midst.[13]

In the rush to legislate, Congress considered more than one hundred anti-alien bills, at least thirty-eight of which would have required noncitizens to register with the federal government.[14] But all the bills had to go through Smith's Rules Committee, so it was Smith's views that dominated the measure that ultimately moved to the full House. Still, the final version was softer than what Smith had envisioned. In March he proposed deporting any noncitizen who advocated a change in the U.S. government or "engages in domestic agitation," which could have been construed as taking part in a raucous Democratic or Republican party gathering or something as simple as leafleting. The proposed law also would have made it illegal to urge members of the military to disobey orders, as some communists had done trying to persuade rank-and-file members of the U.S. armed forces to refuse to fight the Soviet Union if war broke out.

On July 29, 1939, the House finally passed the Alien Registration Act, which became known as the Smith Act. It required noncitizens to register with the U.S. government and barred admission to people who had been active in a Communist party in their native countries. In a little-noted subsection, the law also made it illegal "to knowingly or willfully advocate, abet, advise, or teach the duty, necessity, desirability, or propriety of overthrowing any government in the United States by force or violence." Thus under the Smith Act it would be a crime to print or distribute books or other materials, or help organize any group, that advocated or even taught the "desirability" of overthrowing the U.S. government—a clear conflict with the First Amendment guarantees of free speech and assembly. It was this largely overlooked element of the Smith Act that would rise to such prominence by the end of the decade, and that in some ways presaged the USA Patriot Act more than sixty years later, which was approved in haste and without being read by most members of Congress—many of whom were later surprised to learn the broad investigative powers they had granted to the government.

There was some opposition to the Alien Registration Act as it moved through Congress. One of Smith's colleagues in the House, Rep. John A. Martin of Colorado, argued that expelling immigrants based on political activities was "an invention of intolerance contrary to every principle of democracy and abhorrent to the spirit of Christianity."[15] Rep. Lee E. Geyer of California was even harsher, describing the bill as a "Hitler measure" aimed at West Coast labor leaders like Australian-born Harry Bridges, loathed by shipping magnates but a hero to dockworkers for his militancy leading the International Longshore and Warehouse Union. But those critics' voices were in the minority.

The following spring, the Senate approved the measure, and on June 29, 1940, President Roosevelt signed the Smith Act into law. He sought to soften the blow by announcing that to register as an alien was not a "stigma," couching his defense in paternal terms.[16] "The Alien Registration Act of 1940, which I have just signed, should be interpreted and administered as a program designed not only for the protection of the country but also for the protection of the loyal aliens who are its guests," Roosevelt said. Those who were "loyal to this country and its institutions" had nothing to fear, and with a federal law in place, more onerous local or state regulation of aliens would be avoided, he said. "With those aliens who are disloyal and are bent on harm to the country, the government, through its law enforcement agencies, can and will deal vigorously."

Roosevelt didn't mention the law's potential applications to native-born Americans or its effective gutting of the First Amendment. In fact, little debate around the law addressed those possible ramifications. The Smith Act, much like the USA Patriot Act, would resonate in ways unimagined at the time it was enacted. The law would be used to ruin lives, destroy friendships, and kill careers; it would become a tool of court-sanctioned political repression; it would feed the "hysteria," as President Harry S. Truman called it, that Sen. Joseph McCarthy would harness with such devastating results. In the end, it would give license to the U.S. government to send American citizens to prison for what they believed, rather than for what they had done.

And it all began with a spy story.

TWO

From Spies
to Speeches

August 23, 1945
New Haven, Connecticut

Elizabeth Bentley, moon-faced beneath dark hair, walked past the first-floor Federal Bureau of Investigation office and continued on a few doors down the street, stopped abruptly, then turned quickly and retraced her steps. She was nervous but controlled, watching with sharp eyes for loiterers, unusual movements, or men awkwardly staring into a shop window at some improbable purchase. Bentley did this a few times, on one pass walking with an imaginary purpose and address, and on another pacing as though impatient at a friend's tardiness. It was hot, the dog days, but Bentley couldn't be too careful, or too paranoid. She had invested a lot of time in her strategy. Following her training, she had gamed out different scenarios in her mind, weighed the options and possibilities from every angle, identified all the risks, and then had taken steps to minimize them.

Bentley's first strategic decision: The FBI office at Manhattan's Foley Square was all risk. Too many people in the city knew her by sight. The KGB[1] kept an eye on visitors to the building, and they already had their doubts about her. And doubts in Bentley's business—overseeing Soviet spy networks—came with deadly consequences. Julia Stuart Poyntz was the object lesson. A longtime active communist and occasional spy recruiter, Poyntz returned to the United States in 1937 from a trip to the Soviet Union disillusioned with Stalin and the deadly purges under way. Some friends said later that she had planned to write a book denouncing the Stalinist version of communism she had witnessed. But then Poyntz disappeared.[2] Killed was the word among Bentley's contacts in the underground.[3] Bentley didn't know it, but her own handler, Anatoly Gorsky, feared that Bentley, too, was a potential liability, and was lobbying Moscow to have her killed. Gorsky, the first secretary at the Soviet Embassy but in reality a spymaster who had earlier run the Cambridge Five in England, had already picked out the assassin, a poison expert idling in Paris.

So there was ample risk—known and unknown—for Bentley to be seen venturing into an FBI office. In New Haven, though, Bentley gambled that Soviet spotters wouldn't see her. Even if they did, she had a plausible reason to be in the area. As a little girl she had lived nearby, and over the years she'd returned occasionally to visit relatives and old friends. If someone recognized her here now, an hour north of Manhattan by train, it was unlikely to be anyone who could cause her trouble—as long as no one saw her enter the FBI office itself. And Bentley needed to talk with the FBI. She needed to know what they knew. She needed to begin the delicate process of extricating herself from her own life.[4]

Bentley was an unlikely spy handler. Born in 1908 in nearby New Milford, Connecticut, she was the only child of a retail salesman and store manager, Charles Bentley, and his schoolteacher wife, Mary. As she was growing up, her father chased opportunity after opportunity, moving the family from Connecticut to Ithaca, New York, for a couple of years, then Poughkeepsie for three years before uprooting for McKeesport, Pennsylvania, a drab and poverty-laden steel town of some fifty-five thousand people fifteen miles southeast of Pittsburgh along the Monongahela River.[5] Bentley's mother, a Vassar College graduate, had found ways to keep busy in each city to which her husband moved her, taking small jobs and volunteering with civic groups. In McKeesport, she joined a small private aid agency dealing with the poverty left in the ebb tides of the steel industry. In 1920, the region was mired in a recession as heavy industries recalibrated postwar production levels. Thousands of people in and around McKeesport were out of work, without welfare support or unemployment benefits.

The young Bentley saw the poverty firsthand and heard the stories of desperation her mother relayed at the end of her volunteer shifts. One story came as a revelation to both mother and daughter—a formative moment for a girl not yet in her teens. Mary Bentley returned home one day visibly upset after investigating ways to help a client who had been severely injured when a stairway collapsed in a decrepit tenement house. She discovered that the owner of the house was one of the leading lights of McKeesport, a man who made a show of his support for philanthropic organizations and who, in fact, sat on the board of the very agency for which she worked. In a bit of dark irony, the landlord was donating some of the profits he was squeezing from the legions of his impoverished tenants to an organization trying to help them cope with the miserable living conditions he imposed. The mother made the connection for the daughter: The agonies of poverty were tied to the greed of the wealthy, and the capitalism that rewarded them.

Two years later, Charles Bentley moved his family yet again, this time finding stability working as a general superintendent at the McCurdy & Company department store in downtown Rochester, New York, a city whose health and fortunes were tied to the fast-growing Eastman Kodak Company. Elizabeth Bentley finished her last two years of high school there, then went on to study at her mother's alma mater, Vassar College. At the time, the college was swimming with progressive social and political ideas. Most were circulated by faculty members who came back from tightly controlled tours of the Soviet Union energized by dreams of a society devoted to the good of its people. Slowly the retailer's daughter found her worldview shifting, and she became drawn to the idea that there must be a better way to organize society than through the harshness of profit and loss. She was no theoretician, but she had an emotional response she had trouble repressing, and a growing belief that there was something fundamentally wrong with her country.

Bentley graduated in spring 1930 and embarked on a Vassar-organized tour of Europe—her first trip abroad. Along the way she tumbled into her first taste of romance, a shipboard tryst with a British engineer. That fall Bentley joined the teaching staff at a small, exclusive boarding school in Virginia. It was conservative and insular, and she chafed after the freedoms (and romance) she had felt in Europe. Bentley returned to the Continent the next summer, and after a second school year teaching in Virginia she began working on a master's degree in Italian at Middlebury College in Vermont, then enrolled in the fall at Columbia University. There she won an exchange-program slot at the University of Perugia, in the heart of Italy. When she arrived in late summer 1933, Mussolini was fully in charge. As an American student she was protected from the worst abuses, but Bentley became appalled by the tight control of fascist oppression, the lack of freedoms, the summary arrests, and the simmering violence. Though she was not beyond joining a student fascism club for the associated store discounts and other privileges, Bentley stayed out of politics and focused mostly on her growing sexual awakening, rolling through several more romances, including the rumored seduction of one of her professors. She drank heavily, earning a reputation among her fellow expatriates as "a naughty young woman with a sometimes foul mouth."

Bentley finished her master's degree and returned to the United States, where, in the depths of the Great Depression, teaching jobs were scarce. So she returned to school again, enrolling in business classes at Columbia in hopes of gaining the skills to find secretarial work. By then Bentley's parents were dead, and she had no immediate family. She was a bundle of emotional need. Eager to please and to be accepted, she was susceptible to manipulation and deception.[6] She moved into a rooming house near Columbia on Manhattan's Upper West Side, where she struck up a friendship with a neighbor, Lee Fuhr, whose upbringing paralleled the lives of the people Bentley's mother had once tried to help in McKeesport. Fuhr and Bentley shared stories, including Bentley's time living under fascism in Italy and her fears that the Depression-ravaged United States might be prone to similar extremism. Fuhr enticed Bentley to attend meetings of a group she belonged to, the American League Against War and Fascism, which Bentley would eventually learn was a Communist International front. But by then, Bentley was a willing comrade.

Bentley joined the communists in the spring of 1935 and by 1938 had been recruited into the underground spying apparatus, first keeping track of Italian fascists (she landed a job in the Italian Library of Information), then working as a courier for Jacob "Yasha" Golos, a key Soviet spy handler in the United States. By the time World War II was in full rage, Bentley was a linchpin—and Golos's secret lover. She worked overtly for Golos at the U.S. Service and Shipping Corporation (USS&S), a Soviet front purportedly handling trade from the United States to the Soviet Union, and quickly became a top executive. When Golos died suddenly of a heart attack in 1943—in Bentley's apartment after they had celebrated Thanksgiving together—she took over his spy groups. Prior to his death, Golos had been wrestling with his Moscow supervisors over who would control the American spy networks he had established. Moscow wanted more professional—and Soviet-trained—control. With Golos's death, Bentley continued to resist demands that she turn over their contacts. Earl Browder, then the head of the American Communist Party, was one of Bentley's go-betweens with the Soviets, part of a role Browder played as a referral service for Soviet spy handlers.

Bentley's roster of spies was impressive. It included what became known as the "Silvermaster Group," a loose collection of Soviet sympathizers and anti-Nazis brought together by Nathan Gregory Silvermaster, a midlevel career government bureaucrat. Many members of the group thought that by ferrying classified information to the Soviets—at the time U.S. allies—on German and American troop strength they would help the war effort. Bentley also handled the "Perlo Group," a similar circle of spies within the Defense Department and other war-related divisions, led by Victor Perlo, who similarly believed that helping Soviet Russia was helping an ally and hurting an enemy, fascism. Other group members were less altruistic, selling information for the money. Still others were staunch, underground communists working for a cause.

As the main conduit to the Soviets, Bentley enjoyed a high measure of confidence from her American contacts. They gave her life some context and structure. She enjoyed her position at USS&S, too, as well as the income. But the Soviets were trying to marginalize her, pushing her out of the company as they tried to wrest control of her spy network. Bentley was loath to let go, but eventually the Soviets wore her down, and in June 1944—just after the D-Day invasion at Normandy—she caved in and turned over her contacts. The Soviets had good reason to fear her reliability. Prone to depression and bouts of heavy drinking, Bentley was becoming an increasingly loose cannon. She showed up drunk for a meeting with Gorsky, her Soviet handler, at Alexander's bar in Manhattan in September 1944 and, after a few more dry martinis, exploded in a tirade about the Soviets, calling them "gangsters" and saying she wanted to break off with them. The American Communist Party was "a gang of foreigners," she said, and she hinted that she could cause them problems.[7] Gorsky renewed his recommendation that she be killed, but KGB higher-ups in Moscow rejected the solution. She was still of use, they thought—in fact, she had recently supplied them the name of another potential spy within the U.S. intelligence bureaucracy. But they agreed she needed to be isolated.

In the spring of 1945, after Bentley had been maneuvered into relinquishing control of her spies, she met a man named Peter Heller in the bar of the Hotel St. George in Brooklyn, where she was living in a suite of rooms. After a little talk, a little flirtation, and more than a few drinks, Bentley invited him upstairs to her suite, Room 759. Unlike other men she had picked up, Heller came back to the bar another night, and then another. And back to her rooms. He was a garrulous man, with thinning red hair and glasses, who hinted broadly about his work and his connections. His stories were light on specifics, as though he were hiding something. Bentley guessed he might be a lawyer or some sort of investigator. It didn't really matter to her—until he disappeared for a few weeks, just dropped out of her life, cold, before popping back up with a story about doing secret work for the government.

Bentley hid her fears and chose her moment. One night as he slept after another evening of booze and sex, Bentley quietly went through his pockets. She found an identification card with badge-style insignia in a wallet, but the name of the agency was blurred. Spooked, she reported it to Gorsky, who passed the detail up the chain—with another urgent and secret recommendation that she be killed. Moscow still balked at issuing the directive and instead told Gorsky to insist that Bentley end the relationship with Heller. That wasn't something Bentley was willing to do. Gorsky also encouraged her to defect to the Soviet Union, which she also had no intention of doing, fearing she would be killed once she arrived.[8]

No longer in charge of her spy networks, out of a job, and beginning to fear for her life, Bentley decided it was time to change sides. She ruled out going to the FBI office in Manhattan, then recalled the field office in New Haven. She took the train on "holiday" and scoped the office out, deciding it would do. Still, she stuck to the maneuvers that had become part of her nature, the steps she used to take when picking up documents from her contacts in Washington. After uncounted twists, turns, and double-backs, Bentley—confident she hadn't been followed—finally slipped into the nondescript office building and conducted one final maneuver, taking the elevator to the third floor, then descending the fire stairs back to the first floor and the FBI office. At the reception desk Bentley sounded like any other person with business—or perhaps a tip—for the FBI. "I'd like to see the agent in charge," she said.[9] While she waited her turn on a nearby bench, Bentley's doubts surged and she almost bolted. But she calmed herself and was still sitting there when the receptionist told her the agent was ready to see her.

Bentley had concocted a ruse for the visit, one rooted in the truth, until she could figure out how to turn herself in without getting arrested. She sat down across from Special Agent Edward Coady, who reached for a pack of cigarettes and invited Bentley to join him in a smoke. As they lit up, he waited patiently for Bentley to explain why she was there; in her nervousness, Bentley was slow to begin. Finally she launched into it. She wanted to file a complaint about Peter Heller, she said. He was a lieutenant in the National Guard and had been passing himself off as a government spy. Bentley told Coady that she was an executive for a firm that shipped goods to Russia and that Heller had tried to recruit her as well. She wanted to know if Heller had the bona fides to make such an offer—or if he was an imposter.

Part of her question was sincere—she really was suspicious of Heller and hoped Coady might give her a hint of whether he was working for the FBI. But Coady read Bentley's complaint as a diversion from her real purpose, though he couldn't figure out over the course of their two-hour conversation what exactly she was after. He couldn't tell that, as the temporary face of the FBI, he was essentially being considered for a job as the conduit through which Bentley hoped to move from the shadows into the light.

The session ended with both still playing the charade. Coady later briefed his superior on the odd visit from the enigmatic Bentley, and a report was duly created and filed—and largely forgotten.

Two weeks later, an episode of comic absurdity in Ottawa gave the West its first inkling of the scope of Soviet spying in the Americas—the defection of Igor Gouzenko, an embassy cipher clerk. Gouzenko was born in Belarus two years after the Bolshevik Revolution. At the start of World War II he joined the Soviet Army, where he was trained to encrypt telegrams and other communications. In 1943, Gouzenko, a rising star in the cipher ranks, was assigned to the Soviet Embassy in Ottawa, where he encrypted and decrypted reports back and forth to Moscow that detailed the extent of the communist spy infiltration of Canada and, to a lesser extent, the United States.[10]

In the summer of 1945, with the war winding down, Gouzenko learned that he, his pregnant wife, and their young son were being recalled to Russia. But two years of life in the West had soured him on Soviet living, with its struggles for basic sustenance. He also had come to fear Soviet politics—particularly the sudden and permanent disappearances of old colleagues and friends. Gouzenko didn't want to go home. He thought that if he had something to offer the Canadian government, they would let him stay—and protect him from the KGB. So on the evening of September 5, "an unseasonably hot and sultry" Wednesday night, Gouzenko checked back into work, gathered up 109 pages of documents and code books proving the existence of the Soviet spy rings, slipped them under his shirt, and walked out of the embassy. With a Soviet's ingrained distrust of authority, Gouzenko went first to the *Ottawa Journal* newspaper—where the night editor would have nothing to do with him. Gouzenko similarly couldn't find a sympathetic ear among the guards at various government offices, long since closed for the evening. So he took the sweat-drenched papers home to his wife and toddler son and, after a sleepless night, made a fresh round Thursday morning of government offices, including the Department of Justice, trying to breach the wall of bureaucracy and get someone to listen to him. Increasingly desperate, Gouzenko told stone-faced receptionists that he might as well kill himself because KGB agents definitely would kill him when they caught him. Even that threat failed to get him the ear of someone who could help. Or so he thought.

Within hours of Gouzenko's attempt Thursday morning to meet with the minister of justice, top Canadian government officials were conferring about how best to deal with him without "becoming a party to any course of action which would link the government of Canada up with this matter in a manner which might cause Russia to feel that we had performed an unfriendly act," Prime Minister W. L. Mackenzie King wrote in his journal.[11] Part of the problem: The Canadians didn't yet know the value of the papers Gouzenko was trying to give them. "The man might be only a crank trying to preserve his own life," King said, while suggesting in a meeting with Norman Robertson, his undersecretary of state for external affairs, that they assign plainclothes police to watch Gouzenko until they could figure out their next step. If in the meantime Gouzenko committed suicide, they could have the police grab the papers as part of their investigation into the death. At the very least, King told his underlings, the Canadian government had to have clean hands. "No matter what happened we should not let it be assumed that the government of Canada itself has sought to spy on the Embassy or to take advantage of a situation of the kind to find out something against a trusted ally."

When Gouzenko failed to show up for work Thursday, his colleagues quickly figured out what he was up to—as Gouzenko guessed they would. He was afraid to stay in his own apartment. A neighbor gave the family sanctuary in her flat across the hall, and in the middle of the night Gouzenko watched surreptitiously as the Ottawa KGB station chief—officially an embassy driver—and Soviet Embassy security officials broke into his apartment, looking for the missing papers. The neighbor called police, who rousted the intruders, and the next morning the Gouzenkos were in the protection of the Department of Justice. King was getting regular updates on the "man from [the] Russian Embassy" as Russian diplomats demanded Gouzenko's arrest and deportation because, they said, he had stolen money (there was no evidence of that). The Soviets didn't mention the papers and code books.[12] Over the next few months Gouzenko's revelations—and the papers he turned over—would lead to the arrests of nearly forty people, including a member of the Canadian Parliament, and set in motion a wide range of investigations in the United States into the security of the atomic bomb program (which indirectly led to the arrests of Julius and Ethel Rosenberg and Klaus Fuchs). Most significantly, Gouzenko let the West know exactly how active the Soviets were in recruiting and running spy networks in the United States, Canada, and Great Britain. His revelations accelerated the erosion of trust among the former allies and helped launch the cold war.

Gouzenko's defection hadn't yet occurred when Elizabeth Bentley first approached the FBI in August, and it didn't become public until the following February, but word of his actions quickly spread through the Soviet spying apparatus in the West. Controllers scrambled to extricate spies and insulate as many people as they could from discovery. The FBI, whose agents joined in the investigation, similarly were trying to determine the extent of the spying network. No records detail when and how Bentley might have heard of these developments—or if she did before they became public—or whether Gouzenko could have led the FBI to Bentley. But any revelation such as Gouzenko's had to have made all those engaged in espionage nervous, especially in an environment in which public fears of communist chicanery were being fanned from the White House on down.

In any case, a much higher-profile defection in New York in October couldn't have escaped Bentley's attention. Louis F. Budenz, a Communist Party member since the mid-1930s, had spent five years as the managing editor of the *Daily Worker*, the Communist Party's newspaper. But Budenz, who had been raised Catholic, had been privately wrestling with the urge to return to his faith, trying to reconcile Catholicism with communism (he had been excommunicated for marrying a divorced woman in a civil ceremony but apparently maintained his faith). After a public trading of essays in 1936, Budenz, then an editorial board member of the *Daily Worker*, began meeting occasionally with Monsignor Fulton J. Sheen, the radio priest, who slowly nurtured Budenz's secret transformation.[13] On October 10, 1945, Budenz made a very public and permanent break with the Communist Party, declaring his faith had won out. "Communism and Catholicism are irreconcilable," Budenz said.

"Communism, I have found, aims to establish a tyranny over the human spirit. It is in unending conflict with religion and true freedom."[14] Setting up shop as a teacher first at the University of Notre Dame and then at Fordham University, Budenz became a professional witness against the Communist Party. An overt party member since 1935, he knew little about the spy matchmaking Browder had done for the Soviets, or exactly what Bentley's role was. But he knew there had been spy networks. He knew Bentley. And he had known Golos.

With the newspapers and radios detailing Budenz's conversion, Bentley wasted no time prodding the FBI. She sent a letter to the bureau's Manhattan office ostensibly to renew her concerns about Heller, the lover with the badge. The FBI responded by setting up an appointment with Bentley—and by then she was willing to risk exposure by meeting them in their Manhattan office. She walked in on November 7 and for more than two weeks filled the FBI agents' ears with details of Soviet espionage.[15] Bentley talked about what and whom she knew and about the networks within Washington that were funneling information through her to the Soviet Union. It was a bombshell. And her information jibed with what until then had been the unsubstantiated—and secret—allegations by Whittaker Chambers, a *Time* magazine editor and former Communist Party member who had been talking to the FBI about spies, including Alger Hiss, he had known while in the party.

At first the FBI tried to get Bentley to burrow back into the spy rings to uncover the identities of more moles. But in an era of shadows, the FBI was trumped by one of the Soviets' top spies, Kim Philby, who in his lofty perch at Great Britain's MI6 was in the loop of high-level notifications about Bentley's defection. Philby, part of the infamous Cambridge Five and considered one of the most devastatingly effective Soviet spies, warned Moscow on November 20 of Bentley's defection. The NKVD shuttered its American operations virtually overnight.[16] Bentley couldn't even get Gorsky to respond to requests to meet with her. Unknown to her and the FBI, he had already fled the country. Despite her best efforts, Bentley was destined to "become the least successful double agent in FBI history."[17]

In February 1946, newspapers began reporting on Gouzenko's

defection in Ottawa and the existence of the Soviet spy rings, ratcheting up public fears of the growing "communist menace."[18] When U.S. Secretary of State James F. Byrnes appeared before the House Appropriations Committee that summer to push for an increased budget for the next fiscal year, an annual and usually routine appearance, he was broadsided by questions about the loyalty of some of his underlings and suspicions about spies in the federal government. Over the ensuing weeks Congress added the "McCarran rider," after sponsor Sen. Patrick McCarran of Nevada, to the State Department's funding authorization. It empowered Byrnes to fire anyone whose loyalty was suspect.[19] The fear ratcheted up yet again. On November 25, three weeks after the Republicans swept the congressional midterm elections—in part due to the wave of anti-communist sentiment—Truman established the Temporary Commission on Employee Loyalty to "create a more effective and centralized machinery for purging the Federal pay rolls of communists and other persons suspected of disloyal or subversive tendencies." In March 1947, the administration issued its directive creating the Loyalty Oath program and ordered a "loyalty investigation of every person entering the civilian employment of any department or agency of the executive branch of the Federal Government"—an order that only added to the fear that communists were lurking everywhere.[20]

Mutual distrust between Attorney General Tom C. Clark and J. Edgar Hoover, his supposed underling at the FBI, colored how the Bentley revelations ultimately would be handled. The underlying problem was that Hoover's investigators couldn't corroborate Bentley's claims; Clark wanted to push ahead with prosecutions. Both men wanted political cover from congressional inquiries— particularly the House Un-American Activities Committee—if the Bentley allegations became public and it appeared that the Justice Department had done nothing. Yet Hoover urged caution, an odd position for a man who had built his career on an all-consuming hatred of communists. He believed that a rushed, and failed, prosecution would mean a black eye for the FBI and would cast doubts about the levels of communist infiltration that Hoover believed to be a significant problem.[21] Hoover, who viewed Clark as a political hack, simultaneously feared the attorney general might engineer a case intending to lose, in hopes that a failed prosecution would gut the Republicans' argument that Truman, up for election in 1948, was soft on communism. An acquittal would in effect suggest that the fear of communist spies was overblown. The FBI director also suspected Clark's office was responsible for leaks to the press that Hoover felt imperiled some of his agency's investigations.[22]

Hoover's biggest concern, though, was that the federal government couldn't prove its case. Hoover underling Edward Tamm met with Clark and others at Justice and warned that "success of prosecution in this case would hang by the thread of the testimony of a single informant whose contacts were probably espionage agents who were either dead, returned to Russia, or unidentified."[23] Hoover recommended the bureau end the investigation by turning over its list of suspected spies in governmental agencies to their departmental bosses for "administrative action"—presumably, dismissal.[24] In March, the Justice Department, still concerned about political backlash, considered presenting Bentley's allegations to a grand jury with the express intent of having it offer up no indictments so "that in the event [HUAC] should ever raise a question, it would be possible to answer by saying that the Grand Jury had considered the evidence and had not deemed it sufficient to justify criminal action."[25] In the end, Clark decided to present the case in full, hoping for criminal indictments.

In Washington, the HUAC announced that it would hold hearings in September on the influence of communists on Hollywood, sparking a summer-long debate over propaganda, the subtexts of movies, and whether Hollywood's creative pool was any of Congress's business. "The American free enterprise system will suffer more from the so-called conservatives in Washington than it will from the so-called radicals in Hollywood," said Robert R. Young, chairman of the board of the Chesapeake & Ohio railroad, corporate owner of the film company Pathé Industries. "They should start their investigation of subversives in Washington."[26] His voice was in the minority, though, and in the fall the hearings began, riveting the nation as both stars and obscure Hollywood figures named names, denied knowing anything about communists, or refused to answer—leading to the imprisonment of the Hollywood Ten and launching the movie industry's blacklist era.

By the time those hearings began, the grand jury in Manhattan's

Foley Square courthouse was already two months into its work, the government's case presented by Special Assistant Attorney General Thomas J. Donegan and Assistant Attorney General (and eventual congressman) T. Vincent Quinn. The grand jury proceedings were supposed to have been secret, though they were anything but. On October 16, stories popped up in both the New York City and Washington, D.C., newspapers that a "Red Spy Ring" was under investigation by "the special Grand Jury sitting in New York since last June." The stories were the obvious result of a deliberate leak by someone within the Justice Department and seemed designed to gin up public furor against those who might ultimately be indicted. The *New York Sun*, under the byline Edward Nellor, reported that indictments were coming soon in the case handled by Quinn, Donegan, and the New York City office of the FBI. The story trumpeted that "a communist controlled spy ring which wove its disloyal tentacles into at least six governmental agencies and paid or persuaded at least fifty Americans to serve as espionage agents, will be cracked open soon." It identified the affected agencies as the State, Commerce, and Treasury departments and the Office of Strategic Services (predecessor of the Central Intelligence Agency) and said the espionage had also targeted the government's atomic weapons program. Nellor's story quoted an unidentified federal official as saying, "This case will be the biggest thing that ever happened in the United States."[27]

More stories appeared focusing on the testimony of a mysterious unidentified "woman informant" (Bentley, no doubt) who "gave the FBI the names of a dozen or more persons in Government who, she said, had furnished documents that were passed on to Soviet agents." Much of the coverage was breathless and laudatory of the efforts by the FBI. Some, however, argued that the federal government, rather than ferreting out spies, was engaged in a witch-hunt. O. John Rogge, a former assistant to Clark, was in private practice and defending eleven members of the Joint Anti-Fascist Refugee Committee facing contempt citations for refusing to turn over records to the HUAC. He described the campaign of leaks as "the most porous grand jury investigation in Justice Department history" and placed the blame squarely on Clark's fifth-floor office. "Leaks from the fifth floor of the Justice Department in Washington [were calculated] to place the grand jurors in a position where it would be difficult for them to refuse to return indictments for espionage," Rogge said. "The grand jurors wouldn't go for the trumped up 'treason' stuff so the Federal Bureau of Investigation and the Justice Department have now abandoned that tack."[28] I. F. Stone, the legendarily iconoclastic columnist (and former communist sympathizer), went one step further and concluded in an October 20, 1947, column in *PM* magazine that the prosecutors orchestrated the leaks to pressure their own grand jurors to return some sort of indictment.

In reality, things were not going nearly as well inside the grand jury room as the leaked stories made it seem. Bentley testified willingly and apparently convincingly, but the FBI was still having trouble corroborating her story. Quinn and Donegan subpoenaed several of the people from whom Bentley said she had collected government papers and secrets, but they all either lied and said they had never met Bentley or invoked the Fifth Amendment against self-incrimination. Through the fall newspapers were filled with speculative stories and more leaked items about pending indictments—as many as sixty people, the *Washington Times-Herald* trumpeted on October 17, 1947. The same day, the *New York Daily Mirror* reported that at least four people had already been indicted "with scores more expected," though that was not the case.

By springtime of 1948, the impatient press began turning against the process. *New York Journal-American* writer Howard Rushmore, a former party member and generally a gung-ho backer of the anti-communist campaign, reported that the HUAC might launch its own investigation into the grand jury process to determine if it had been sabotaged by politics. "Although more than 200 witnesses have appeared before the jury at Foley Square since last summer, not one indictment has been returned. This week the grand jury was called in for half an hour and dismissed for another ten days. This procedure has been followed for several months and jury members are known to be indignant at Justice Department officials over the obvious stalling tactics. Although more than 100 New Dealers, many former or present high officials in such key agencies as the State department, have been named as members of Soviet espionage network, no action has been taken. . . . In Washington political circles, the rumor is that Clark, acting on Administration

1. Elizabeth Bentley's revelations of spy-handling for the Soviet Union launched the grand jury investigation that led to the indictments of the twelve leaders of the Communist Party–USA. WPA Film Library. Image courtesy of MPI Home Video.

orders, will keep the Jury sitting until November"—after Truman's reelection campaign for the White House.[29]

By the time Rushmore's scathing article appeared, Donegan and Quinn knew their case was in trouble. They began contemplating a face-saving measure. If they couldn't indict the spies, they might be able to go after the more visible enemies—the leadership of the Communist Party, under charges they had violated the 1940 Smith Act. It had only been used twice before, but the Smith Act could be construed as making it illegal to advocate communism, since as a political theory it called for the violent overthrow of governments—like the U.S. government—built on capitalism. It could be just the tool the feds needed to crack down on the party. But again, one of the few voices against pursuing indictments against the party leaders, at least until the case could be vetted by outside attorneys to ensure they could get convictions under the Smith Act, was Hoover himself. "I told Quinn last week that I thought it was a mistake to present Communist Party case [until it] had been most carefully reviewed and digested and a determination made as to whether a 'case' existed," Hoover scrawled across the bottom of one field report.[30]

Meanwhile, Bentley, realizing the grand jury would not be indicting the people she had named, began taking her own steps to ensure her story got out. Public revelation, she believed, was the only thing that would keep her safe from Soviet assassins. On April 1, she called Frederick Woltman, a reporter for the *New York World-Telegram* who had won a Pulitzer Prize the previous year for articles exploring the communist infiltration of labor and political organizations. She identified herself only as a Vassar graduate who had known Woltman's former wife, another alum, and wanted to meet with him to discuss something he might find interesting.[31] Woltman set up a meeting for the next day and drew in a colleague, Nelson Frank. Both reporters were former communists, and Bentley later said—somewhat disingenuously—that she was hoping to get their advice on how to handle her own switch. In truth, she planned to use them.

They met for three hours, and Bentley gave the reporters an overview of her experience and her testimony before the grand jury. Bentley mentioned a few specific names of people she had dealt with. She seemed confused and told the men she thought she was being followed, perhaps by communist agents out to silence her. Ultimately they told her they had no advice to give and couldn't publish her story because the grand jury was still in session, but they would be back in touch. Frank also told her they planned to call the FBI, and "she interposed no objection," telling the reporters that she had a "fine" relationship with the bureau.[32] Woltman called FBI agent Joseph Kelly a little after nine o'clock that night. Kelly, coincidentally, had met that morning with Bentley, who did not mention her pending appointment with the newspapermen. Kelly quickly spread the word within the Justice Department and the FBI by phone and telegram.

Donegan immediately saw trouble and approached the management of the *World-Telegram* to pressure them to drop the story, arguing that they might find themselves in legal trouble if they published details from what was supposed to be secret grand jury testimony. The paper, apparently going along with Donegan's demand, agreed to hold off. In reality, the reporters were still trying to verify Bentley's story and weren't ready to publish yet. They hoped that seeming to promise to delay publication would earn them a chit to redeem with the government later on.[33]

Still, the "communist threat" was a top story. As Donegan and Quinn were trying to save their case, Eugene Dennis, general secretary of the Communist Party, gave a speech carried on the ABC radio network the evening of April 7. The next evening, U.S. Rep. Karl E. Mundt of South Dakota responded over the same airwaves that he would introduce a new set of laws that would require communists like Dennis—U.S. citizens—to register with the government, bar them from government employment, deny them passports, exclude them from federal labor law protections, and require them to submit fingerprints to the FBI. Noncitizen communists would be deported. Mundt said he stopped short of calling for an outright ban on the Communist Party, acceding to concerns by Hoover, among others in Washington, that it would be harder to keep tabs on communists if draconian laws sent them underground.[34] (In early May, the two leading contenders for the Republican nomination to take on Harry Truman in the November presidential election would hold the first-ever nationally broadcast debate between presidential candidates. The topic: Whether the Communist Party should be banned. Former Minnesota governor Harold E. Stassen, a backer of what became known as the Mundt-Nixon Bill, argued that it should. Thomas E. Dewey, the New York governor and eventual Republican nominee, argued that it should not.)

The Thursday morning between the Dennis and Mundt speeches, Quinn, in Washington, called John F. X. McGohey, the U.S. attorney in Manhattan, and asked him to review a top-secret 1,850-page dossier the FBI had prepared against the Communist Party leadership and recommend whether it was solid enough to present to a grand jury.[35] It was, in essence, a job feeler—Quinn wanted McGohey to take over the case. That afternoon McGohey talked with Donegan in New York extensively about the Bentley and Communist Party cases to get a sense of what he might be getting himself into. On Monday, he called Quinn in Washington and told him that he would handle it, but that if the plan ultimately was for him to prosecute the Smith Act case, he thought it ought to be presented to a different grand jury than the one Donegan had convened to hear the Bentley revelations because "I do not want to be identified with [the Bentley] case presented during [the] last ten months."[36] McGohey lost that behind-the-scenes fight.

In Washington, a different and wide-open fight was under way as communist leaders engaged in a dramatic battle with the HUAC over the legitimacy of the congressional hearings. The HUAC had subpoenaed Dennis, the party's general secretary, after he earlier refused in voluntary testimony to tell the committee his real name (he was born Francis Xavier Waldron Jr.). Dennis failed to appear on April 9 and instead sent a statement via his lawyer in which he argued the HUAC "was not a body which may lawfully subpoena a witness to appear before it." The committee disagreed, and at the urging of Rep. Richard M. Nixon, who was just beginning to establish his reputation as a staunch anti-communist, the HUAC voted to hold Dennis in contempt of Congress, a showdown reported in most major newspapers.[37]

"What to do about the communists?" was a dominant question in Washington. Legislators jockeyed to create laws to answer the question. Mundt, Nixon, and others in Congress offered up proposals that would bar "subversive aliens" from entering the country, broaden anti-espionage laws, and require communist-dominated organizations to register their membership rosters with the U.S. attorney general's office, which maintained the "subversive groups" list. Other proposals would bar communists from running for office. Protests cropped up periodically in Washington and elsewhere, primarily by leftists arguing that such moves were tantamount to fascism.[38]

While the drama played out in Washington, McGohey was trying to read and digest the massive FBI dossier contained in "eight heavy black cardboard folders." It took him two weeks to get the basics down. On April 29, he traveled from Manhattan to Washington to meet with Donegan and Quinn in a conference room off Clark's fifth-floor office in the Department of Justice on Pennsylvania Avenue, midway between the White House and the Capitol. Also on hand were Deputy Attorney General Peyton Ford and Herbert A. Bergson, Clark's executive assistant (who in a few weeks would be tapped to head up the department's antitrust division). Clark opened the meeting about 1:00 P.M. by asking, "What are you going to do about the Commies?" and made it clear he was more interested in accelerating the prosecution than dissecting the case.

McGohey, after reading the report (he admitted he had only skimmed portions of it), felt the strongest case against the communists would be on "the basis of proving 'overthrow by force and violence' and that I should not get into a wide range of economic theory." He suggested the lawyers prepare the hoped-for indictment based on the FBI brief, but then reinterview witnesses and find fresh ones since some of those included in the brief related details of events that had occurred decades earlier. Quinn and Donegan argued that the brief was thorough and that McGohey could present the case immediately. McGohey dug in, threatening to quit: "If it was decided to go forward now, I would have to withdraw because I could not, in justice to myself or the government, proceed with such little preparation." They argued through the afternoon, with Clark slipping out for a series of appointments—most of them apparently the "meet and greet" variety, including having his photograph taken with visiting Salvation Army officials.[39] They finally agreed on a compromise: McGohey would present the case before the already sitting grand jury, but the jurors would be asked to take a two-month adjournment so he could get ready.

The Communist Party's fractious history, including its various name changes, has been written about in depth from the right, the left, and the ostensibly impartial. That history isn't important to the story of the 1949 trial, except for a few crucial details that framed the case McGohey put together—beginning with the tight relationship between the American leadership and the Kremlin. While the American party might have had an American accent, its policies—and a large part of its funding—came from Moscow. In the late 1930s, as Hitler was driving Europe to war, the American party was staunchly anti-fascist, which ended when the 1939 Molotov-Ribbentrop Pact established an arm's-length détente between the Soviet Union and Nazi Germany. The American party then struck a pacifist tone, arguing against American engagement in Europe—until Hitler reneged on the pact and invaded Russia. Then the American party shifted and lobbied for the war effort, including no-strike pledges in key industries, which weakened its support among more militant labor activists. It even changed its name to the Communist Political Association, with its intimations of being a club rather than an active political party. With the end of World War II and the resurgence of tensions between the communist Soviets and the capitalist United States and Great Britain, the American party again veered to toe the Moscow policy line.

Most of those switches came under the tutelage of Earl Browder, who led the party from 1932 until 1945. He (with occasional help from Eugene Dennis) also acted as a spy-scout for the Soviets, picking out potential turncoats in the U.S. government, and for a time handled a string of spies himself, some of whom eventually wound up on the Golos-Bentley list.[40] But as the war neared its end, Browder sought to distance the American party from the Soviets, arguing that communism and capitalism could coexist. His stance was famously denounced in a 1945 letter by French communist leader Jacques Duclos—who was generally viewed as delivering informal Kremlin orders for the American party to get rid of Browder. Foster, Dennis, and other top American leaders were happy to do so. In 1946 Foster, who had preceded Browder as chairman, became chairman again, and Dennis became the general secretary; Browder was kicked out of the party. But with the exception of Browder's role—and Dennis's assistance—as a spy recruiter and occasional handler, the party leadership limited its actions to politics. Their alliance with the Soviet Union was clear, but they were not engaged in covert acts against the United States.

Key to the indictment was a conference that began in New York City on June 2, 1945, at which the Communist Political Association was dissolved and replaced by the CPUSA, re-embracing Soviet policies. That decision, McGohey would argue, was the beginning of the conspiracy. The defendants adopted a constitution based on Marxism-Leninism, created a network of district-level subsidiary organizations, and established training programs and schools to teach Marxist-Leninist policies. Proving that violated the Smith Act, though, would be dicey. The U.S. Supreme Court had already ruled in two other cases, including one against Harry Bridges, the West Coast dockworker and union leader, that mere membership in the Communist Party or espousing communist beliefs was not sufficient to deport aliens. It would be hard, McGohey reasoned, to argue that membership was tantamount to calling for revolution. "They require, to me, proof of actual teaching and advocacy of forceful overthrow," McGohey wrote in a memo as he mulled how to proceed. "Mere membership, or affiliation with the party is not enough. It must be shown that there is knowledge of its purpose."[41]

Who should be charged was another question. McGohey and George Kneip, an appeals expert brought in to help "bulletproof" the indictment against legal challenges, decided the best course was to aim for the top, and limit the scope to avoid creating a circus in the courtroom.

By early June, though, McGohey found himself facing a bureaucratic wall: The FBI said it could not amass the evidence he thought he needed in the time allotted. Quinn, McGohey's boss, directed that the case be presented to the grand jury based on the existing dossier—which McGohey and Kneip felt was insufficient and failed to include overt acts that moved the case beyond the "affiliation" threshold the Supreme Court had already thrown out. As good soldiers, McGohey and Kneip dug into the report for overlooked nuggets. McGohey lined up Budenz, the former *Daily Worker* managing editor, as a key witness to lay out the goals and ambitions of the Communist Party and set June 22 as the day to begin presenting the case. McGohey thought the decision to go ahead with the FBI dossier case had been made at the highest levels in Washington and handed down to him through Quinn. On June 18, however, in a phone conversation on other matters, Peyton Ford asked about the case "and was surprised to learn we are going ahead . . . at Q[uinn]'s direction." McGohey, by now committed to presenting to the grand jury, headed for Washington the next day for a meeting with Clark, who was less concerned with the merits of the case than with the timing. "He asked if we could not hold up presentation until after July 20, e.g., after the Dem[ocratic] Convention." McGohey, put off by the overt political considerations and questionable ethics, told his boss that wouldn't be possible. McGohey told Clark that he believed he could get the indictments in the next two weeks and arrest warrants could be issued to pick up the defendants on Tuesday, July 6—the day after Independence Day would be celebrated. A few days later, Clark—who had told the White House the indictments wouldn't come before the convention—sent the file to the solicitor general's office, which handles the department's appeals, ostensibly for review. In effect, it put the case on ice for three weeks.

The political concerns from Washington were considerable. Truman had ascended to the Oval Office in 1945 when FDR died of a brain hemorrhage less than three months into his fourth term.

He had had an unremarkable legislative history, and as president he struggled with a wide range of domestic and foreign issues. As McGohey and Clark wrestled over the timing of the indictments, the Soviet Union began its blockade of ground routes into occupied Berlin, a strategy aimed at asserting Russian control over the East German city still divided among the Allies. The showdown dominated news coverage, and speculation ran rampant about a possible war with the Russians. Conservatives already were harshly critical of Truman's Marshall Plan to rebuild Europe. Congress was in the hands of the Republicans after the disastrous (for the Democrats) 1946 midterm election. Truman was also having trouble with political friends. He had earned the enmity of unions in 1946 when he threatened to nationalize the railways to end a strike. And Henry Wallace, Truman's predecessor as Roosevelt's vice president, was contemplating a Progressive Party campaign for the White House that, at a minimum, would siphon off liberal Democrats. All in all, Truman was considered ripe for unseating in November 1948. With former New Dealers putting together a "draft Eisenhower" movement, it was not a sure thing that Truman's own party—fragmented in the void left by Roosevelt's death—would even give him the nomination.[42]

The Democratic National Convention began July 12 at Philadelphia's Independence Hall. It would be a momentous convention, marked by a deep split over segregation between northern liberals, such as Minneapolis mayor Hubert Humphrey, and southern Democrats. In a moment of historic eloquence, Humphrey, then running for the Senate, demanded in a speech on the convention's second day that the Democratic Party adopt a "morally sound position" on race and civil rights. It was not a popular call. The Alabama delegation and half of the Mississippi delegation walked out in protest, leading to the States' Rights Democratic Party—the Dixiecrats—and its presidential candidate, South Carolina governor Strom Thurmond. But by the time all the dust had settled, Truman had won his bid for the Democratic nomination.

The Republicans, though, smelled blood in the water, particularly after taking control of Congress two years earlier. Dewey, who had been soundly beaten by Roosevelt in 1944, won the Republican nomination over challenges by Ohio's Sen. Howard Taft, former Minnesota governor Harold Stassen, California governor Earl Warren, and General Douglas MacArthur. Dewey then picked Warren, a popular figure in electoral-vote-heavy California, to be his running mate. Given Truman's low appeal to voters and the fracturing of the Democratic Party, it looked to be a Republican year. By Labor Day pundits had written Truman off, and the only question was how bad would it be.

The week after Truman won the Democratic nomination, the grand jury reconvened on the fourteenth floor of the U.S. Court House at Manhattan's Foley Square and was presented formally with the legal charges, now "scrubbed" by the solicitor general's office. Just before noon July 20, the jury handed up the two-count indictment to U.S. District Court Judge Vincent L. Leibell charging twelve leaders of the CPUSA with violating the 1940 Smith Act. No one was accused of spying, the crime the grand jury had been convened to investigate. The indictment alleged that, beginning around April 1, 1945, the twelve leaders of the CPUSA "unlawfully, willfully, and knowingly did conspire with each other" to form the Communist Party as "a society, group, and assembly of persons who teach and advocate the overthrow and destruction of the Government of the United States by force and violence." It further said the men conspired to "advocate and teach the duty and necessity of overthrowing and destroying the Government of the United States by force and violence" through the convening of meetings, organization of schools and seminars, and publication of books and journalistic articles "advocating the principles of Marxism-Leninism." Conviction could mean up to ten years in prison on each count, as well as fines.

There were no overt acts, no detailed plans to attack the government. The evidence would be the twelve men's roles as leaders of the Communist Party, the books they read, the political schools they supported, and, in essence, their thoughts.

THREE

A Sudden and
Violent Storm

As native Chicagoans, Gil Green and his brother Ben knew all too well how hot and miserable July could be in the Windy City, when humid Gulf of Mexico air would settle in a noxious, suffocating stew of factory smoke, exhaust from ill-tuned cars, and soot from coal-fired electric plants. The air had its own texture, its own bitter and cloying taste. Nighttime brought little relief inside sweltering apartment buildings. Merciful thunderheads could boil on the updrafts and bring short blasts of drama and coolness before drifting eastward over Lake Michigan, but the storms were short and the relief temporary.

In late spring of 1948, knowing those days were coming, the brothers made plans to get their families out of the city for a week in the middle of the summer. Through a friend of a friend, they found a bargain—ten dollars for seven days at a small lakeside cabin in Wisconsin, about sixty miles northwest of Chicago. The heat and humidity could be just as oppressive there, but at least the air would smell of grass and trees, not exhaust and ash. So the brothers arranged for a day off work and on the morning of July

32

20 roused their wives and children early to beat the traffic. The fathers wanted to get to the cabin with enough of the day left to play with their children before returning to the city—and their jobs—the next morning, leaving the women and kids to their own devices until they picked them up again the next week.[1]

The drive was uneventful. The adults kept the children distracted with road games like counting cows and graveyards and singing songs. After quickly unpacking the car, they took to the lake and played all day, breaking for meals and conversations. By dusk they were exhausted. With the kids sent off to bed and the evening chores done, the adults—Gil and his wife, Lil, and Ben and his wife, Florence—sat in the cooling night air and tried to stay awake late enough to catch the 10:00 P.M. radio news out of Chicago, to hear what they had missed during the day.

As the hour approached, someone fiddled with the dial until the announcer's voice flowed out of the speaker. The top story was about indictments out of New York City under the 1940 Smith Act: Several of the leaders of the Communist Party had been arrested, several of the accused were still at large—and one of the warrants was for Gilbert Green of Chicago. The couples listened in shocked silence as the radio newscaster reported raids that afternoon on the Greens' apartment at 806 Independence Boulevard and the North Wells Street office where Green worked as chair of the Midwest district of the Communist Party. Reporters had gone to the Greens' apartment building, where neighbors reported that they were quiet people, the kids polite, and that Green could sometimes be found outside playing ball with his oldest son, Danny, ten, or taking the younger kids, Josie, six, and Ralph, three, for rides on the handlebars of his bicycle. But when the FBI came calling, none of the neighbors knew where the Greens had gone.

The newscast ended. The anxious couples talked for a bit, wondering if the FBI could trace Green to the cottage, ultimately deciding no—if the FBI knew where he was, they would have swooped in and grabbed him already. They talked some more about the "repressive wind [that] was blowing" and how they should have realized there would be some action by the government, though they also recognized they had no way of anticipating exactly what.

It wasn't as though Green was a spy or had been working in some sort of underground capacity. He was an overt leader of a political party; he got his name in the papers, traveled to conferences, and gave reports and wrote articles. He had even run for mayor of Chicago. Green tried to sort through it all. It was disorienting to hear his life discussed on the radio, to learn he was a wanted man, to realize that he could be going to prison. It was "as if a sudden and violent storm had burst into our lives."[2]

The couples' four-way conversation eventually ran out, and they headed off to bed. There was little sleeping in Gil and Lil's room, though. They pillow-talked about their lives, their children, and the uncertainty they faced as the political turned personal. "I'm frightened," Lil admitted at one point during the restless night, the breeze in the trees making "startling and ominous sounds."[3]

That the FBI didn't know where to find Green caused a bit of a stir within the bureau. And he wasn't the only defendant they couldn't track down. Before the indictments were handed up, McGohey had urged the FBI to assign agents "who are familiar with each of the persons involved" to serve the warrants and make the arrests, a job usually handled by U.S. marshals. McGohey wanted all the defendants rounded up at the same time and believed that the FBI, which was monitoring the men, was better equipped to do that. But the FBI balked, fearing potential legal and public relations fallout. "The Department is desirous that the handling of this case be no different than that of any other routine case," fellow prosecutor Raymond Whearty advised McGohey. McGohey appealed to Attorney General Clark—ostensibly both his boss and the overseer of Hoover and the FBI. "It is my considered opinion," McGohey wrote, "that it will be a serious mistake and an indefensible waste of our efficient manpower not to have these warrants executed by agents of the FBI, who alone have the facilities for the full coordination and synchronization required."[4]

In the end, the FBI did serve the warrants—but it was hardly an example of "efficient manpower." The decision was made at the last minute, and the job rushed after the *Washington Times-Herald* reported the morning of July 20, before the grand jury reconvened and made the indictments official, that "at least twelve of the highest officials of the American Communist Party will be indicted this week for 'advocating overthrow of the United States by force and violence.'"[5]

In a postmortem of the operation, Daniel M. Ladd, assistant director of the FBI, reported to Hoover that late on July 19 the bureau had notified agents in New York, Cleveland, Detroit, and Chicago that they needed to start surveillance of the twelve party leaders and be ready to arrest them on the morning of July 21, the day after the sealed indictment was expected to be signed. But the *Times-Herald* story forced their hand. Were it not for the story, Ladd told his boss, the field agents would have nabbed all twelve men. Passing on details from George R. McSwain, head of the Chicago FBI office, Ladd told Hoover that "the premature publicity in connection with this case had caused Green to disappear from his normal haunts and stated that had this unfortunate publicity not taken place, his office would have been able to locate Green without any difficulty. Green's habits are well-known to the Chicago office but, according to Mr. McSwain, [Green] has not made contacts with his intimate associates nor frequented his usual haunts since the aforementioned publicity." The presumption was that Green had gone underground. There's no indication the agents ever considered that Green was simply on vacation, and McSwain didn't pass along the fact that, despite regular surveillance of Green, they had no inkling he had left town.[6]

Hoover didn't buy the explanation and ordered formal reprimands be placed in the personnel files of the agents involved. In a handwritten note on the bottom of Ladd's report, Hoover said, "I don't agree at all. While the premature publicity was certainly prejudicial yet we ought to have had the members of the Co. Board pegged at *all* times. We knew these arrests were brewing for some time & while it had not been decided FBI would make the arrests yet as the Investigative Agency responsible we should have had a definite line on the members. N.Y., Chicago & Cleveland as well as Security Div. are to be censured. Such lapses cannot be tolerated."

The arrest warrants were signed at midday July 20, and the FBI began the roundup just before 6:00 P.M.[7] In Manhattan, at least six agents, led by Special Agent Edward Scheidt, arrived at the Communist Party headquarters in a nine-story loft building at 35 East Twelfth Street, off Broadway a couple of blocks due south of Union Square. On its lower floor, the former garment factory housed the

Daily Worker and the Yiddish-language *Morning Freiheit* newspapers, a shipping operation for communist books and literature, and offices controlling the network of local and regional party apparatus. The national office was on the top floor. Scheidt and his agents rode the "wheezing elevator" and stepped out into a sparse reception room decorated with portraits of Franklin Roosevelt, George Washington, Thomas Jefferson, and Abraham Lincoln along with Lenin, Marx, and a pantheon of American communist "pioneers." The agents passed a railed-off reception desk, went through a door to the back offices, and entered a meeting room where five men had gathered: William Z. Foster, the party chairman; Eugene Dennis, the general secretary; and national board members Jack Stachel, John Williamson, and Henry Winston. It was clear the men knew the agents were coming. Their lawyer, Abraham Unger, was on hand to witness the arrests, as was a reporter for the *Daily Worker* and Marion Bachrach, the party's public relations director.

The party leaders had a statement prepared for the reporters accompanying the agents. In harsh terms, they decried the arrests as a political ploy by Truman to "win the election, by hook or by crook." The party leaders also accused the government of using fear to rally support for confrontations with the Soviet Union. "All that is known of the history of the blue ribbon grand jury which reportedly returned these indictments confirms our charge. For a full year the Justice Department has apparently been planting in the ultra-reactionary press tales about its alleged investigation of a 'gigantic spy plot.' Clearly the purpose of these inspired newspaper accounts was to bring pressure on the grand jury, while at the same time whipping up an atmosphere of public hysteria. In the Congress, the courts, and above all before the bar of public opinion we communists will press our case against the pro-Fascists and war mongers in the GOP and the Truman Administration."[8]

The agents tried to question the men in the party office but didn't get very far. Scheidt asked Foster to tell him where the FBI could find two other defendants, *Daily Worker* editor John Gates and Robert Thompson, a decorated war hero and national board member who also led the New York State party. Foster, at sixty-seven the oldest of the defendants and suffering from serious heart ailments, said he "absolutely would give no information of any kind" to the FBI. After the men were taken away in cars, the agents searched the entire nine floors.

Foster and the other defendants were arraigned at 7:35 P.M. before federal Judge Vincent Leibell at the U.S. Court House and released in their lawyers' custody a little before 8:00 P.M. pending the posting of $5,000 bail each the next morning. The evening was still hot and muggy, and not all of the building was air-conditioned. After the bail hearing, Foster, feeling weak, was led to a chair in one of the cooled areas. "I have a bum heart," Foster told a reporter. "This heat does me no good." But he recovered quickly, and the defendants went as a group to "the small, broiling hot press room" in the courthouse, where "they sat behind a big table under the strong white movie lights and denounced the frame-up in a fighting mood."[9] Before an array of two dozen still and movie cameras, Foster and Dennis stated emphatically that the party "never has, and does not advocate the forceful overthrow of the government of the United States."[10] Cognizant of the importance of their press conference, they read the statements a couple of times to give the cameras and microphones a better chance at capturing the moment.

At some point a reporter asked McGohey about the *New York World-Telegram* reports that the indictments had been sparked by the grand jury testimony of a "blonde spy queen." McGohey opted to lie. "I know nothing about any woman before this grand jury—blonde or otherwise."[11]

Progressives and other leftists immediately denounced the indictments. Wallace, who would accept the Progressive Party's 1948 presidential nomination two days later in Philadelphia, issued a scathing condemnation. "It is significant to me that after this prolonged investigation, the indictments make no charge of the commission of acts of force and violence. They are limited to a charge that these men teach a doctrine. This is not a new allegation. J. Edgar Hoover has made it before, yet I recall that Hoover quite rightly opposed the very objective the indictments seek to accomplish—the objective of outlawing the Communist Party."

Wallace went on to argue that once political repression begins, it becomes dangerous for all. "Defense of the civil rights of communists is the first line in the defense of the liberties of a democratic people. The history of Germany, Italy, Japan, and Franco Spain

2. Mug shot array of the six defendants arrested in the initial roundup in New York City. New York City Councilman Benjamin Davis Jr. (top left), party leader William Z. Foster, Eugene Dennis, John Williamson (bottom left), Henry Winston, and Jacob Stachel. Library of Congress, Prints & Photographs Division, *New York World-Telegram* Collection, LC-USZ62–111437.

should teach us that the suppression of the communists is but a first step in an assault on the democratic rights of labor, national, racial, and political minorities, and all those who oppose the policies of the government in power." As did the defendants, Wallace accused the Truman administration of using fear to try to win the coming election. "We can expect further Red Scares and attacks on minority groups with charges that their views are hostile to the government."

Wallace also cut to the heart of the shaky legal foundation of the Smith Act itself—its inherent conflict with the First Amendment— and said he expected the courts would rule it unconstitutional because the allegations against the men involved no acts and did not constitute a "clear and present danger" to the government. "Such an application of the Smith Act clearly violates the First Amendment and infringes the American right of free speech."[12]

The American Civil Liberties Union (ACLU), despite having recently purged itself of communists, also rose to defend the indicted men, writing in an open letter to Attorney General Clark that the indictment "violates every principle of freedom of speech and press."[13] And the Civil Rights Congress (CRC), which had formed two years earlier in the merger of three other leftist organizations, rose to post the bail for the defendants and announced that it would try to raise $250,000 for a legal defense fund. In a joint statement by George Marshall, the chairman (not Truman's secretary of state), and Len Goldsmith, the CRC's national director, the organization accused the government of indicting the men "to suppress the Communist Party of the United States. This political persecution is contrary and repugnant to American law and democratic tradition." The statement also accused the government of leaking details of the grand jury proceedings to the press. "A close perusal of the record will indicate that whenever the administration was faced with a foreign policy crisis, this Grand Jury and the 'leak' technique was used to create a witch hunt atmosphere."

The CRC tied the indictments to the Mundt-Nixon Bill, arguing that by ratcheting up fears of communism the government would create a public hysteria that would lead to the bill's passage and the outlawing of the Communist Party. "We believe this is a fight to maintain our democratic institutions. We believe that there has been no country in the history of the world which suppressed [the] Communist Party or any other political party and remained free and democratic. . . . We recognize that defense of the Constitutional and civil rights of communists and other minorities is the first line in the battle for democracy."[14]

As the committees and political figures wrangled, the FBI continued trying to round up the other accused men. Benjamin Davis Jr., a civil rights lawyer and elected New York City councilman from Harlem, was nabbed at home while working on a column for the *Daily Worker*.[15] Agents in Detroit caught up with Carl Winter, the state leader, as he was driving home with his wife a little before 6:00 P.M. The agents pulled up to Winter's 1947

Ford Tudor sedan and motioned him to the curb. Winter told the agents he would go with them but his wife was uninvolved and should be allowed to go home. "The agent assured me that his companion would drive my car and my wife directly home from the point where I was arrested. Instead, my wife was forcibly and, against her will, driven to the headquarters of the FBI." The agents detained Winter while they searched the car, confiscating a small black leather "Daily Reminder" notebook and more than three dozen other items, mostly political pamphlets, notepads, and a mimeographed copy of Gil Green's speech to the Illinois Communist Party convention from the previous November. The agent didn't get around to showing Winter the arrest warrant until 11:00 P.M.—five hours after he was taken into custody. He spent the night in the nearby Wayne County jail.[16]

The other defendants proved more elusive. Agents in New York City missed Gates in Manhattan—he had left the party headquarters on East Twelfth Street moments before they arrived. Gates later said he spent the night with a friend and turned himself in at the federal courthouse the next morning after hearing about the indictment, though it's hard to believe he had been in the office with the others and didn't know the FBI agents were on their way. As it was, Gates had to borrow a jacket and tie for his court appearance, which came just after the CRC posted bail for the men who had already been arrested.

The others trickled in slowly, as though to make a show of it. Irving Potash, a member of the national board and manager of the Furriers Joint Council of New York, appeared at the Foley Square courthouse two days after Gates. Thompson sent word that he would turn himself in shortly, but he remained at large for a week before finally popping up at the FBI office with his lawyer and no explanation. Green surfaced in Chicago on July 30. The last of the defendants, Gus Hall, the Ohio chair, walked into the FBI office in Cleveland on August 4, tanned and relaxed and silent as to where he had been for the previous two weeks.

Ultimately, the desire of Donegan and other Justice Department officials to use the indictment of the party leadership to deflect attention from their failure to indict alleged spies based on Bentley's revelations didn't work. On July 21, the *New York World-Telegram* finally dropped its story under the banner headline "Red Ring Bared

3. Carl Winter with his wife, Helen, and daughter, Michele, around 1948. Photo courtesy of Michele (Winter) Artt.

by Blond Queen," detailing what Bentley had told the grand jury, and followed up the next day with "Super-Secrecy Veiled Russia's Spy Cells Here." A week later she was testifying before the HUAC in Washington and naming names.[17]

But there was plenty of publicity to go around, and the arrests of the top twelve leaders of the Communist Party became one of the driving stories of the year. They embodied a growing fear within the nation—that the communists were getting the upper hand through subterfuge and guile. And the variety in their backgrounds added to the sense that anyone could be a communist, and thus an enemy. One man—Davis, a Harvard-educated lawyer and native of Georgia—was an elected member of the New York City Council. Two of the leaders—Davis and Winston—were black. Three of them—Potash, Stachel, and Williamson—were foreign born and subject to deportation. Most had working-class roots, and several had combat experience in World War II and with the Abraham Lincoln Brigade in Spain. All were true believers. And most, like Green, were drawn to communism by their own life experiences.

Of the twelve defendants, Green left the most detailed and personal record.[18] He was born in 1907 in Chicago, the first of three children to Isaac and Lizzie Greenberg, Jewish Russian immigrants who worked as a team in their own small tailoring business off Archer Avenue in South Chicago. The shop was in the front; the family lived behind a wooden partition in the back. It was a hardscrabble existence—Isaac Greenberg was debilitated by diabetes and often unable to work, leaving his wife to hold the small business and family together. When the father finally succumbed to the disease in 1915, Lizzie closed the shop and moved the young family—Gil, then nine, Harry, eight, and infant Bennie—into a first-floor flat at 3318 West Thirteenth Street and hung a sign in the window: "Dressmaker." Demand was light in the heart of what was then Chicago's Jewish ghetto, and Lizzie Greenberg applied for "home relief" to help feed her children, an experience her son would look back on later as integral to his sense of economic justice.

Lizzie Greenberg was embarrassed by her need, a humiliation young Gil felt despite her efforts to hide it. And the relief check came with a caseworker who, to the Greenberg children, seemed a character carved from a fairy tale, a grim figure with the Dickensian name of Mrs. Law who delighted in catching the family in such wasteful spending as occasional candy treats and a movie. "How we hated Mrs. Law! Any little thing that was not on her list of permissible Spartan necessities put us into a sweat."[19]

When he was thirteen, Green's mother secured for him a "respectable" after-school job—one with a potential future—as an errand boy and soda jerk at a local drugstore. In his memoir, Green paints the druggist as an empathetic figure and implies the older man became a surrogate father. Part of the druggist's business was selling bottles of "medicinal" alcohol with faked prescriptions from friendly doctors to avoid Prohibition-era controls. As the 1919 holiday season approached, the druggist's sales outpaced his supply of faked prescriptions. Fearing exposure, he reported an imaginary break-in at the drugstore, the burglars making off with his supply of medicinal liquor. "I knew there'd been no bottles left to be stolen. I said nothing, for I still needed the job. But it was never the same again. My youthful, wide-eyed illusions had been shattered. If this was how nice people acted, did I want to be like them?"[20] Green eventually quit.

There was little money in the household, and education after high school was out of the question. But Green found plenty of exposure to the wider world along nearby Roosevelt Road, where soapbox orators fought each other for the ears of passersby. One weekly speaker in particular caught young Green's attention—a blind man who held forth on socialism and history. His arguments resonated with Green, who while still in high school moved from job to job, wrapping packages in a mail-order house, washing restaurant dishes, aiding a millwright in a bedspring factory, poking holes in leather at a belt factory. His worldview took root, aided by conversations with a socialist uncle and books by Jack London, Upton Sinclair, Émile Zola, and others. He admired Eugene V. Debs, the Socialist Party presidential candidate who served federal prison time for opposing World War I. Eventually, when Green was seventeen, a friend invited him to a gathering of the Young Workers League (YWL), the precursor to the Young Communist League (YCL), and he joined soon after in January 1924. Just two years after the 1922 Palmer Raids had sent many radicals into hiding, the YWL was largely aboveground but limited in scope, topping out at about four thousand members concentrated in New York and Chicago. Several of Green's future fellow defendants—Stachel, Williamson, and Winter—would also join.[21]

Belonging carried risks. Around the same time he joined the YWL, Green landed a job in the shipping department at the Sinclair Refining Company, whose gasoline-production business was growing rapidly along with the nation's car culture. "An important objective of the Communist Party and the Young Workers League at the time was to help in the unionization of production workers. That became my objective," he would recall. Although he worked in shipping, he began spending time with the production workers. When the manager announced one Saturday that there would be a mandatory Sunday shift—meaning no day off for the six-day-a-week workers—Green spoke up, saying that making the men work on Sunday would be unfair. "You are too young to know what you're talking about," the manager replied. "You'd be a lot smarter if you kept your mouth shut." The following Monday, Green was called into the manager's office and dressed down again. The exchange apparently concerned the bosses enough to spur them to learn more about Green. They discovered that he was regularly attending communist gatherings after work—and ordered him to stop. Green stayed away from the gatherings for a few weeks but then resumed, and was promptly fired. "I never did learn the identity of the stoolpigeon."[22] Fearing that his political activities might hurt his family, he dropped the "berg" from the end of his name.

Green had trouble settling into another job. He became a drill press operator, then left shortly afterward to become a mail carrier, but was fired in 1927 for excessive absenteeism. He reapplied using an alias—George Gilberts—but someone in the employment office discovered Gilberts was Green and rejected the application. So Green went to work full-time for the party.[23] In 1928 he traveled to New Bedford, Massachusetts, where a violent textile strike was under way, and eventually landed in New York City, where he became editor of the YCL's *Young Worker* newspaper. By the early 1930s, Green's devotion to the cause had moved him into the YCL leadership, which took him to Germany and Moscow in 1932, and to the 1935 Seventh World Congress of the Communist International, also in Moscow, where he was elected to the executive committee and, later, secretariat—in short, into the upper echelon of the YCL. He was part of a trio of American communist leaders—the others were Foster and then–general secretary Earl Browder—who delivered an update on communist activities in the United States to the international gathering, and their glowing reports of making gains prompted a diplomatic protest by Ambassador William C. Bullitt over the Soviets' "flagrant violation of the pledge . . . to non-interference in the internal affairs of the United States."[24]

In 1936, Green traveled to Geneva, Switzerland, for a World Youth Conference and made a side trip to Spain, where civil war had broken out weeks before between the communist-backed Republicans and various right-wing and fascist rebel groups. Green returned to Spain a year later, under false papers and in violation of a State Department travel ban, and visited with members of the Abraham Lincoln Brigade, many of them fellow American communists volunteering to fight the fascist forces. Green's use of false names would become a key part of the case against him. And Thompson and Gates, with whom Green would be indicted, were part of the Brigade, though there's no indication their paths crossed in Spain.

Green's life wasn't all politics. Around 1927 he met Lillian Gannes, the Cleveland-born daughter of Russian immigrants who was also a young party activist (her brother, Harry Gannes, would eventually become foreign editor of the *Daily Worker*). They married a decade later, on March 12, 1937, and began having children despite warnings from Foster and others that the life of a communist revolutionary didn't leave much room for family.

The Greens made room, and managed to balance out their lives. During the war years Green rose to state party chair in New York, and in 1944 he was elected national vice president of the Communist Political Association—the reorganized wartime version of the party. But at war's end Green sided with Browder in the showdown with Moscow and, once Foster replaced Browder, was sent back to Chicago to be Illinois state chair. It wasn't a complete exile. Green still spoke at national conventions and was quoted in the newspapers. But he tended to toe the party line, urging the United States to share its atomic bomb technology with other nations—notably the Soviet Union—because he believed such a military monopoly was dangerous for the world. And he urged a resumption of wartime rationing so Americans could share their food largesse with impoverished nations.[25] In the spring of 1947 Green ran for mayor of Chicago on the Communist Party line, part of a crowded field of candidates. When the polls closed, Green's vote tally barely registered. Despite their work, their international travels, and their visions of forging a new America, Green and his colleagues were living on the political margins.

But did they represent a threat? Leaving aside for the moment the First Amendment problems with the Smith Act, the political organization the twelve men led was not exactly finely tuned;

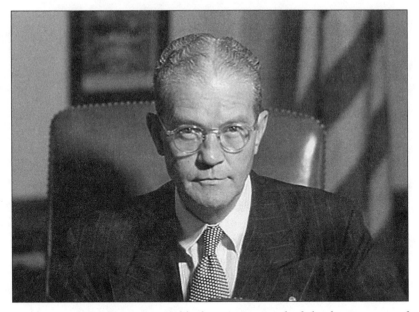

4. John F. X. McGohey was tapped by his superiors at the federal Department of Justice to handle the Smith Act case after it became clear they could not obtain indictments of alleged spies based on Bentley's revelations. WPA Film Library. Image courtesy of MPI Home Video.

nor was it a mass movement. In a nation of just under 150 million people, Communist Party membership peaked at about eighty thousand—a negligible voting bloc. And the party members were far from radicalized worker battalions. Fewer than a third were laborers or industrial workers; most were white-collar workers, and about half lived in the New York City area—not the kind of distribution or national penetration likely to gel into an armed uprising. The party was unstable, too: Membership turnover was about one-third per year, exacerbating organizing problems. As the British historian David Caute summed up the case against Green, Foster, Dennis, and the others, "The government took a sledgehammer to squash a gnat."[26]

McGohey, the prosecutor, wanted the trial to begin in October, which supporters of the indicted men viewed as further evidence that Truman—trailing Dewey in the polls—engineered their indictment in a cynical attempt to woo voters in the November election.

Republicans and other critics were trying to paint Truman as soft on communism, alleging that many of the New Dealers still in government service were closeted Reds. Two days after the indictments, Rushmore, the former party member turned anti-communist columnist for Hearst's *New York Journal-American*, testified before a Washington state legislative committee that the nation's capital was riddled with communists, apparently taking his cue from Bentley's reported revelations to the federal grand jury in New York City. "Units have been set up in Government buildings, including the State department," Rushmore said. "Workers deliver copies of the document to 'cell leaders' who relay the material to reliable messengers to the Soviet Embassy."[27] He stopped short of waving a list of supposed names, but Rushmore's testimony followed a template similar to the one Sen. Joseph McCarthy would use three years later.

Rushmore wasn't the only one talking about communists in high places. On July 31, Bentley took the stand publicly before the HUAC and repeated the basics of the story she had told the grand jury, which had been published in the New York papers. Chambers followed a few days later with a "rather flamboyant description of his years as a communist revolutionary, his subsequent change of heart, and his new role as the defender of America against Communism."[28] Chambers reinforced much of Bentley's testimony, including identifying Assistant Treasury Secretary Harry Dexter White, whom Bentley had named as a spy, as a communist. He added a few other names of people he said he remembered from his days within the party, including Alger Hiss, a former top State Department official who had a significant role in establishing the United Nations, participating in the Dumbarton Oaks Conference, the wartime meeting of the Allied leaders—Roosevelt, Churchill, and Stalin—at Yalta, and the founding convention in San Francisco. Hiss, Chambers told the HUAC, was a communist assigned to infiltrate the top levels of the U.S. government. Several of the people Chambers named were also Wallace campaign advisers, fueling conservative beliefs that the Progressives were closet communists.

"The purpose of this group at that time was not primarily espionage," Chambers testified. "Its original purpose was the communist infiltration of the American government. But espionage was certainly one of its eventual objectives. Let no one be surprised at this statement. Disloyalty is a matter of principle with every member of the Communist Party. The Communist Party exists for the specific purpose of overthrowing the government, by any and all means, and each of its members, by the fact that he is a member, is dedicated to this purpose."[29] But the people he named were not spies, he said.[30]

The incendiary allegations only added to the political furor, leaving the White House scrambling. In a press conference the day after Chambers's first hours of testimony, Truman dismissed the hearings as a "red herring" tossed out by the Republicans, who controlled Congress, to divert attention from economic proposals he was pushing.

"No information has been revealed that has not long since been presented to a federal grand jury," Truman said in a statement. "No information has been disclosed in the past few days by Congressional committees that has not long been known by the Federal Bureau of Investigation. The Federal grand jury found this information insufficient to justify indictment of the Federal employees involved. All but two of the employees involved have left the Federal government and these two have been placed on involuntary leave. The public hearings now underway are serving no useful purpose. On the contrary, they are doing irreparable harm to certain persons, seriously impairing the morale of federal employees, and undermining public confidence in the government."[31]

One of those who had already left the government was Hiss, who at the time of the HUAC hearing was president of the Carnegie Endowment for International Peace. He first learned of Chambers's allegations in phone calls from news reporters looking for comment. Chambers had barely mentioned Hiss—he focused on White in his testimony—but said that he had visited Hiss at home after his own rejection of communism and tried to "break him away from the party. As a matter of fact, he cried when we separated, when I left him, but he absolutely refused to break." Chambers testified that he was "very fond of Mr. Hiss."[32]

Hiss's initial inclination was to ignore Chambers's allegations as a nuisance. But the more he mulled it, the more he became convinced that he needed to respond to the committee itself; otherwise no one would believe his denial that he was working for the communists. Hiss had been hearing similar whispers for a couple of years, that the word around Washington was that he was a communist. This was his chance to face that down.[33]

Hiss voluntarily appeared before the HUAC two days later and denied Chambers's allegations that he had been an integral piece of a prewar organization to infiltrate communists into top federal positions. He also said he did not recognize Chambers's name and didn't believe he had ever seen the man whose picture was filling the newspapers, despite Chambers's claim that he had visited Hiss at home. Hiss did acknowledge knowing some of the other people Chambers had named, mostly through his work in government or as a lawyer.

After the hearing, Nixon, a freshman member of the committee, began digging deeper into Chambers's story and learned that he had used an alias—Carl—while a party member. Hiss, he realized, wouldn't have known Chambers by his real name. Nixon and a small contingent from the committee arranged to interview Chambers again, under oath, to explore how he had known Hiss; they arrived at the Foley Square federal courthouse sometime before 10:30 A.M. on Saturday, August 7. There, in the same building where the Communist Party leaders had been arraigned just two weeks before, Nixon gathered the bait for the trap that eventually led to Hiss's indictment on perjury charges—handed up by the same grand jury that had indicted Foster and the others—in a case that, for many, still defines the era.

While Nixon worked on Chambers, three of the indicted communist leaders—Green, Winter, and Hall—sought court permission to return to their homes in Chicago, Detroit, and Cleveland. On August 25, Unger, their lawyer, expanded the list of those who wanted the freedom to travel to include Foster, the chairman, Dennis, the general secretary, and Winston, the organizational secretary. But those defendants weren't looking to return to distant homes until the trial. They wanted to go back to work.

"As the leading officers of a national political party, our normal duties require us to travel in the various states of the Union for the purpose of carrying on the legitimate activities of the Communist Party," they said in a court filing. The petition also took aim at the indictment itself and indicated that they would fight the charges not just in court but in the media. "This indictment threatens the very existence of the political party which we have the honor to head. It is our duty, not only in defense of our persons, but in defense of our political party, that we discuss the issues in this case with our fellow citizens throughout the country, the nature of the charges against us having to do entirely with our political opinions, principles, doctrines, make this doubly necessary and appropriate. The enormous hostile newspaper and radio publicity against us and our party inevitably influences the course of this case. In fact, it has that precise purpose. We and the Communist Party cannot combat this through similar channels, since the press and the radio are not available to us."

They also said they needed to travel to raise money for their defense, and they scoffed at suggestions they might jump bail. They intended to wring every bit of publicity from the court battle they could. Further, they argued, to deny them the right to travel would also deny them the right to participate in the upcoming presidential election. "The Communist Party has repeatedly asserted that these indictments are part of the aim of the Republican and Democratic parties to carry out their political program which, if successful, would lead this country to fascism and to the brink of war. . . . More is at stake than our individual fates. We look upon this case as raising the most serious question that confronts a democratic people in this period—the issue whether people have the right to associate, form a political party of their choice, and to advocate its principles and programs without interference by the government. We are fighting the battle of constitutional democracy versus fascism, and there is no danger that we will have run away from that battle."[34]

McGohey had opposed letting any of the defendants leave the district unless they were traveling home, and Judge Samuel H. Kaufman, who handled the travel request filed on Hall's behalf, agreed. "What you are asking this court to do is license the activities of this defendant so that he may engage in the very activities the government complains about," Kaufman said. Unger fired back, "This court cannot license him to commit unlawful acts any more than it can limit his activities within this jurisdiction." He said Kaufman's decision was "tantamount to holding that an indictment is a conviction." Kaufman held firm and limited Hall's travel to the

Southern District of New York and Ohio. But Unger tweaked his argument, refiled it, and on September 9 persuaded Judge Simon H. Rifkind that there was no indication the men would flee and that, since there were no allegations of overt acts, there was no threat to public safety. The defendants were free to roam the continental United States.

For the first month or so of the proceedings, Unger worked largely alone. A cofounder of the National Lawyers Guild, Unger was a well-known Manhattan attorney with a long list of radical clients—from the Communist Party to the controversial Father Divine, a Harlem-based evangelical. As a staff attorney for the communist-dominated International Labor Defense (ILD) group in the 1930s, a predecessor to the CRC, Unger helped with pretrial preparations defending the Scottsboro Boys, nine young black men accused in Alabama of gang-raping two white women. The ILD's involvement in that long-running case marked a strategic landmark for the Communist Party, which took up the plight of African Americans at a time when many mainstream political organizations would not. In New York City, Unger also represented Department Store Employees Union Local 1250, which launched a sit-down strike in March 1937 against the Green and Woolworth chains. And in 1936 he ran unsuccessfully as the All Peoples Party candidate for a city judge post.

But it was clear that a dozen defendants would be more than one lawyer could handle. The day after the party leaders were arrested, the CRC convened a meeting in Manhattan and laid plans to raise money, draw unions and other progressive organizations together to defend against the government's action, and distribute two million handbills "to educate the public on Tom Clark and President Truman." The CRC was already on the attorney general's list of subversive organizations, and the group's alliance with the Communist Party would eventually destroy it.[35]

It took a while to build the legal defense team. On September 20, Harry Sacher of New York City—one of the nation's most highly respected trial attorneys—signed on to represent Gates, and Louis F. McCabe of Philadelphia agreed to handle Dennis's defense; he already was Dennis's lawyer in a contempt of Congress case after Dennis refused to testify in April 1947 before the HUAC.

Slowly, the rest of the team came together. On October 15 Abraham J. Isserman appeared as Williamson's attorney, and he later took up Green's case, too. He was followed on November 8 by San Francisco lawyer Richard Gladstein, representing Thompson. The last of the main lawyers to sign on was George W. Crockett Jr., a black lawyer from Detroit who first appeared November 17 on behalf of Winter, the Michigan defendant. Unger's partner, David M. Freedman; Crockett's friend from Detroit, Maurice Sugar; and Mary M. Kaufman of New York—all civil rights activists and members of the National Lawyers Guild—rounded out the defense. The last three rarely, if ever, spoke in court, though Freedman did handle some of the pretrial appearances.[36]

While Unger was the first lawyer to represent the defendants, he soon was replaced as lead counsel by Sacher, a high-profile figure in Manhattan legal circles who served both as a criminal defense lawyer and as attorney for a mix of leftist labor groups. In fact, two weeks before he signed on to the Smith Act case Sacher had been dismissed from his $8,500-a-year job as general counsel for the conservative Local 892, American Federation of Musicians, AFL, because of his leftist beliefs—the second such job he'd lost in the previous year as the union movement continued to oust communists, real and imagined.[37] With a slight build and a tempestuous, antagonistic courtroom style, Sacher had a reputation for occasionally defending his clients with a bit too much enthusiasm.[38]

Gladstein, of San Francisco, also had a history of defending leftists and was the longtime attorney for longshoremen's union leader Harry Bridges. The federal government had been trying to deport Bridges to his native Australia under the Immigration Act of October 16, 1918, which called for the expulsion of noncitizens who belonged to groups working against the U.S. government. In a case that reached the Supreme Court in 1945, Gladstein persuaded the judges that there was insufficient evidence that Bridges had been a communist, so he couldn't be deported—and, in fact, was eligible for citizenship.

Gladstein and Sacher were the most flamboyant of the defense attorneys—"actors," Isserman called them, and they often jockeyed for control of the defense team. McCabe was the most taciturn. A vice president of the National Lawyers Guild, he was a practicing Catholic and in the 1930s had chaired a church organization formed to oppose communism. Crockett, the team's only black lawyer, had a long background in labor law—he had served in the federal Department of Labor and also had represented the United Auto Workers. In 1951, he would open a practice in Detroit with Ernest Goodman—believed to be the first interracial law firm in the country. Crockett was also far outside the communist fold in his own political beliefs. In fact, he had debated political ideas with Winter, his new client, three months earlier in Detroit.[39]

The Belgian-born Isserman also was a longtime attorney for leftist unions and labor agitators. In the 1930s his clients ranged from radical activist Edith Berkman, who fought a deportation order after she helped lead the 1931 Lawrence Textile Strike, to the North New Jersey CIO. He waged legal challenges to anti-picketing ordinances and filed suit against Roosevelt's Works Progress Administration, arguing that its beneficiaries were not aid recipients but federal employees entitled to accrue vacation and other employee benefits. He also served for a time as counsel for the American Civil Liberties Union. He resigned in 1941 after the ACLU ousted Elizabeth Gurley Flynn as a communist and then blocked Isserman's renomination to the board of directors unless he gave his word that he did not belong to a "totalitarian" organization.[40] The year before signing on to the Smith Act case, Isserman defended Gerhart Eisler in a high-profile passport fraud trial in which the German native was accused of hiding his role as the Soviets' top agent in the United States. Eisler skipped bail and slipped out of the country by stowing away on a Polish freighter—which would fuel fears about the twelve indicted men.[41] He eventually became a top East German propaganda official.

Although the defendants were all charged with the same crimes, stemming from the same events, there was only loose agreement on how to fight the government's charges. And with that many lawyers, there were plenty of ideas—and egos. Gladstein wanted to challenge the jury selection process that led to the indictment, believing that the federal system drew potential jurors primarily from the upper classes and from white neighborhoods, thus violating the constitutional guarantee of due process. He saw that as part of a broad and aggressive attack on the foundations of the government's case. Isserman wanted to follow the template of Bulgarian commu-nist Georgi Dimitrov, whose calm demeanor and piercing questions

5. Defendants Jacob Stachel (back row, left), Irving Potash, Carl Winter, Benjamin Davis Jr., John Gates, Gil Green, Robert Thompson (front row, left), Henry Winston, Eugene Dennis, Gus Hall, and John Williamson. WPA Film Library. Image courtesy of MPI Home Video.

as his own defense attorney helped win a surprise acquittal in a Nazi show trial after the 1933 burning of the Reichstag. At another point Isserman lobbied the legal team to quit en masse, arguing that the trial was about politics, not criminal acts, and thus the lawyers were unable to mount a defense. When that was rejected, he decided, with Crockett, to focus on building a strong appeal by making sure the defense followed court procedures and filed proper and detailed objections to give the appeals court issues to chew on. McCabe suggested another tack. He wanted to focus on the witnesses, attacking their credibility by painting them as spies and turncoats more interested in justifying their own actions than in testifying truthfully. Sacher zeroed in on the core argument: that the defendants were engaged in constitutionally protected political activities.

But the overriding factor in establishing the tone of the defense came from the defendants themselves. They micromanaged, and some three decades later Gladstein said the defendants "should

never have had lawyers at all; they should have defended themselves." The defense lawyers "were not our own masters," and the
defendants insisted even on editing Gladstein's eventual summation
to the jury.[42]

Ultimately, the defendants believed that they were guilty of
nothing. The government was twisting the decades-old words of
Marx, Lenin, and Stalin—written in radically different political
climates—to conclude that the modern American Communist Party
was bent on armed revolt. It was a political trial, they believed, so
they decided to defend their politics. They ordered their lawyers
to counter the government's case argument by argument. When the
government cited an excerpt from a work by Marx, the defense
would offer a fuller explanation of what Marx meant. The court
battle would become a literal war of words—and interpretations
of the evolution of the Communist Party.

FOUR

The Judge,
and the Mood

As the size of the defense team grew, so too did the scope of their arguments, and the legal papers flew. Several judges had handled the early shotgun blasts of motions and proceedings, from bail hearings and arraignments to the requests for permission to travel. On August 16, Judge Harold Raymond Medina, whom Truman had appointed to the bench the previous summer, got his first taste of the case—a fairly routine request from Unger seeking an extension of the length of time he had to file motions. Unger wanted ninety days instead of the usual thirty. Medina, unfamiliar with the case, asked to see a copy of the indictment. He later professed to have been stunned to see that the case involved allegations of teaching revolution.[1]

Unger told Medina he needed the time because he planned to challenge the constitutionality of the 1940 Smith Act, which would raise issues that "have been recognized as perhaps the most important types of cases upon which the court can pass. This case presents such issues perhaps to a greater degree than any that has come before the court in a hundred years." He also said he

56

planned to seek dismissal of the indictments because leaks to the press may have influenced the jurors to indict where the evidence didn't warrant it. "It is a matter of public record that there has been a concerted aim on the part of many forces to outlaw the Communist Party by hook or by crook; the newspaper columns are full of evidence of this lawless purpose."[2]

Medina rejected Unger's assertion that the news leaks might have influenced the grand jurors and said the legal issues, despite Unger's claim of complexity and historical heft, were straightforward. He also made it clear that the presumption of innocence was a formality. "I think the case is important to these defendants, but I think the interests of the government and the people are a little more important," Medina said. "If the difficulty and complexity has to do with this idea of overthrowing the government by force, I should think that public policy might require that the matter be given prompt attention and not just held off indefinitely where perhaps there may be more of these fellows up to that sort of thing." Unger argued that the indictment did not allege that violent acts had been planned or talked about, but Medina cut him off. "No, they want to wait until they get everything set and then the acts will come," Medina said. "The quicker this case gets disposed of with finality, the better for all concerned." He also accused the defendants of using "weasel words" to mask their intentions. He denied the ninety-day extension and gave the defense until September 27 to file their motions.[3]

A week later, Medina ordered the trial to begin on October 15, eliciting howls of protest from Unger. But Medina said the case was "just another criminal case and I don't see why it should be treated differently." Unger argued that it was a politically motivated set of charges, and a speedy trial served political ends, not judicial ends. Medina warned him to stick to legal arguments and once again cut him off when he accused Medina of setting the October date "to suit himself." "Just a minute," Medina interrupted. "I recommend to you that you leave out those cracks. They are extremely offensive to me. I get these little innuendoes very quickly and I don't like them."

Medina's comments prompted the *Daily Worker* to publish an

6. Judge Harold R. Medina in his chambers on the first day jurors were questioned in the trial. The Smith Act trial would be his first criminal case as a federal judge, and the friction between him and the defense team helped define the case. Associated Press/Anthony Camerano.

editorial denouncing him—which Medina privately found amusing. "Things have been very hectic for me in the court house; and it looks as though this week would be even tougher," he wrote to his brother, Richard Medina, in Fairlee, Vermont, on August 23. "I am managing to survive, however, and now have the distinction of an editorial against me by the *Daily Worker*, which I have not seen yet, but which I am informed says in effect that I am the worst Judge in the United States. Quite a compliment, considering the source."[4]

Although Medina's letters and his autobiographical writings contain no overt declarations of prejudice, there are enough comments like the "considering the source" and his in-court reference to the defendants in effect biding their time to act to suggest he was less than the dispassionate judge he thought himself to be. In fact, he was proud of his performance during a court hearing earlier in the year. In March, Medina was one of three federal judges to hear unrelated writs of habeas corpus filed by several communists—including Irving Potash, one of the current defendants—being held without bail as they appealed deportation orders over their communist affiliations.[5] In a private letter to fellow Princeton alumnus Ripley Ropes, a lawyer in Meredith, New Hampshire, Medina bragged that "things have been most exciting here in my court and I had one very thrilling day in connection with one of these alleged communists who was before me on a writ of habeas corpus. There must have been about a thousand people in the courtroom, including a large number of cops and FBI men in disguise and I can tell you that the sparks were flying. I really gave the guy the works and I wouldn't have been surprised if one of the spectators had pulled out a gun and taken a shot at me."[6]

Medina's reputation with fellow jurists was mixed. Supreme Court Justice Felix Frankfurter privately described Medina, whom he had first encountered as an appeals lawyer, as "the most insufferable egotist by long odds" ever to appear before him.[7] And Medina made an art of subtle self-aggrandizement, reveling in anecdotes that on the surface held him up as the butt of a joke but that on a deeper level affirmed his sense that he always knew better than anyone else how best to resolve a situation.[8]

Barrel-chested and always meticulously dressed, he was compared by journalists at the time with Hollywood actor Adolphe Menjou, who had named names before the HUAC and was a member of the Motion Picture Alliance for the Preservation of American Ideals, composed of conservative Hollywood figures eager to aid in expelling communist influences from entertainment.[9] Medina was conscious of his image—he hired a clipping service to keep track of coverage of his cases—and, once he ascended the bench, lent a theatrical flair to the courtroom. He relished engaging with the lawyers before him and used a strong hand in moving trials and proceedings along—including rephrasing questions for witnesses when he thought it might help clarify a point—and "had a powerful personality with ego to match."[10]

In October, Southern District Chief Judge John C. Knox decided to assign the case and its flood of motions to a single judge who would also preside over any eventual trial. Knox settled on Medina. A fawning post-trial biography, *Judge Medina*, by Hawthorne Daniel, attributed the selection to Medina's physical hardiness and the fact that he was not Catholic, and thus presumably not susceptible to Vatican opposition to communism. It's more likely that as one of the newest judges on the bench, Medina was predestined to get the short straw in what everyone expected to be a long, arduous trial. Knox knew how Medina worked—he had once assigned Medina to represent a client before the Supreme Court in a high-profile treason case. At the time Knox picked Medina for the Smith Act case, the former appeals lawyer was a virtual unknown outside New York City law circles. That would change quickly.

Medina was born in Brooklyn on February 16, 1888, to Joaquin A. Medina, who had emigrated from Mexico's Yucatán city of Mérida, and Elizabeth Fash, "from an old Dutch colonial family" in the New York City area.[11] The elder Medina, born in 1858, grew up in a well-to-do plantation family, which had sent him at age fourteen to boarding school at Seton Hall in South Orange, New Jersey. Three years later, after graduating, he returned to the family plantation in Mérida but chafed under his autocratic father. He ran away, back to New York City, and landed a job as an office and errand boy for R. H. Allen & Co., which made agricultural tools. He quickly learned the import-export side of the business. After becoming a naturalized citizen in 1880,[12] Medina started a small side business filling hardware and grocery export orders for friends in Mérida, which he eventually built into the highly successful J. A. Medina Company, handling soap for a predecessor of Colgate-Palmolive and yeast for Fleischmann, among others. At the same time, he imported Yucatán sisal fiber, used for making twine. In 1922, as the Mexican revolution disrupted much of his export business, he began importing coffee from Central America, which came to be the firm's dominant business until it merged with the Anderson Clayton Company in 1955.

In 1886, Medina married Elizabeth Fash, the sister of a friend; he had first met her when they roomed near each other in Brooklyn, and she had worked for him for a time. Medina's success came with rewards—he raised his family in a three-story brownstone at 273 Jefferson Avenue in Brooklyn (now the heart of Bedford-Stuyvesant) in the neighborhood where his wife had grown up.[13] The family employed a live-in Irish housekeeper, as did most of the families on their street.[14]

The younger Medina was an occasionally mischievous boy who

once threw dirt on a chocolate cake a neighbor was cooling on a windowsill. "The lady wrote an awful letter," his mother recalled. Harold Medina attended P.S. 44 at Throop Avenue and Monroe Street, near Putnam Avenue, which he later held up as "a cross-section of America." "Every nationality was represented at that school," he said. "I'm grateful to P.S. 44. You understand America only if you live with its varied people." But it wasn't exactly a mini United Nations. Medina was ten years old when the Spanish-American War broke out, and his Spanish surname made him a schoolyard target. He recalled other kids calling him "greaser," and his inevitable response: a fight.

Medina didn't stay among the "varied people" very long. A bright and ambitious student, he moved from P.S. 44 to Holbrook Military Academy, a military school in Ossining, then on to Princeton University, where he excelled in modern languages and won admission to the Phi Beta Kappa academic honor society, captained the fencing team, made the swim team, and was goalie for the water polo squad before graduating summa cum laude in 1909. He contemplated a career teaching languages but became engaged to Ethel Forde Hillyer of East Orange, New Jersey (they married June 6, 1911), and decided a law career would bring in more money.[15] So Medina went on to Columbia University and earned his law degree in 1912. He was active in alumni efforts, including fund-raising, for Columbia (where he would eventually teach) and Princeton, but even late in life he considered himself a Princeton man first, maintaining regular contact with fellow members of the Class of '09. At the time he was assigned the Smith Act case, Medina was deeply involved in arranging for the class's fortieth reunion the next summer. Both of his sons would eventually attend Princeton, too, and follow him into law.

And the law was good to Medina. He joined the law firm Davies, Auerbach & Cornell directly from Columbia, moving from the Upper West Side to downtown, at 34 Nassau Street, between City Hall and Wall Street. By 1918 he had stepped out and opened his own practice. A loyal Democrat, he worked on various committees to help get Democratic judges elected, though he seemed to stay out of nonjudicial campaigns.[16] His law practice evolved into handling mostly appeals, and he became the attorney to whom other lawyers brought their "tough work."[17] But he made his biggest mark as the founder of a tutoring dynasty, helping law school graduates cram for the bar exam. At the time he was named a federal judge, at age sixty, Medina was making somewhere between $85,000 and $100,000 a year ($835,000 to $982,000 in 2008 dollars). Most of it was from the tutoring business.

Medina enjoyed the money. He and his wife had an apartment at 14 East Seventy-fifth Street but considered home a fifty-five-acre compound on Westhampton's Apaucuck Point at the edge of Moriches Bay. Medina bought the land in 1923, and his first house, which he named "Windward," was completed there in 1925. The house, along with his fifteen-thousand-volume collection of books, was lost in the Great Hurricane of 1938. Medina rebuilt, calling the new mansion "Still to Windward," and added a house each for his two sons and their families and another for his mother, who was ninety-one at the time of the trial. A few hundred feet from the main house, on the far side of his wife's elaborate garden, Medina built a separate library for himself, more of an academic lawyer's playhouse than a den. There was one room for his law books (including a 245-volume "stout, specially bound" collection of his appeals cases), another for his rebuilt collection of Greek, Latin, French, and English texts, and a third for his billiards table.[18]

Despite Medina's self-perception as a tolerant man of the world, there are clues that he was hungriest for status. He played billiards once a week at the University Club, was an avid golfer at a private club in the Hamptons (at least twice winning the President's Cup in club tournaments), took regular sailing trips on his yacht, *Spindrift II*, to Cape Cod, where he would meet up with other Princeton alums, and made a show of being present at the key Princeton football games. He and his wife often vacationed over Christmas in Bermuda or the Virgin Islands.[19] After the Smith Act trial Medina would waver publicly between spending a month or two in Southern California or Florida. He eventually picked Bermuda, where the Medinas had the loan of an admirer's sailing boat and guest passes at private country clubs. Medina complained in letters to friends about the grueling nature of the job as a federal judge. "They have me tied hand and foot here and I shall be lucky if I squeeze a few days of vacation sometime in September for a little trip in my boat up to the Cape," he wrote in August. "This is beyond all question the damnedest job in the world." Still, he managed to get out on the golf course at least three days a week to work on his game.[20]

The upper-class normalcy of Medina's career and the trappings of his private life obscure an unusual and seldom noted element. When he was appointed to the bench, Medina became a ground-breaking rarity for the era: an Ivy League–trained Mexican American federal judge.

Judge Knox's selection of Medina to preside over the Smith Act trial was not a popular choice with the defense lawyers, who assumed he got the case because of his strong anti-communist beliefs.[21] Unger immediately challenged the decision, arguing that Medina displayed his prejudice during the August 16 motion hearing on whether the defendants could travel. Medina, not surprisingly, denied Unger's motion that he recuse himself and rejected the argument that he couldn't be impartial. "Had I been conscious of any personal bias, or prejudice against the defendants, or any sign, I would, without waiting for any suggestion by counsel or the filing of any affidavit, have disqualified myself when the case first came before me," Medina said.[22] But it wouldn't be the last time the defense would challenge Medina's impartiality, and the ruling helped cement a rancorous relationship between the defense lawyers and Medina that defined the trial to come. "My guess is that he had all the prejudices of his class," Isserman, one of the defense lawyers, said years after the trial. "I think he was probably oblivious to it."[23]

Outside the courtroom, a propaganda war was raging. Anti-communist papers, such as the *New York World-Telegram*, savaged the defendants while the *Daily Worker* portrayed them as heroes of the people and targets of a Truman-directed political witch-hunt. In late August, the paper focused on Davis, already well known as the only elected black communist member of the New York City Council. Davis first won office in 1943, taking the seat Adam Clayton Powell vacated to run for Congress, on a campaign to end police brutality against his black neighbors in Harlem and to outlaw real estate covenants that precluded the sale of homes to blacks and other minorities. Davis was a dignified-looking man, a poised and forceful orator. A few nights after their arrests, Davis,

Winston, and Stachel were the main speakers at a street rally at Lenox Avenue and 125th Street, where they railed against the indictments as a calibrated political maneuver by, as Davis said, "that pipsqueak Truman."[24]

The *Daily Worker* also profiled Thompson under the headline "How a Communist Defended America." Thompson, in fact, was an American war hero. A veteran of the Spanish Civil War, Thompson enlisted in the U.S. Army to fight Nazis but was deployed to New Guinea instead, as a staff sergeant in Company C, 127th Infantry, 32nd Division. Thompson saw extensive combat and won the Distinguished Service Cross—second only to the Congressional Medal of Honor—after risking his life to help his patrol of five men cross the swollen Konombi River near Tarakena.[25] According to an eyewitness account by Tally Doyle Fulmer, a second lieutenant in the same division, Thompson slipped alone into the river dragging a line and swam, under enemy fire, to the far side, which held "a heavily fortified position. . . . Clad only in shorts, armed with a pistol and three hand grenades, Sergeant Thompson alone remained under cover of the hostile bank, in order to direct the crossing of his platoon. With utter disregard to his personal safety, he not only directed the crossing of his platoon but led them in successful attack against two dominating pillboxes, thereby securing a small bridgehead."[26] What the Japanese soldiers couldn't do, disease did. Thompson was sent home in 1943 after being debilitated by malaria and tuberculosis.

At home, Thompson faced a different kind of enemy. Three months after the Smith Act indictment, a little after midnight on September 22, Thompson left his garden apartment at 3940 Forty-sixth Street in Sunnyside, Queens, to walk a couple of blocks to 3977 Forty-fourth Street and meet with William Norman, secretary of the party's New York State branch; Thompson was the state chair. Thompson, who was six feet two inches tall and weighed 190 pounds, noticed a car following him and assumed it was the FBI, whose agents had made no secret of their surveillance of the twelve defendants. When Thompson cut down an alley as a shortcut, at least two men hopped from the car and caught up with him. One grabbed at him as the other swung something at Thompson's head, stunning him momentarily and knocking him to the ground. Thompson clambered back to his feet, punching at his attackers until one of them stabbed him in the upper left abdomen. The assailants ran off, leaving Thompson bleeding on the ground.

Thompson regained his footing and made his way to Norman's house, where Dr. Joseph Shapiro, who lived a couple of blocks away on Forty-sixth Street, was summoned to treat a one-and-a-half-inch cut. Thompson also suffered bruises and a concussion, injuries Shapiro described as "unpleasant but not serious." Thompson said he was carrying about seventy-five dollars in cash that the men made no effort to take. A $15,000 reward was offered for information, but no one was ever arrested, and police officials told reporters that there were "inconsistencies" in Thompson's statement to them and that he had refused hospital treatment—intimating they suspected Thompson may have staged the attack and suggesting that they had little intention of investigating the incident.

The party blamed the attack on public backlash over the indictments and released a copy of a threatening letter postmarked September 21 and mailed to the party headquarters. "If war starts with Russia I will go gunning for the bigwigs in this country. I read the papers. I got names and addresses. I'll pay those bastards a visit." The letter went on to threaten to "shoot, poison and burn them." It was one of dozens of such letters the party said it had received, as well as threatening phone calls.[27]

Despite his injuries—or perhaps because of them—Thompson was one of the main speakers at a "Smash the Frame-Up" rally the next night at Madison Square Garden that drew some twelve thousand people. The attack on Thompson became the main subject of the night, with Norman, the state party secretary Thompson was walking to visit, telling the crowd "the hand that wielded the knife was the hand of a low-down scoundrel, but the brain that incited and directed it is to be found in the high circles of finance capital." The event was billed in part as a campaign appearance for Simon Gerson, a party member and publicist running for New York City Council from Brooklyn, who spoke first for about fifteen minutes.

The party had bought a half-hour slot on the American Broadcasting Company's WJZ radio station to air the rally, but the station cut the broadcast short as Davis, the indicted council member, linked the attack on Thompson to a national mood of anticommunist hysteria. "Red-baiting haspassed over into the stage of violence, of physical brutality at the hands of storm troopers who have become drunk and inflamed by the vile campaign of war hysteria and red-baiting now assaulting the American people through the monopoly press and the monopoly controlled radio." Davis complained about being cut off the air, but the station said it had sold the time for Gerson's campaign speech, not the rally—a spurious excuse, since the time was paid for.[28]

There were other rallies as well, many of them organized around the country by the CRC to gin up political support for the defendants—while, presumably, pressuring the prosecution—and to raise money for the defense. In Philadelphia, some seventy-five people picketed outside the federal courthouse, and other throngs marched in front of the White House in Washington, D.C. In Chicago, Pearl Hart, a cofounder of the National Lawyers Guild and a state leader (and occasional candidate) of the Progressive Party, led a rally at 116 South Michigan Avenue, near Grant Park. "If you are progressive, if you believe in the Bill of Rights, if you believe in your right for political action, do not be tricked into believing that this is an attack on the communists," Hart said in the flyer announcing the rally. "The first attack is directed toward the communists. The next attack will be against you." Another Chicago meeting was scheduled as a fund-raiser for the defendants, featuring the CRC's William L. Patterson.[29]

On September 22, a delegation from the CRC tried to take the issue inside the White House. The closest they got to the Oval Office was meetings with aide Philleo Nash, Truman's special assistant for minority affairs (he would later repel attacks by Sen. Joseph McCarthy that he was a communist), and Raymond Whearty of the Justice Department's internal security office (one of the government lawyers who obtained the perjury indictment against Hiss). The delegation urged the president to dismiss the Smith Act indictments and instead order the prosecution of "those who use legalized force and violence in an effort to destroy labor's right to organize, bargain collectively and to strike." Nash told the delegation he "would convey their request to the president"—a polite brush-off.[30]

In fact, Truman had no intention of intervening. For weeks, the Republicans had been trying to paint his administration as soft on communism, seeing that as the key wedge issue to try to dislodge him from office. Hovering in the background was the fear of another war, this time with Russia. In 1947, pollster George Gallup reported that the nation's postwar economy was the top issue on voters' minds, in the wake of the lifting of price controls and the resulting spike in the cost of a wide range of basic goods. By April 1948, as the cold war intensified, fears of another shooting war emerged as the top issue, with 38 percent of respondents listing "avoiding war" as their main concern and 27 percent listing "getting along with Russia." Communism ranked fifth, with 7 percent—just behind high prices and inflation at 8 percent.[31] Even so, with the newspapers and radio filled with reports of spies and secret communists infiltrating Washington, arguing about who would be the communists' tougher nemesis—Truman or Dewey—became an undercurrent of the campaign.

Truman had already dismissed the hunt for communists as a "red herring" the Republicans were using to take the focus off the economy. But Dewey, on a swing through California in late September, accused Truman of ignoring a crisis. Speaking before a packed Hollywood Bowl on September 24—stars such as Gary Cooper, Ginger Rogers, Hedda Hopper, Charles Coburn, and Harold Perry were in the audience—Dewey said that the American "way of life is . . . being challenged and threatened. A vast, disciplined worldwide organization of unscrupulous men is bent upon the wholesale perversion of the loyalties of people everywhere, abroad and right here at home." Dewey made a direct plea to Hollywood—whose support was going primarily to Truman and Wallace—to reject communist propaganda about a workers' paradise in the Soviet Union and to focus on combating lies with truth. He accused Truman of "shutting his eyes to the rampant evil" of communism with his "red herring" comment. But Dewey also said the best way to combat communism domestically was through an open approach to politics and dialogue. "We must neither ignore the communists nor outlaw them. If we ignore them, we give them the cloak of immunity they want. If we outlaw them, we give them the martyrdom they want even more. . . . In this country we'll have no thought police. We will not jail anybody for what he thinks or believes." He called for a campaign of truth and insisted that the ideals of American democracy would win out in the political process.[32]

Truman, trailing in the polls, responded four days later in Oklahoma City, downplaying the scope of communists' political strength in the United States while simultaneously blaming the Republicans for policies that would make it easier for communism to grow. "I regret to say that there are some people in the Republican Party who are trying to create the false impression that communism is a powerful force in American life. These Republicans know that this is not true. . . . Our government is not endangered by communist infiltration. It has preserved its integrity, and it will continue to preserve its integrity as long as I am president." But the Republican Congress, he said, was making the soil richer for communism by rejecting legislation he had proposed to enhance housing, health care, education, and Social Security. "This is the best way to kill communism at its roots. People who are well-fed, well-clothed, well-housed, and whose basic rights are protected, do not become victims of communism."

Truman cited his loyalty program as proof that the communist menace was overblown. "Only in the case of one in six thousand Government employees has loyalty been found doubtful," Truman said. Left unsaid, though, was why Truman felt compelled to subject some two million federal employees to the loyalty test in the first place.[33]

On November 9—a week after Truman surprised everyone but himself and won reelection—McGohey announced that he had summoned three hundred people to the Foley Square courthouse the next week to serve as potential jurors in the trial, which was scheduled to begin November 15. That start date, however, was written in sand. The same day as McGohey's announcement, the defense team was arguing before the U.S. Court of Appeals that Medina had erred in denying the motion that he recuse himself, and Gladstein had already indicated the defense planned to challenge the jury selection process itself.

A more pressing issue was Foster's health. Foster had suffered a heart attack in 1932, which forced him to step down as the party leader, replaced by Browder. The attack was debilitating—Foster spent the next four or five years recuperating (most of it in the Soviet Union) and by the late 1930s had resumed his normal life with unspecified physical restrictions. In the early morning hours of September 2, Foster was awakened by "a tingly and numb feeling in his entire right side including his face, mouth and extremities, accompanied by weakness of said extremities." Dr. Louis Finger, a wonderfully named cardiologist at Harlem Hospital, was summoned to the Fosters' apartment in the Bronx. Foster told him that he had suffered a similar attack the week before but recovered quickly and that a physician who looked at him then had "diagnosed the condition as a spasm of the cerebral blood vessels." Foster, the head of the CPUSA and the lead defendant in the case, had suffered two strokes.[34]

Finger examined Foster and found "a marked hypertension, some weakness of the right upper and lower extremities, and considerable sensory disturbances involving the right side of the face and the right upper and lower extremities. These findings indicated that damage had been done to the brain as a result of a cerebrovascular accident." Finger ordered bed rest for the month of September and minimal movement afterward. On October 27, he examined Foster again and concluded the attacks were a result of his "extreme degree of arteriosclerosis and markedly high blood pressure." He called in three specialists: Dr. Foster Kennedy, the chief of neurological service at Bellevue and a neurology professor at Cornell; Dr. Leo M. Davidoff, a professor of neurological surgery at Columbia University and chief of neurological surgery at Montefiore Hospital; and Dr. Alexander Wolf, another Manhattan neurologist. After they all weighed in, Finger told the court Foster was too frail to go on trial. "For at least the next three months Mr. Foster's condition requires complete rest, that he be at bed rest for most of the day, and that he go out only for short airings preferably by car riding once or twice a day." Finger warned that "any breach of the routine . . . will create a strong probability of a recurrence of the cerebrovascular accident which would probably be more severe than the last one and which may even prove fatal."

Medina wasn't willing to take the defense's word for the state of Foster's health. He assigned two physicians—Henry Alsop Riley of Columbia Presbyterian Medical Center and Cary Eggleston of New York Hospital—to examine Foster and review Finger's diagnosis. They agreed with Finger, and on November 12 Medina postponed the start of the trial, eventually pushing it back to January 17, well after the holidays, in hopes that Foster's health would stabilize and he could be tried with the rest of the defendants. Medina noted that McGohey had said he would be ready to proceed then with or without Foster, and the judge volunteered that he would consider severing Foster's case "at such time as the matter is presented to me for decision"—all but inviting McGohey to file the motion.[35]

Medina was also concerned about his own health. Though he was hale and hearty, he was well aware that one of the two earlier uses of the Smith Act probably sent a judge to an early grave.

The government first invoked the Smith Act in 1941, when twenty-nine Minneapolis unionists—most of them Trotskyites—were indicted in the midst of a brutal Teamsters' union fight. The case was perceived in many quarters as President Roosevelt doing a favor for a political friend. Dan Tobin, the longtime leader of the International Brotherhood of Teamsters, was facing a rebellion from leftists leading Minneapolis Local 544. Most of the trouble was coming from members of the Socialist Workers Party, who had gained some political clout within the union after the successful 1934 Teamsters strike that paralyzed Minneapolis and much of the upper Midwest (a defining event in the evolution of the Teamsters into the national force it was to become). Tobin had tried to oust the Trotskyites but backed down in the face of their local popularity and support from other Minneapolis-area unions. He parsed the union rules oddly to do that. The Teamsters' constitution barred communists from being in the union, which Tobin eventually declared meant that only Stalinist communists were barred—the Trotskyites were all right. But by 1941, with war in the wind, Tobin wanted the Teamsters' board to sign off on a "war-preparedness" program, and he feared the Trotskyites, who opposed war, would cause trouble. So they had to go.[36]

Tobin worked with a group of Local 544 dissidents, who called themselves the Committee of 99 and were mostly politically ambitious and disenchanted socialists. The group met and passed a resolution asking the Teamsters International to step in and take over the local. The opposition Trotskyites were led by the Dunne brothers—Vince, Miles, and Grant—who caught wind of the maneuver and mounted a preemptive strike, seceding from the Teamsters and seeking to align themselves with the local CIO. A full-scale local labor war broke out—this was where Jimmy

Hoffa, a young Detroit organizer, honed his skills. In the midst of the battle, Tobin asked Roosevelt for help, charging that union subversives were targeting him because he supported FDR in the 1940 election. Roosevelt obliged.[37]

In June, the Socialist Workers Party offices were raided by the FBI, and the indictments came in July. The ACLU saw it as a blatant political move, not a response to criminal behavior, and pointed out that the only change in Local 544 since the 1934 strike was the assertion of control by the Teamsters International. It cited communication from Tobin to Roosevelt stating that "we feel that while our country is in a dangerous position those disturbers who believe in the policies of foreign, radical governments, must in some way be prevented from pursuing this dangerous course." But the Dunne brothers and their fellow Trotskyites weren't following any foreign radical government.

"It seems reasonable to conclude that the government injected itself into the inter-union controversy in order to promote the interests of the one side which supported the administration's foreign and domestic policies," the ACLU concluded. "Our conclusion is reinforced by the fact that it has been a matter of common knowledge for some years that the Socialist Workers Party, an insignificant little group of extremists, has been strongly represented in the Minneapolis labor movement—alone of any city in the country. Nothing charged in the indictment is of recent origin. The situation in Minneapolis is no different now from that obtaining over the past five or ten years."

In the ensuing trial, the FBI revealed that it had been working clandestinely with the Committee of 99 to try to oust the Trotskyites. The evidence led the judge to dismiss the charges against five defendants, and the jury acquitted five others, including Miles Dunne. Grant Dunne had shot himself to death a couple of weeks before the trial began.[38] The rest of the defendants were convicted on December 2—five days before the attack on Pearl Harbor—and sentenced to up to eighteen months in federal prison. The Trotskyite menace was destroyed. The CPUSA—following the Moscow line on the Stalin-Trotsky split—applauded the government's prosecution of the Minneapolis radicals, an ironic stance given the case that would later emerge against them.

The Smith Act was again invoked in 1942, this time in a high-profile move against fascists in Washington, D.C.—another use of the law propelled more by personal desire than a need to criminalize behavior. This time Roosevelt, antagonized by right-wing critics, prodded the Justice Department to act against Nazi sympathizers in the United States. It obtained indictments against a roster of pro-Nazi activists, and after a couple of years of wrangling over the legal weakness of the original indictment, the trial—with twenty-six defendants—opened in Washington, D.C., in April 1944. It immediately dissolved into an uncontrollable farce, with Judge Edward C. Eicher proving incapable of corralling the proceedings. After seven months, the prosecution still had not finished presenting its case, and on November 30, 1944, Eicher—a former member of Congress and onetime chair of the Securities and Exchange Commission—died in his sleep two weeks shy of his sixty-sixth birthday. The legal community concluded that Eicher, who had suffered a heart attack five years earlier, had been harassed to death in his own courtroom. The case was declared a mistrial. In 1946, with the war over and the government dragging its feet in deciding whether to proceed, the charges were thrown out for violating the Sixth Amendment guarantee of a speedy trial.[39]

Medina knew about the 1944 case and the fate that had befallen Eicher. Some of his friends were warning him to tread carefully, believing that the communist leaders could be just as challenging as the fascists. Spencer Gordon, a friend in Washington, D.C., mailed Medina a copy of the book *A Trial on Trial*, by Maximilian J. St. George and Lawrence Dennis—two of the accused. "It has a wealth of information about the trial, much of it you will take with a grain of salt as it is written by one of the defendants," Gordon wrote. "If you are going to try these communists, you should certainly familiarize yourself with what was done. Counsel for the defendants in the Sedition case made Judge Eicher look like a monkey and finally killed him. I am sure that no one is going to make you look like a monkey, but I want to preserve your health as well."

Medina wrote back a few days later that he had read the first one hundred pages, "which seem filled with repetition and not very informative. Doubtless the good material will come when I get down to the actual proceedings. Goodness knows I shall need all the help and good advice that I can get. It does not look to me as though the two situations were comparable, but that may be due to my own ignorance. In any event, you may be sure that I will go over this material and the cases referred to in your letter with a fine tooth comb." Medina also reminded Gordon to send him some unspecified magazines they had apparently discussed by telephone a few days earlier. "What I am looking for, of course, is data that will help me to avoid pitfalls; and don't forget that I can look like a monkey just as well as the next fellow can. All I can reasonably ask is to reduce the chances thereof to a minimum."

Gordon responded that the common thread he saw was the scope of the two trials. "There were a number of defendants and probably a pretty hard lot of lawyers. By working in unison the lawyers in the Sedition case made objections in such a way that the trial was practically broken up." Medina didn't write back, but the idea that the defense lawyers in Eicher's courtroom had worked in concert to disrupt the trial lodged itself in his mind. Medina would eventually make that same accusation against the lawyers in the communist trial.[40]

Two months after the attack on Thompson, no arrests had been made—not to anyone's surprise. At the time of the attack police intimated to reporters that it might have been staged, something Thompson and his backers vigorously denied. But there was no doubt about a second targeting of Thompson.

Thompson had made plans to go out with his wife on the evening of November 19, and asked a friend, Mildred Cheney, twenty-three, to come babysit their seven-year-old daughter, Ellen, and thirteen-month-old son, James. Cheney, in turn, invited a friend, Harry Rainey, to sit with her.[41] Sometime after midnight, one of the Thompsons' neighbors, Robert Burke, twenty-five, showed up at the door, drunk. For some reason Cheney let him in and, when he asked, agreed to make Burke a cup of coffee. While she was in the kitchen he wandered into the girl's bedroom, where Cheney found him a short time later with his clothes in disarray. Burke then went into the bathroom and eventually left the apartment, about ten minutes before Thompson and his wife returned home (newspaper accounts offer no details on why Rainey didn't intervene). Cheney told Thompson what had happened, and Thompson called the police, who arrested Burke that afternoon at his apartment two buildings down the street and charged him with impairing the morals of a minor, indecent exposure, and unlawful entry. Burke, who identified himself as a freelance private detective, told police he had gone to Thompson's apartment drunk and ready to "give him a hard time" over his role in the Communist Party.

Thompson was livid. He believed that failure by the police to arrest anyone in the September attack on him had, in effect, declared it open season for vigilantes to target the defendants. The molestation of his daughter was "a direct consequence of the failure to arrest and punish the assailants" and "a product of the savage campaign of violence against communists and all progressives unleashed by press and radio and organized big business."

Burke was convicted on the morals and indecent exposure charges on December 27, though the illegal entry charge was dismissed. But in an odd and unexplained turn of events, on January 6 the court set aside its verdict and ordered a new trial after Queens Chief Assistant District Attorney J. Irwin Shapiro told the judges that there was something wrong with Burke's admission of wrongdoing. Thompson called it "open collusion" between Burke and the district attorney's office. On January 13, four days before Thompson and his codefendants were to go on trial themselves, Burke returned to court, denied all the charges, and was quickly acquitted as scores of people in the gallery hissed their disapproval.

But by then, few members of the public were paying attention to the case in Brooklyn. The big show was getting ready to open in Medina's courtroom in downtown Manhattan.

FIVE

Battle Lines
and Battle Scars

The trial opened on January 17, 1949, a warm—fifty-four degrees—and cloudy Monday on the cusp of a cold snap that would sweep into New York City by the middle of the week. During the six months of pretrial hearings, groups of Communist Party supporters had mounted regular demonstrations on the sidewalk outside the federal courthouse and across the street in Foley Square. The crowds were usually orderly but sometimes converged in numbers so large that Judge Medina complained he had trouble getting to work. On this morning, the authorities were anticipating the largest demonstration yet, so by 8:00 A.M. a cordon of more than four hundred police officers had already surrounded the courthouse. Most were in uniform and on foot. Eleven other officers on horseback helped with the crowd control. Still more officers mingled undercover in the crowd and in the courthouse. It was the largest such deployment in the city's history, and police officials said they intended to repeat the show of force every day of the trial, expected to last at least two months.[1]

All twelve of the defendants were out on bail, and all but the ailing Foster arrived at the courthouse that morning. Some came alone, while a few arrived in clusters, waving to supporters as they mounted the steps. Medina got there early, eyeballing the jeering protesters and the line of police as he walked up the marble steps and entered through the front door. A pool of 592 potential jurors had been summoned, and they, too, made their way past the throng.[2]

Medina's usual courtroom was on the twenty-second floor, near his office. To accommodate the expected crowd the trial was moved to the building's biggest space, Room 110, on the first floor. The room was sixty-one feet long and forty-three feet wide, with a nearly thirty-foot-high ceiling from which hung four massive chandeliers. Medina had ordered about half of the 140 seats to be reserved for news reporters—the biggest press gallery for a trial since the 1935 Lindbergh baby kidnapping and murder case.[3] The remaining seats were split roughly in half between relatives of the defendants and members of the public. Scores of people lined up hoping to get one of the public seats and to be eyewitnesses to the spectacle.

And it was, indeed, a spectacle. For weeks the newspapers had been filled with stories about the "Reds," both those headed for trial in New York and those trying to spread communism overseas. In China, Mao Zedong's communist forces were on the verge of seizing the northern section of the country, and it was clear that it was only a matter of time before the Kuomintang nationalist forces of Chiang Kai-shek would be annihilated or driven to the sea. Diplomats feared that the Soviets were arming North Korea, extending the chess match over Eastern Europe to another part of the world. In the United States, a month earlier, the same grand jury that indicted the Communist Party leaders had indicted Alger Hiss on perjury charges, less than two weeks after Whittaker Chambers had revealed his "pumpkin papers"—evidence that purportedly proved Hiss had lied about not being in contact with Chambers since the early 1930s.

The opening of the trial dominated the news, particularly in New York City. In some quarters, such as the *New York World-Telegram*, it was reported with gleeful anticipation—the Reds would be getting their due, was the general sentiment. But others were more thoughtful. The *Christian Science Monitor*, under a neutral "Twelve Communists and the Law Go on Trial" headline, warned: "The outcome of the case will be watched by governments and political parties around the world as to how the United States, as an outstanding exponent of democratic government, intends to share the benefits of its civil liberties and yet

7. The trial of the Communist Party leaders drew near daily protests and was followed closely by the major New York media as well as the communist *Daily Worker*. WPA Film Library. Image courtesy of MPI Home Video.

protect them if and when they appear to be abused by enemies from within." William L. Shirer, the veteran CBS radio newsman who, as one of Edward R. Murrow's "boys," became a national fixture for his dispatches from Germany in the 1930s chronicling the rise of Nazism, also sounded a note of caution about the full heft of the case against the twelve men. The *New York Star* (which was to fold two weeks later) previewed a midday radio talk by Shirer, quoting his warning that the trial "may set a precedent for this country's attitude toward the whole communist movement. No overt act of trying to forcibly overthrow our government is charged. . . . The government's case is simply that by being members and leaders of the Communist Party, its doctrines and tactics being what they are, the accused are guilty of conspiracy." And he said the ACLU, "while in no way sympathetic to the communists, holds that the trial is—to quote it—'an unwarranted use of the only peacetime sedition law in American history since 1798.'"

Medina planned to ignore the politics and treat the trial as just another criminal case—though it was, in fact, the first he would handle as a federal judge. Medina prided himself on being prompt, but on this morning he was more than ten minutes late. At 10:42 A.M., dressed in his flowing black robe, Medina finally entered Room 110 through a side door, stepped up to the bench, and settled into his seat, a high-backed, red-leather swivel chair that when he leaned back left him nearly hidden behind the massive desk. He kept a green binder in front of him, which over the course of the trial he would fill with tiny, cramped handwriting, jotting down legal points and other notes.[4] The wall behind him was nearly covered by a deep-red velvet tapestry with a large bald eagle embroidered in gold. To Medina's right the Stars and Stripes draped limply from a pole anchored by a floor stand.

It was an imposing room, the lower walls covered with dark marble and the upper part paneled in walnut. The wall to Medina's right, across from the jury box, was topped by a high row of windows that let in the thin wintry sun, and yellow bulbs in the chandeliers helped fill the shadows. As Medina settled in, nearly all the gallery seats were filled, half of them, per Medina's order, by newspaper and radio reporters, who also had their own room nearby wired for instant access to their editors and networks. Court officials and extra bailiffs for security were arrayed along the walls.[5]

The scope of the trial—a dozen indicted men—called for unusual physical arrangements. Rather than being placed side by side, the prosecution and defense tables were arrayed in rows. The court clerk and court stenographer sat with their backs to Medina at a small table in front of the judge's bench. The prosecutor and his team— about seven people altogether—faced Medina from behind a polished rectangular table of dark wood. The defense lawyers—usually six people—sat at a larger table behind the prosecutor and spilled over onto a row of wooden chairs lining the wall beneath the tall windows, facing the jury box. The defendants themselves were relegated, almost as an afterthought, to a row of wooden chairs backed up against the low rail that separated the court from the gallery. The pool of potential jurors was out of sight in nearby Room 108, waiting to be summoned—a wait that would try their patience.

Medina wasted no time on pleasantries. The docket—the list of actions and motions in the case—already covered five single-spaced pages. And the trial would prove to be even more contentious than the preliminary skirmishing had been.

Court was called to order, and McGohey, with his slicked-back steel-gray hair and conservative dark suit, rose to ask Medina to sever the case against the ailing Foster so that the case against the other eleven men could go forward. Foster, he said, could be tried later, once the doctors said it was safe to do so. But McGohey had barely launched into his motion when Sacher, one of the leaders of the defense team, leaped to his feet. "Before your Honor proceeds to consider any proceeding in this trial we wish to call to the Court's attention a matter of gravest importance," Sacher said, then went on to denounce the heavy police presence as a signal to potential jurors that the men on trial were dangerous. He cited morning newspaper accounts portraying the courthouse as "an armed camp" protected by a squad of what he referred to as "military police."

"This detail, this two and a half companies of military police, have been thrown around the court house and into the court house solely for the purpose of creating a Hitler lie that there is some danger in the conduct of this trial which has to be suppressed or met by the police," Sacher said. He asked Medina to order the city police removed from the federal courthouse—implying a jurisdictional conflict—and to delay the trial for ninety days to let "the vicious impact" of the deployment dissipate. It wasn't the first, nor would it be the last, time that the defense found cause to demand a delay or mistrial. In fact, it would be a recurring theme of the defense.

Medina, not surprisingly, rejected the arguments. "I am not accustomed to take the statements in the newspapers as determining matters before me," he said archly. "I have seen no evidence of any armed camp around here when I got here this morning, or in the courtroom here. I have some recollections myself of rather substantial picket lines on various previous occasions. It rendered it a little difficult for me to get in and out of the courthouse myself. But however that may be, I can't see anything to justify the comments that you have made. And the motion is denied."

Sacher offered to walk Medina "around the corner in this building" to see the "couple of hundred policemen whom I saw with my own eyes in a room right next to the press room, right on this floor, so that you need not take, your Honor, the statements contained in the press. You can have visual evidence of the truth of what I say."

Gladstein joined in, arguing that "I am aware of the fact that trigger-happy men are included among those who wear the uniform of the police. I am aware of the fear, the sense of terror that is imbued at the sight of a tremendous cordon of police." He said potential jurors walking through the line "saw something they have never seen before and which immediately they rationalized as justified by some menace or threat" posed by the defendants. "So there are hundreds of jurors whose minds are already poisoned. . . . This was a deliberate, purposeful effort to intimidate and to create an atmosphere . . . to poison the minds of those potential jurors." Gladstein also indicated the basic course the defense intended to follow—that the twelve accused men were on trial not for actions they had taken but for their beliefs.

The rest of the defense ensemble rose in a daisy chain of arguments, including reviving a pretrial request that the proceedings be moved to a larger venue to accommodate the public interest. Crockett, the only black lawyer on the defense, told Medina that he had partici-pated in trials in the South, which he viewed as precedent. "I know exactly what happens when a trial is held under conditions resem-bling mob conditions. I am convinced, and I think this court should be convinced, that a mob is no less a mob merely because it is clothed in uniform and has a pistol on the side." Crockett added that "there is no difference between the atmosphere surrounding this trial and the atmosphere surrounding the infamous Scottsboro trial." Crockett conveniently didn't mention that the bulk of the crowd outside the courtroom that morning was demonstrating against the trial and for the defendants. Isserman finished up the flood of arguments by demanding Medina conduct an inquiry into who ordered the police presence.

Medina would have none of it. "We are here to try the main charge of this indictment, not a trial of the police department or someone else," he said, adding a few moments later: "All this talk about intim-idation here in the courtroom is absurd. Now, you gentlemen and your clients have not shown the slightest evidence to me of really being intimidated in the slightest degree, and I just don't put any stock in it."

Gladstein jumped up. "Is your Honor judging by the fact that we protest against the show of force and violence by the police and the prosecution—is your Honor judging on that basis that we therefore are not intimidated?" he said. "Must we reach the point that we are so paralyzed that we can't speak before your Honor will say, 'That is sufficient, that is adequate proof?'" Then Gladstein shifted points to argue that the public should have access to unused seats reserved for the media, and then changed tack once again and asked Medina to order the removal from the prosecution table of a man in "a muffler, an overcoat, and a hat in his lap" who he said was connected with Robert Burke, the man who had been first convicted, then acquitted, of attacking Thompson's daughter. Gladstein called the man a "two-bit stool pigeon" who had "come into the house of my client and committed an assault on a child." Medina rejected the request, and he and Gladstein wrangled a bit more until Gladstein got deeply under Medina's skin.

"Your Honor will certainly permit me to call your Honor's attention at least to the facts that I want to complain about, even though I am told that your Honor is not going to do anything about it."

Medina shot back: "You know, Mr. Gladstein, I don't like that crack. . . . I am going to decide these motions as best I can with such light as God gives me to do what is right, and if you make any comments insinuating something else you are making a big mistake."[6]

The trial was barely under way, and the judge and the lawyers would argue like that through the afternoon.

On the trial's second day, the two sides picked up on the debate over whether the case against Foster should be cut loose from those against the other eleven men. The defense argued that since all twelve were charged with the same conspiracy it would be prejudicial to Foster to have the case proceed without him. He wouldn't be present to defend himself or to weigh in on points of law about the conspiracy—rulings he likely would have to live with in his subsequent solo trial. Better, Gladstein argued, to dismiss the charge against Foster altogether, especially since the government had had ample time to pursue the charges over the previous several years and chose not to. Crockett urged a different path, delaying the case until Foster could rejoin, because Foster, as the head of the party, was the key defense witness. Siding with the prosecution, Medina rejected those arguments early in the afternoon, severed the case against Foster, and ordered the trial of the remaining eleven defendants to move forward.[7]

The courtroom debate over the issue also illustrated what would become a persistent problem during the trial. With five attorneys representing one or more of the individual defendants, each had to rise on behalf of his client or clients to make a motion, join a motion, raise an objection, or adopt an objection made by another lawyer. On a few occasions, the lawyers would disagree about arcane details of arguments, but mostly they mounted a unified—if redundant—defense. Gladstein, Sacher, and Isserman were particularly adept at stretching what should have been a succinct point into a near-Shakespearean soliloquy. Medina tried to accommodate by ruling that each motion or objection raised by a single lawyer would be presumed to apply to all, but it didn't help.

The first element of the defense's courtroom strategy was to attack the process itself. Gladstein and other members of the team believed that the system used to select jurors—both for the grand jury that indicted the men and for the trial itself—was designed to weed out the communists' presumed peers: working-class people and racial minorities. They had spent weeks poring over old jury rolls, zeroing in on twenty-eight jury panels going back to 1940 that they believed showed that a preponderance of jurors hailed from such "silk stocking" neighborhoods as Park Avenue, Fifth Avenue, Sutton Place, and Gracie Square. Conversely, they found few jurors on those panels from the working-class and minority neighborhoods of Harlem, the Lower East Side, and the West Side below Seventy-second Street and down into Hell's Kitchen.

They had first raised the issue the previous October and been rebuffed by U.S. District Court Judge Murray Hulbert, who ruled that the defense lawyers had failed to make their case. The team polished up the arguments and filed a special petition directly to the U.S. Supreme Court, asking it to void the indictments of the twelve communists because of what they argued was an unconstitutionally tainted jury pool—an argument the Supreme Court rejected as well, without comment, on January 10, a week before the trial started. But the defense was not ready to take no for an answer and announced it would tweak its argument and renew the challenge at the start of the trial. "We shall prove by a wealth of incontrovertible facts that Wall Street and Park Avenue control the jury system here and have converted it into a conviction machine," Henry Winston, one of the defendants, told reporters after the Supreme Court decision.[8]

Despite the court defeats, the defense raised a compelling point. If the defendants hadn't been communists, and if Medina and their attorneys hadn't been so bent on irritating each other, the defense might have persuaded Medina that they were right, that the jury deck was stacked against them. Their argument echoed, in fact, a legal challenge that Medina himself, before he ascended to the bench, had pursued in 1947 against a similar system used by the New York State courts. Medina used the argument in the appeal of two labor leaders convicted of conspiracy and extortion. (In fact, the courts would change their system a few years later.) The defendants in that case had been convicted by a specially convened "blue ribbon" jury, which their lawyers argued was designed to weed out the defendants' peers and thus denied them their Fourth Amendment guarantees to due process. They lost the argument in the lower court, and Medina was brought in to handle the appeal.

The "blue ribbon" juries were essentially a prescreened pool of jurors that in theory speeded up the voir dire—"see-say" in French—segment of a trial in which potential jurors, under oath, answer questions designed to weed out those with biases, conflicts of interest, or other issues that made them unsuitable to sit on a jury. Potential jurors were restricted to local citizens between the ages of twenty-one and seventy who owned or were married to the owner of property worth at least $250. Those with felony or "moral turpitude" misdemeanor convictions and those who could not read or write English were ineligible. The pool was further limited by a wide range of exemptions including "clergymen, physicians, dentists, pharmacists, embalmers, optometrists, attorneys, members of the Army, Navy, or Marine Corps, or of the National Guard or Naval Militia, firemen, policemen, ship's officers, pilots, editors, editorial writers, sub-editors, reporters, and copy readers." And women were granted a blanket exemption if they chose to take it. From that pool, court officials gleaned a second, the "blue ribbon" jury pool, of about three thousand people who were already vetted by the time they were brought in for voir dire in specific cases—did they know the defendants or any of the witnesses, the lawyers, or the judge?

But the convicted union leaders' lawyers argued that the distilled pool of jurors denied the defendants their due-process protections because it in practice excluded their peers from the jury. The panel was designed "with a purpose to obtain persons of conservative views, persons of the upper economic and social stratum in New York County, persons having a tendency to convict defendants accused of crime, and to exclude those who might understand the point of view of the laboring man."[9]

Medina argued the case before the U.S. Supreme Court on April 3, 1947. "If these defendants were tried before a proper jury—one made up of a true cross-section of the community—we are confident they would be acquitted," he told the panel of nine judges. "Official statistics show that these special juries are prone to convict. When a prosecution builds a defendant up to be a Public Enemy Number One, it must win a conviction. This case was a perfect set up for this special jury system."

While the Supreme Court deliberated, Medina was nominated on May 15 for a seat on the U.S. District Court in New York. The Supreme Court handed down its decision upholding the convictions—and rejecting Medina's jury challenge—on June 23, as the secret grand jury was beginning to hear testimony by Elizabeth Bentley about the spy rings she had handled for the Soviet Union. Medina lost the argument in a narrow 5–4 ruling in which the Court said that it was not persuaded by Medina's statistical analysis of the makeup of the jury pool, and that there was nothing inherently prejudicial in requiring potential jurors be able to read or to own property.

The Foley Square defendants' argument about the federal jury selection process was similar in theory to the one Medina made about the state court's jury selection process, and that may be why he decided to grant the defense some leeway in making its challenge. On the second day of the trial, after all the wrangling over security, over whether the defense might subpoena Medina to testify as part of its jury challenge, and over a raft of other mostly diversionary complaints and motions, Medina directed the defense to make its case that the system was fundamentally—and unconstitutionally—flawed. But Medina also indicated that the defense had a hard sell: "My disposition has been to grant the prosecution's motion [denying the jury challenge], but this will give me time to study it further." What Medina didn't anticipate was the length of the defendants' argument, and how the next six weeks played out cemented his belief that the defense was on a mission to wear him down. The late Judge Eicher was never far from his mind.

Gladstein led the charge with a roiling, long-winded, and at times stultifying argument. Part of the line of reasoning was that none of the federal judges in New York City, including Medina, should hear the argument because they were all honorary members of the Federal Grand Jury Association of the Southern District, a voluntary group of current and former grand jurors that had been integral in the jury selection system. Beginning in 1938, the association created and sent to the court administrator lists of potential jurors culled from *Who's Who in New York*, *Who's Who in Engineering*, the *Social Register*, *Poor's Register of Executives*, and the *Directory of Directors*. It also gathered names of potential jurors from the alumni directories for Princeton, Columbia, Harvard, Yale, and Dartmouth and added still others based on the recommendations of members of the association itself. There were not, the defense argued, many names offered from the working-class neighborhoods and the Lower East Side tenements.[10]

On the third day of the trial, Gladstein cut to the heart of the defense's complaint. "A system of jury selection should be democratic, should be impartial, should seek to obtain neutral cross-sections of the people so that the jury, as an ultimate body . . . is truly representative of all the people, without discrimination," Gladstein said. "Our proof will show that here, here in this courthouse, the jury system has been captured by Wall Street and by Park Avenue, and that that capture has been carried out . . . under the direct supervision and instigation of the chief judge."[11] Gladstein brought up Medina's argument before the Supreme Court, pointing out that Medina as a lawyer had relied on a similar analysis of jury pools to argue that "there was discrimination against classes and races and groups of people." Medina cut Gladstein off: "Well, you know, I got licked in that case."[12]

Medina was losing patience. McGohey had opposed the defense's request to challenge the jury system and had moved that Medina strip out part of the defense motion about the grand jury because the Supreme Court had previously rejected the similar defense petition. But Gladstein argued that in the interim the defense had uncovered new evidence—an internal court analysis called the Tolman Report—that bolstered the defense's claim that the system was unconstitutional. That launched a lengthy discussion over whether the defense lawyers had had access to the Tolman Report before they first broached the subject. The debate came to a head in the afternoon of the fourth day of the trial, with Medina threatening to cut off the defense's argument opposing McGohey's motion, primarily because Gladstein, only the first of the five defense lawyers to make their arguments, kept steering the argument down cul-de-sacs.

"I am getting pretty to the point where I am going to decide it," Medina said, which sparked a fresh round of outrage from the other defense lawyers, who said Medina was prejudging the motion before they had a chance to weigh in on behalf of their clients. Isserman rose first. "I think it is absolutely unfair for your Honor to begin to decide motions before we state our grounds of objection," he said, as some of the other lawyers chimed in. Medina cut them all off and urged them not to talk all at once. That drew Crockett and Sacher out of their seats to complain that they had not been talking at all.

The comedy of the moment hid the raw emotions Crockett was feeling. Crockett knew he had been added to the team in part because of his race, and he intended to make sure fellow African Americans had the same opportunity to be heard as white Americans.[13]

"I feel this subject very, very keenly and very personally," Crockett said, his voice breaking with emotion when it was his turn to enter an objection. "I hope that before the hearing is over I will be given an opportunity to speak . . ." Crockett stopped, removed his black-framed glasses, and wiped his eyes before continuing. "I will be given an opportunity to speak not only as a member of the bar of this court but also as an American citizen who for once is ashamed to see a representative of my government trying to cover up the rotten situation that exists right here in the Southern District of New York. I hope also that I would be given an opportunity to speak on behalf of the three hundred thousand black people who have been segregated right here in the Southern District of New York and who, because of their segregated condition, have been made the victims of this despicable system that has just been described by Mr. Gladstein. That is all I have to say at this time."

Crockett's tearful moment was trumpeted in the evening and morning newspapers, and the next day he apologized, after a fashion. "If the court please, perhaps it would be appropriate for me to begin my statement in connection with this challenge by expressing, shall I say, my regret over my emotional outburst yesterday," Crockett said. "I offer no apologies, of course—"

"What was that motion?" Medina interrupted, mishearing Crockett's use of the word "emotional." "I don't remember you making any motion."

"I did not refer to a motion, your Honor," Crockett replied. "I said, to express my regrets because of my emotional outburst yesterday. I was about to state that I offer no apologies for it, and I am satisfied your Honor does not expect any apologies. However, I do regret—"

"Well, I think if counsel can avoid weeping in the courtroom, it is generally better," Medina interrupted.

"I agree, your Honor," Crockett replied, clearly ruffled by Medina. He went on to argue that McGohey's opposition to their challenge of the jury system was discriminatory, and that Medina's indication that he was going to cut off the defense arguments added to a history "of subtle discrimination, and it is bound to call forth some emotional expression."

"You certainly wept," Medina said, "and wept profusely and plainly in the sight of all, and, as you say, you think you probably will not do it again."

Crockett interjected that he had made no such promise.

"Well, then," Medina said, "if you feel like doing it again, or your emotions overcome you, you will do it again. I don't make any objection to it. I just suggest that generally speaking it is better for counsel to refrain from weeping in the courtroom. But that is a matter which sometimes is beyond one's control."

"Thank you, your Honor. I appreciate your permission for me to give vent to my emotions whenever I feel inclined to do so."

"In moderation."

"In moderation, of course," Crockett said.

Outside the courtroom, the CRC and other supporters of the defense held regular rallies and protests and beseeched their followers to lobby the government to end the trial. Medina himself received a flood of letters, telegrams, telephone calls, and in-person visits, a full frontal lobbying assault. He quickly found it overwhelming.

"The worst experience I have had is running into a mass of about five hundred photographers when I went out to lunch on the first day of the trial," he wrote a week after the trial began to his old Princeton friend Ripley Ropes in Meredith, New Hampshire. "They were right on top of me popping these bulbs and taking pictures in front of me, from the right and from the left and even under my legs and I felt like the biggest damn fool you ever saw. I know I must have looked very silly and I certainly felt that way. By now I am beginning to get used to having my picture taken and act a little more natural."[14]

Despite the nonchalant attitude, Medina was concerned about the repercussions of his role presiding over the trial. He initially balked at, then was talked into, around-the-clock guards at his office and home, and a bodyguard was at his elbow whenever he moved around the city. The notoriety led some old friends to abandon him, telling him they feared being out in public with him, sure that he would be attacked by a communist fanatic.[15]

Almost overnight Medina became a household name. As a private attorney, and as a rookie federal judge, Medina liked to keep track of his press mentions. And there were quite a few, ranging from his bar committee appointments to Princeton and Columbia alumni events to his wife's social engagements on Long Island and else-where. But the onset of the trial unleashed a flood of coverage, and Medina—now on a federal judge's salary—decided to cut some expenses, beginning with Burrelle's Press Clipping Bureau in New York, which apparently charged by volume. "I am beginning to get a little worried about the large number of clippings due to this communist trial and I do not want to get in over my head," he wrote to the agency just days after the trial began, hoping to negotiate a lower, undisclosed rate. "I am anxious to continue to receive the clippings but now have limited resources to draw on as a U.S. District Judge and hope you can perhaps give me some special arrangement to lighten the burden." Medina apparently didn't see any problems with converting his status as a federal judge into some freebies. He also enjoyed free passes to movie houses, stage theaters, and the occasional ball game, all supplied by people happy to curry favor. But Burrelle's was apparently less amenable and didn't offer the judge a discount, or at least a sufficient one. Medina dropped the service.[16]

The attention also flooded into his chambers. As Medina arrived at eight thirty each morning, he would find delegations waiting for him, and again at lunchtime. They were invariably progressive labor activists or political leftists, and some were from the CRC. Medina made time for them all, including skipping lunches to hear them—an odd ethical decision for a judge overseeing a trial. To a team, the visitors lobbied on behalf of the defendants and against the trial. In early February, one group of seven union leaders showed up and met with Medina "to add their objection to the way the jury pool had been formed," complained about the paucity of black jurors in the pool, and urged Medina to move the trial to a larger courtroom to accommodate more of the public—parroting the key elements of the defense's stance. Medina told the visitors that "I can understand why working people and trade unionists are concerned about this jury question" but that his hands were tied and they should approach the U.S. attorney general.[17]

After a few weeks, though, Medina abruptly stopped receiving the emissaries. And once they realized the audiences were over, the delegations stopped coming. At the same time, the pace of the letters and telegrams picked up, most of them straightforward and courteous but some weighted with insults and threats, including calling Medina "a degenerate from the bowels of hell," a "son of a bitch," and a "fiend incarnate."

Medina's response to the public uproar was, in essence, to sequester himself. He notified friends and his own grown children that he would not be in regular contact until the trial ended. He suspended his busy social calendar, including shooting pool with fellow Princeton and Columbia alums at private clubs, and turned down invitations to card parties and dinners out—a sacrifice for a man who deeply enjoyed the conviviality of friends and a few cocktails (martinis, especially). He put himself on a daily regimen of arising at 6:30 A.M. for breakfast and reading the morning papers. By 8:30 A.M. he was in his chambers preparing for the day, and by 10:30 A.M. he was on the bench, the court in session. He lunched alone in chambers, napping for a half hour before he returned to the bench. He ended court at 4:30 P.M. each day and, after finishing up in chambers, stopped at a health club for a workout around 5:15 P.M. on the way home to the apartment at 14 East Seventy-fifth Street. After a quiet dinner with his wife, he would take a mild sedative before retiring at 9:30 P.M.[18]

Eventually, harassing telephone calls led Medina's wife to ask the judge's secretary to talk with the telephone company about finding a way to make them end. The Medinas ultimately switched to an unpublished number.[19]

The defense planned to make its point about the inequities in the jury selection process in excruciating detail. It became a six-week-long farce as the lawyers subpoenaed dozens of former jurors and court officials, warning that they might subpoena Medina himself (he told them he would not testify in a case he was overseeing) and nearly a dozen of his fellow judges. The defense eventually called more than thirty witnesses, from former jurors to court officials to U.S. Rep. Vito Marcantonio, a Communist Party supporter and New York chair of the American Labor Party, who represented Manhattan's Upper East Side and East Harlem.

They began with former members of grand juries and in the first week called eighteen of them—including thirteen of the people who had indicted the defendants and Hiss—to the witness stand. The lawyers probed their lives, their livelihoods, their affiliations, and anything else they could think of to reinforce their contention that the jurors were not drawn from the same world as the defendants. Medina ran out of patience, and on January 27 he ended the parade of jurors, telling the defense lawyers that they had exhausted the argument and ordering them to move on to more "tangible" testimony. He threatened them with sanctions if they persisted in this "new technique" of "willful, deliberate, and concerted delay."[20]

The tactic was obvious. Each of the five lawyers rose to examine nearly every witness called. Objections were raised as if by choir, and points of law were argued to the point of distraction. Despite Medina's occasionally sharp-edged prodding, the defense lawyers meandered in their questions and sought to find ways around Medina's rulings upholding prosecution objections that their questions were irrelevant and thus should be stricken from the record. On February 4, Marcantonio took the stand, and Isserman tried to elicit testimony from him on the evolution of housing in his congressional district, which at the time held a large number of tenements. Medina agreed with McGohey that the housing conditions were immaterial to the charges against the defendants, launching a three-way discussion with Isserman and Sacher about what lines of questioning Medina would allow. Isserman kept trying to slip his point about the poverty endemic in Marcantonio's district into the trial record anyway—much to Medina's annoyance.

"Mr. Isserman, you are doing just what I told you not to do," Medina said, cutting off Isserman in midcomplaint. "That has happened so persistently here in this trial that it has made a very definite impression on me. You may remember that some time ago I had occasion to remark that I felt that there had come into my mind for the first time a thought that a willful, persistent, and deliberate attempt was being made for delay. I can find no other explanation for the way counsel have been conducting themselves in dragging this matter out and in paying no attention to my rulings." Then Medina warned Isserman to tread lightly. "I may be literally forced to take some sort of action here merely to protect the administration of justice from frustration."

Isserman wouldn't back down. "I object to your Honor's characterization of the conduct of counsel, to the statement that this is an effort to drag this matter out," he said.

Gladstein rose to suggest some court cases for Medina to consult, but the judge cut him off, too. "I have had that suggestion addressed to me a little while ago and I have rejected it," Medina snapped. "Now I think perhaps you gentlemen would do well to let the matter rest as it is now and proceed with the interrogation of the witness, so that we may get some testimony relevant to the issue that is before me."

"If the court please," Gladstein said, "there are cases and cases which show that unless counsel makes an offer of proof—and the offer is not required to be in writing—"

"Mr. Gladstein," Medina said sharply, "did you understand that I indicated that I did not desire to hear any further argument on the point?"

After a little more back-and-forth Sacher rose to add his objection to Isserman's about Medina's characterization of the defense trying to drag out the proceedings in a courtroom that held "forty or fifty newspapers" awaiting Marcantonio's testimony. "This is not according us a fair trial when throughout these proceedings you persist in characterizing testimony whose materiality and relevancy you have not yet ascertained—you proceed to characterize it on its threshold as constituting stalling and delaying," Sacher said.

"Well," Medina replied, "you and your colleagues have apparently adopted a new technique in criminal cases by which instead of the defendants who are indicted being tried, the Court and all the members of the court are the ones who must suffer the excoriations and accusations of counsel. But I think, perhaps, with patience there will be an end."

Medina told Isserman to resume his questioning of Marcantonio—but Isserman prefaced his questions by continuing his objection to how Medina was conducting the trial, saying that it was affecting the defense attorneys' ability to represent their clients. "You have been at it three weeks now," Medina snapped, exasperated. "I think possibly if you go on arguing this way we will be here the rest of the year on this challenge. But I think I shall take some steps to prevent that."[21]

All of this was watched closely by the press, who began holding up Medina as a paragon of patience. In one broadly published Associated Press story—it was carried by the *Washington Post* and the *Los Angeles Times*, among others—writer Saul Pett described Medina in glowing terms. "Objections come fast. The judge overrules or sustains them quickly, quietly, positively. Although this is his first criminal case on the bench, he exudes confidence in his knowledge of the law. Also patience and good humor. Even in rebuke, the thunder in his voice is only implied. His tone is invariably gentle, almost cooing at times. Like a progressive school teacher, firm but careful not to scar the pride of her pupils."[22]

The defense lawyers had a different view. Much as Medina detected a pattern among the defense lawyers to try to badger him and delay the trial, the defense lawyers began viewing Medina as the enemy—an impression fed by the judge's decisions almost invariably upholding prosecution objections while rejecting defense objections. The showdown between the defense team and the judge began to overshadow the trial itself, with more time given to the back-and-forth over legal issues and defense complaints than to the hearing of testimony itself.

The reports of the defense team's behavior didn't help the defendants' public images. "If I had my way, I wouldn't even bother to try them," one onlooker said as the court headed for an adjournment. "Certainly no one is as good to them as we are," another court-watcher said. Both were quoted in a *Christian Science Monitor* article that drew comparisons to the 1919 Palmer Raids.[23]

Medina, in a private letter, struck his habitual tone of ego swaddled in self-deprecation. But there was no doubt that the conduct of the trial, and his inability to control it, were bothering him.

"I am really giving these defendants a fair trial in the best American tradition despite all the tremendous effort to get me to kick them around," Medina wrote. "The vast bulk of the American people believe in fair play and I think they feel proud to see a judge who keeps his temper and his dignity and makes things run smoothly with a little touch of humor now and then. But it is a frightful strain that is bound to get worse as time goes on. They have thrown every kind of legal question known to man or beast at me and it is hard for me to get a good night's sleep when I am worrying about some of the maneuvers. Thank goodness I have a pretty good legal background; otherwise I would have been in Bellevue before this."[24]

If Medina's decision to let the defense attorneys challenge the jury selection system could have been read as a good sign for the defense, their utter failure to make the case had to have been seen as a harbinger of problems to come. And some of the problems with the case were self-inflicted.

On February 9, three weeks into the trial, the defense's key witness, Doxey Wilkerson, admitted on the stand that he had messed up the statistical analysis of the jury pools—the key point underlying the defense's challenge. Wilkerson, a former party education director who was teaching at the Jefferson School of Social Science (on the attorney general's List of Subversive Organizations), acknowledged that he had reclassified self-employed tailors as executives, since they ostensibly ran their own firms. So with a pen stroke they had gone from working class to capitalist class, skewing the numbers to reinforce the defense's point about the narrowness of the jury pool. Medina had already thrown out 149 maps and other illustrations Wilkerson used in his eight days of testimony because Wilkerson had not prepared them himself and couldn't identify who had actually put them together and under what criteria.

"It doesn't make a very favorable impression on me that all this data, which was supposed to be so carefully and accurately assembled, was actually got together by such a miscellaneous assembly of people, some of them who just happened to come into the office, and some of them people whose names he doesn't even know," Medina said.

At the same time, and reminiscent of a first-grade teacher, Medina was zeroing in on the defense lawyers' refusal to obey his courtroom orders to end challenges and to stop talking—at one point blasting Sacher for his apparent attempt to suggest an answer to Wilkerson when McGohey pressed him on his definition of tailors and how they affected the statistical analysis. "I don't want to have these stalling tactics and suggesting tactics here," Medina said. Sacher kept talking anyway, and when he was finished, Medina warned: "Mr. Sacher, you've done precisely what I've told you not to do, and I'll have it noted on the record. I ask all counsel to desist from making comments which suggest answers to the witness in the guise of objections." Sacher objected to Medina's admonition, drawing another rebuke: "Nothing seems to shut you up, Mr. Sacher, so I merely indicate to you my desire that you desist."[25]

Through it all, the eleven defendants sat quietly behind the defense table, occasionally taking their own notes or whispering into their lawyers' ears. The court battle so far had had little to do with them—it was a fight among lawyers over the court system, and dissolving rapidly into personality clashes between the defendants' legal team and the judge.

Outside the courtroom, the anti-communist fervor was picking up steam—propelled by the trial in Hungary, then a Soviet satellite, of Roman Catholic Cardinal Joseph Mindszenty, who was convicted February 3 and sentenced to life for treason in a show trial aimed at solidifying the communists' control of the country. The case sparked international outrage and public protests, including a special sermon by Francis Cardinal Spellman at Saint Patrick's Cathedral in Manhattan. Spellman, who rarely took to the pulpit—his previous sermon marked V-E Day on May 8, 1945—called on Americans not only to push back against communism internationally but to fight it at home before the showdown between West and East turned into the century's third major war.

"Unless the whole American people, without the further ostrich-like actions and pretenses, unite to stop the communist floodings of our own land, our sons, for the third and last time, shall be summoned from the comforts, tranquility and love of their own homes and families to bear arms against those who would desecrate and destroy them," Spellman said. "It is full time that a strong and vigilant America unite in prayer and protest against wasting the youth of her own nation, and try to help save civilization from the world's most fiendish, ghoulish men of slaughter."[26]

Even judges were weighing in. Speaking before the Queens County Grand Jurors Association—similar to the group that had helped select federal jurors—Municipal Court Justice John F. Scileppi scored the daily picketing outside the federal courthouse as "a form of intimidation not only to the judge but to the jurors who are sitting in the case"—seemingly oblivious to the fact that no jurors were yet sitting. But Scileppi's dislike for acts that could be construed as jury manipulation didn't extend to himself. He advised the still-unselected jurors to "abolish the Communist Party as soon as you can."[27]

President Truman also chimed in, calling Foster and Dennis "traitors" after they issued a statement March 4 condemning any move by the United States toward war with the Soviet Union—a standard policy remark for the Moscow-connected American party. When asked about the statement during a press conference the next day in Washington, Truman, said, "I have no comment on any statements made by traitors." The exchange gave further impetus to moves in Congress to try to muzzle or outlaw the Communist Party.[28]

By then, Medina had tried to seize control of his own courtroom, limiting the defense team's tactic of drawn-out cross-examinations of witnesses by taking the highly unusual tack of questioning the witnesses himself. After giving the defense a deadline to finish presenting its witnesses, Medina forced the proceedings to a close at the end of court on Tuesday, March 1, saying he would deliver his decision by noon Friday. And it was clear he would rule against the defense and reject its request that the case be thrown out because the jury selection system was biased. He told the court that he expected to start trying to seat a jury the following Monday and that both sides should submit questions they would like him to ask potential jurors during the voir dire process. He also said that he would ask the questions, not the lawyers for the prosecution or the defense, which was the custom. Implied in his decision was that he wasn't about to let the defense drag the process out.

On Thursday afternoon, the defendants mounted another effort to fan public sentiment and try to marshal pressure on the court to dismiss the charges. All but one of the defendants mounted the back of a flatbed truck parked at Madison Square Park, at Broadway and Twenty-sixth Street, as part of a two-hour midafternoon rally that drew some three thousand people. Speaker after speaker—including Davis, the city councilman who was one of the defendants—demanded the jury selection process be thrown out and a more representative system be put in its place. Someone also read aloud a telegram to be sent to the White House demanding "the immediate dismissal of the indictments against the communist leaders," a message the crowd made a show of endorsing unanimously by voice vote.[29] The rally drew a private rebuke from Victor Lasky, a conservative columnist for the *New York World-Telegram* who had worked with Frederick Woltman on the Pulitzer Prize–winning series about communist infiltration of a wide range of American organizations. "I would like to call your attention—if you don't know already—that councilman Benjamin J. Davis Jr., one of the defendants in the communist trial, spoke at a rally protesting the trial in Madison Square Park Thursday night," Lasky wrote to Medina. "And according to an Associated Press account Mr. Davis was quoted as having said that Judge Medina was 'one of the Ku Kluxers who draped themselves in the robes of judges.' I believe that even for a Soviet stooge this is going too far." Lasky typed the letter but signed it by hand, in pencil. There's no indication whether Medina responded.[30]

The next day, Medina delivered a thirty-two-page opinion ruling that the defense had failed to make its case—mainly because of the problems with Wilkerson's testimony—and that an alternative system it proposed of proportional representation by race, gender, and class would be unworkable. The ruling was greeted with the predictable denunciations by the defendants' supporters and cheers by the anti-communists. But it cleared the way for the real fight to begin.

SIX

The Trial Opens

If Medina thought that by questioning the potential jurors himself he was going to derail the defense's play-it-slow strategy, he was mistaken. When the trial resumed on Monday, Medina entered Room 110 a little after 10:30 A.M., as had become his custom. With the bailiff ordering, "All rise!" Medina ascended the bench and settled into his big red leather chair. In the trial's opening days people waited in line to snag one of the few seats reserved for the public. But as the often intensely boring debate over the legality of the federal jury process dragged on, the courtroom had attracted fewer and fewer curious members of the public. Some days, the seats that had once been the hottest ticket in town weren't even filled.

The public seats were empty again this morning—but not through lack of interest. In fact, with the jury challenge over and the trial set to start, interest had spiked, and a noon protest rally had already been planned. Medina had barred the public from the courtroom for the jury selection, deciding that the court needed those seats for potential jurors. His plan was to bring the pool of contenders in, about sixty at a time, and go through the laborious voir dire process. When Medina took the bench, the prosecution and the defense teams were at full staff. McGohey had four other lawyers at his side; the usual array of five defense lawyers swelled with the addition of Mary Kaufman, as well as Abraham Unger and David Freedman, the partners who had initially represented the party leaders.

Medina might have had his plan for how the voir dire would proceed, but the defense lawyers had their plans as well. Medina had barely started, telling the court that he had a couple of points he wanted to address, when McCabe rose and asked, "May I interrupt your Honor?" Medina sat him down: "No, you just wait a moment, Mr. McCabe." Medina went on to chide the defense attorneys for not getting their suggested voir dire questions to him until Saturday, giving him little time to prepare. The prosecution, he noted, had complied much sooner. Still, he was ready to proceed. But he also intended to maintain control of the questioning, as promised. If a potential juror's comment triggered a follow-up question from either side, he said, the lawyer should write out the question. Medina would decide whether it was pertinent and then proceed.[1]

Medina finally turned back to McCabe, who, rather than discussing the voir dire, renewed a defense motion that Medina recuse himself from hearing the case. "It has seemed to me that the circumstances which arose during the course of the trial of the challenge more than justified our allegation that your Honor's state of mind was not one of detachment and freedom from bias," McCabe said, adding that he had compiled a list of Medina's comments that "indicate both the bias which your Honor showed, and the sarcastic approach which your Honor adopted toward the argument of counsel and toward our evidence." In a moment of presumably unintentional irony, as McCabe argued that Medina had regularly cut the defense team off in midargument, Medina cut McCabe off. "Do you think you need to elaborate very much longer?" Medina asked. McCabe told him no, and Medina warned both teams that he was done with listening to "lengthy arguments or repetitive arguments . . . when I have the jury present."

Medina's attempt to browbeat the defense into submission didn't work. Over the next couple of hours the defense attorneys raised twenty-two objections; their complaints included Medina's conduct and their belief that he was biased, the media coverage they thought created an atmosphere in which it would be impossible to find unbiased jurors, and Truman's labeling the defendants "traitors"—an improper action, they argued, by the boss of the attorney general overseeing the case. Medina denied all the major motions, cut the defense off, and ordered the jury selection to begin with the afternoon session. "I am beginning to get the impression that you gentlemen are trying to keep talking so long we won't be able to get the jury in today," Medina said. But they did. After lunch, with an hour or so to go before the end of the day's session, and as McCabe, Crockett, and Sacher each tried to wedge in additional last-minute motions and objections, the first group of sixty potential jurors filed into the courtroom, filling the seats usually reserved for the public.

The prosecution had notified Medina that it planned to call sixty-two witnesses during the trial, and the defense said it planned to call twenty-eight witnesses. The names included Elizabeth Bentley, Whittaker Chambers, and Howard Fast, among others, including the singer Paul Robeson, who was also a high-profile civil rights activist. A few days earlier Robeson had announced that he would cut short a European tour to return to New York to testify on behalf of the defendants. "Marxism is on trial," he told reporters in Glasgow. "It is a way of life, a philosophy. The trial should be very interesting. I am going to take the view that Marxism is a cultural philosophy."[2]

With the potential jurors present, Medina struck a friendly, somewhat paternal pose in the courtroom and warned that the trial could last as long as two months (he was off by seven months). He began by trying to weed out those with time conflicts and asked if serving on the jury would pose a significant hardship. One woman, Hannah D. Feldman, told Medina she would have trouble with after-school care for her young child if court stayed in session until 4:30 P.M. each day, as Medina planned. Medina dismissed her. Ralph M. Low persuaded Medina that his business would suffer were he to be out of reach for that length of time. Regina W. Frieber asked permission to tell Medina something privately, and after a whispered exchange she was dismissed, too—as was court for the rest of the day.

The jury selection went on for nine days. As if intended to rebut the defense's opening challenge to the selection process, the

8. The defense legal team: Abraham Isserman (left), George Crockett Jr., Richard Gladstein, Harry Sacher, and Louis McCabe. Photograph courtesy of the Southern California Library for Social Studies and Research, Los Angeles, Richard Gladstein Papers.

pool of potential jurors was sprinkled with working-class people, African Americans, and women. The first juror to be seated, in fact, was an African American woman, Thelma Dial, a part-time dressmaker who lived with her musician husband on Edgecombe Avenue, a couple of blocks north of Harlem in Washington Heights. In keeping with court tradition, as the first juror to be seated she became the de facto jury foreman.

The rest of the jury that eventually was selected represented a cross-section of the city: Russell Janney, a famous white theatrical producer and author of the best-selling novel *The Miracle of the Bells*; Ida F. Howell, a black beautician and cabdriver's wife who lived down the street from foreman Dial; Kathryn E. Dunn, an unemployed brokerage house clerk who lived on Riverside Drive; George L. Smith, an African American real estate agent and furrier who court records said lived on East 165th Street, though the *Amsterdam News* reported he lived on Edgecombe, near Dial and

Howell; Lillian Berliner, a woolen salesman's housewife living on upper Broadway; Patrick Reynolds, a retired beer salesman living on East Twenty-first Street; Henry E. Allen, an unemployed civil engineer living on the Upper East Side; Lillian Schlesinger, a store clerk living in the upper reaches of Washington Heights, a few blocks south of the Bronx; James F. Smyth, a wireman and assembler for Bell Telephone Laboratories who lived in the new Stuyvesant Town a few blocks north of Tompkins Square Park; Carrie L. Robinson, a Washington Heights widow employed by an eyeglass-case manufacturer; and Gertrude L. Corwin, a housewife living in Hell's Kitchen whose husband was a women's sportswear salesman.

The selection of Janney likely wouldn't have occurred had the defense stumbled across details from a speech he had delivered in February in Macon, Georgia. During his voir dire interview on March 16, Janney—as had the other potential jurors—told Medina that he held no prejudice toward communists. But three weeks earlier the *Macon Telegraph* had reported on the celebrity author and producer's visit there for National Brotherhood Week, quoting him on February 22 as saying that "communism breeds on intolerance. People who want communism should go to Russia and live." On February 25 the paper quoted him again, from a talk before the Macon Exchange Club in which he predicted communists, who had recently arrested Cardinal Mindszenty in Hungary, would next target Jews. "We are in a war whether we think we are or not," Janney said, citing other recent arrests of Protestants in Bulgaria. "Communism cannot have brotherhood" but instead "tries to stir up un-brotherhood. If by talk we help to stir up religious or racial hatred then we are worse than communists. We are Joseph Stalin's fifth column."[3]

Those weren't isolated admissions by Janney.

The week before Janney sat down in the jury box and answered Medina's questions, performer Carol Nason (her real name was Carole E. Nathanson) stopped by his office for one of her regular drop-ins to let Janney know what she was up to and, she hoped, to keep her in his mind as he sought performers for his productions. It's unclear whether she was a Communist Party member, but she was a sympathizer. She wanted to talk with Janney that day about an anti–Mundt-Nixon Bill program in which she planned to perform but found him in a foul mood. So she went to lunch with Janney's partner, Royal Cutter. Janney, Cutter told her, had received his jury summons and was anxious to be seated because he was working on a new detective novel and wanted to use color from the courtroom for his book. On a later visit, Cutter told her the only reason Janney made the jury was because the defense team had run out of challenges. But his presence would lead to problems.[4]

The jury was set. Its twelve members, as the *New York Times* noted in its headline March 17, the day after the last juror was picked, included seven women and five men. Of the total, three were black, two were unemployed, and two were "toilers"—the sorts of people the defense had argued were systematically excluded from the jury selection process.

And finally, two months almost to the day of when it was supposed to begin, the trial of the eleven leaders of the Communist Party was ready for opening arguments.

———————————

Throughout the jury challenge and the jury selection process, the eleven defendants remained nearly silent in the courtroom, letting the lawyers do the talking. But outside the courtroom, several of them sought to build momentum for their cause, scheduling speaking engagements in various cities and at colleges—though they often found themselves silenced before they could begin. John Gates, the *Daily Worker* editor, arrived in Chapel Hill to give a talk January 12 at the University of North Carolina, only to find the college had canceled the speech while he was traveling. He gave two speeches on city streets instead. Ten days later, Hall was added to and then dropped from the speakers' roster for a meeting of the American Labor Party on January 23 in Yonkers after the manager of the Jewish Community Center threatened to cancel the event.[5]

One defendant whose pulpit could not be taken away was Davis, the New York City Council member who joined the party because he saw it as the best hope for American blacks to find something akin to equal footing.

Davis was born in the Deep South, in Dawson, Georgia, in 1903, the grandson of slaves. As he pointed out in his posthumously published and unfinished memoir, *Communist Councilman from Harlem*, the Emancipation Proclamation was barely forty years old when he entered the world, and the legacy of slavery still permeated the community—and family—into which he was born. One of his grandmothers, who died in 1924, couldn't bend one knee; it had been wrecked in one of the frequent beatings by her slave master. The father of her first two children—who, she later told her grandchildren, could never accept his own slavery—was regularly beaten and eventually sold away as a troublemaker. She never saw or heard from him again, chilling family lore that embedded itself deeply in the young Davis.[6]

Davis's father was a successful man in, as Davis described it, three fields: "as a Negro fraternal order leader, as political leader, and as editor and publisher of the Atlanta *Independent*." The elder Davis rose to a position of significant—for a black man in the early twentieth century—influence in Republican politics in the South, built in large part through his leadership within the International Order of Odd Fellows. He also led the National Negro Publishers Association, and his editorial calls for enfranchisement of blacks drew several Ku Klux Klan protests, delivered one burning cross at a time.

But the elder Davis was not an easily dissuaded man, a lesson of character for his son. One day the father called Davis, then about sixteen years old, into his office to show him a stack of about eighty mail-delivered *Independents* that had been returned by the Covington, Georgia, postmaster with a scrawled note: "Nigger Ben, we don't allow this paper in this town stirring up trouble among our niggers. Keep it out of here and stay out of here yourself." Davis urged his father to lodge a complaint with the postal authorities. Instead, about three weeks later, the father drove with his son to Covington to hand-deliver his papers.

In a prearranged session with Odd Fellows members, the local courthouse was reserved for a discussion of the U.S. Constitution—the local policy was to make the space available for anyone, regardless of color, wishing to speak on the issue. The Davises arrived to find nearly two hundred black men, many from the surrounding rural area, and about fifty whites. The father and son entered the two-story red-brick courthouse and made their way to the second-floor courtroom, the crowd—black and white—following them in. The black men all took off their hats as the whites arrayed themselves against walls. After a brief introduction, the elder Davis rose to speak, telling the crowd, "I'm glad to see that my people respect this courthouse by removing their hats." Then he stood still, and silent, and waited. After a few moments some of the white men began removing their hats; a few filtered out in disgust. But the tension had been broken. The elder Davis spoke for about an hour about the black struggle for dignity, respect, and equality, and at the end he handed out copies of the *Independent* to anyone who wanted one—including several of the white men.

The younger Davis didn't learn until the drive back to Atlanta how carefully Davis and his local supporters had planned the event—and planned for his safety. Many of the black men in the crowd were armed and ready to act if the whites moved toward Davis, and several remained outside, weapons hidden, as they nonchalantly awaited any threats.

It's safe to assume that Davis, writing this account decades later and after the death of his father, with whom he often quarreled, embellished. But the strength and courage of his father manifested themselves in many other occasions. When the elder Davis won election as a national committeeman for the Republican Party in the mid-1920s, the windows in his home were stoned off and on for the better part of a month, the tires on his car repeatedly shredded, and two crosses lit afire in his front yard. He remained unbowed, and eventually the harassment faded away.

The younger Davis attended high school and a year of college as a boarding student at Morehouse in Atlanta, where he led a successful showdown with administrators over a requirement that students attend a two-hour evening study hall. However, Davis was suspended three weeks for his involvement (scaled back from full expulsion after his father intervened). He went on to study at Amherst College in Massachusetts and graduated from Harvard Law School in 1930. After a short stint working for a newspaper syndication service, Davis began practicing law in Atlanta, handling mostly minor cases for black clients.

In the spring of 1931, the arrest and first trial of the nine Scottsboro Boys riveted civil rights activists. The African American youths were accused of raping two white women while riding a freight train in Alabama, and the speedy conviction of eight of them exposed the lack of justice available to black defendants in the Deep South (the ninth defendant's trial ended in a hung jury, but he was not released from jail until 1937). Davis watched the trial unfold from afar and was impressed by the postconviction work by the Communist Party and the International Defense League to rally political and legal pressure aimed at overturning the convictions and death sentences.

In July 1932, Davis read an Atlanta newspaper report about the arrest of a young communist organizer named Angelo Herndon, who had been grabbed by police as he picked up his mail at a local post office. The charge: insurrection, based on an antebellum law enacted to thwart slave uprisings before they could erupt. The maximum possible sentence was death by hanging. "A brief conference with my law partner," Davis wrote, "and I was off."[7]

Davis met with Herndon in the Fulton County Towers, the local jailhouse, and signed on as his lawyer. Herndon's life was a common one—born into a large, poor black family in Alabama, he struggled as a teen to find work and over time "learned the value of organization and collective action" through local unemployment groups. He eventually joined the Communist Party in Alabama, then was transferred as an organizer to Atlanta, where he led demonstrations agitating for a program of "jobs or relief" for the poor. Public support grew, and in early July several dozen protesters led by Herndon launched a demonstration on the steps of the Fulton County Courthouse. Local police swooped in and broke it up. On July 11, indictment in hand, police arrested Herndon.

The case was to dominate Davis's life, and practice. As if anticipating the Smith Act trial, much of the evidence against Herndon came from his papers and books, which the police confiscated from his apartment. Davis pored over the seized documents, getting a crash course in a political theory and history that until then had been far outside his range of interest in segregation and Jim Crow laws. At the same time, Davis was taken with Herndon's devotion to communism. Once he had been released on $5,000 bail, Herndon moved in with a circle of fellow believers—an integrated circle, Davis noted—and resumed his organizing activities while carving out time for trial preparation with Davis.

Davis and his law partner, John Geer, settled on a multipronged strategy that would surface again in the Smith Act case. They first moved to have the indictment tossed out for lack of evidence. The judge—a rural racist (he referred to blacks, in open court, as "darkies") assigned to the case after all the Atlanta judges had begged off—denied the motion before Davis could even make his argument. Then Davis sought to introduce evidence challenging the jury selection system in Atlanta, which excluded blacks. Again the judge denied the motion, though at the nudging of the prosecutor (who recognized the judge had committed an error an appeals court could use to overturn the eventual verdict), he allowed Davis to call witnesses who testified that no blacks had served on a jury for decades. Then the judge confirmed his opinion that the practice did not amount to a denial of due process and adjourned court for the day.

As Davis and Geer left the courtroom and made their way to the elevators, they were accosted by a throng of armed white men. "Watch yourself or we'll string you up," one said. "We'll be here tomorrow and the next day," another said, as a third man flashed a knife. "That red nigger better be convicted." The next morning, as Davis left his house to return to court, he found a white, unburned cross on his front lawn with the sign: "The Klan Rides Again. Get out of the Herndon case. This is a white man's country." But Davis had his supporters, too. A small group of black men led by a local minister assigned themselves as bodyguards for Davis and Geer and stayed with them for the short duration of the trial.

It was a frustrating, one-sided affair for Davis and came with a preordained verdict. Yet Herndon, testifying in his own defense, warned that he was but a single man and that his conviction would do nothing to stop the tide. "No matter what you do with this Angelo Herndon, thousands more will arise to take his place, to fight the battles of the negro people and the workers until they are free." The jury returned with the expected verdict, guilty, but recommended mercy. He was sentenced to eighteen to twenty years in prison and served two of them before winning his release on appeal. In 1937, the U.S. Supreme Court ultimately voted 5–4 to overturn the conviction, ruling that there was no evidence that Herndon had incited insurrection.

The experience radicalized Davis, who saw the Communist Party as one of the few organizations willing to stand up for blacks. In fact, the party was far ahead of most of American society in pressing for an end to segregation and for the full extension of civil rights—stances that won the party a warmer reception among African Americans than among the general public. The night of Herndon's stirring testimony, Davis signed his own membership card in the Communist Party and handed it to his client.

Davis eventually left Atlanta for New York City and settled in Harlem. He became more politically active, including joining with the International Labor Defense and other groups pushing for a federal anti-lynching law[8]—one of eventual CRC leader William L. Patterson's main causes. Davis ran for several offices, including district attorney, on the Communist Party line, only to be shellacked each time by the city's Democratic machine. But after the 1940 Census, congressional redistricting carved out a seat dominated by Harlem. The Rev. Adam Clayton Powell Jr., the first black elected to the New York City Council, immediately took aim at it. Backed by a labor-heavy coalition, Davis won the local election to succeed Powell on the city council in 1943, becoming the second communist—Peter Cacchione from Brooklyn was elected in 1941—to win a seat.

Davis and Cacchione formed a small but vocal voting bloc, sponsoring scores of laws aimed at ending segregation in housing. They vehemently opposed the new Stuyvesant Town development—where one of the Foley Square trial jurors lived—because of the covenants barring blacks from living there, and were able to get a watered-down measure eroding such covenants in future developments. But most of their ideas and issues died.

As the Smith Act trial got under way, Davis was a regular speaker at rallies, and in the city council chambers he sought to force his colleagues to support the communists. On January 18, Davis took his seat and at the end of a debate over a city charter amendment rose as a point of "personal privilege" to denounce the deployment of some four hundred city police officers to stand guard at his trial, calling the array an "affront" to his "dignity and status" as a sitting member of the council. After lengthy wrangling, Davis was ruled out of order and the council took no action. A few days later, he introduced a measure that would have the council demand an inquiry from federal officials into the jury selection process—then under challenge in the courtroom. It was sent to a legislative death: assignment to a committee for further review.[9]

The trial itself was becoming a challenge for Davis. He was

required to be in the courtroom, and also to take his seat on the city council when it convened every Tuesday at 1:30 P.M. Several council members—political opponents—began looking for ways to oust Davis, but the body eventually agreed to meet at 5:30 P.M. for the duration of the trial, a generous conciliation that gave Davis time to get from his court seat to his council seat.

When court reconvened on the morning of March 17, the jury and four alternates finally selected and seated, the plan was for a light day of motions and a private meeting among Medina and the two legal teams to go over ground rules for the opening statements. But before Medina could, in effect, move beyond taking attendance (Gladstein was absent, ill with the flu), McCabe handed a motion to the bailiff to present to Medina, who scanned it. "I would like to submit this to Mr. McGohey," Medina said, handing the papers to his bailiff to pass along to the prosecution, "so that he may have occasion to make any observation that he desires." McGohey, as it turned out, had several observations to make.[10]

The papers were a notice that Dennis had fired McCabe as his lawyer and wanted to represent himself for the duration of the trial. Scowling as he read the petition, McGohey saw a trick—he was afraid Dennis might later seek to rehire a lawyer, adding yet another delay to the proceedings. And he warned Medina that the case law was still unsettled on whether Dennis could later come back, if convicted, and appeal on the grounds of inadequate counsel, or that he had not been fully aware of the consequences of serving as his own lawyer.

Medina asked Dennis to stand and began questioning him. Yes, Dennis said, he understood that he was choosing to fire an expert in favor of hiring an amateur, himself. Medina wanted to make clear that Dennis knew what he was doing and the risk he was taking. "There are so many things in the law that some people call technicalities, but which are rules of law that have grown up over the years that lawyers know about . . . that an ordinary layman would not know about," Medina said. "And he might possibly sacrifice some of his rights by not knowing these things. Now, have you taken that into consideration?"

Dennis, who had represented himself in court before, had indeed considered that, he told the judge in his tight, clipped voice. And he made it clear that he saw the trial was focused not on his guilt but on his beliefs. "I am called upon to defend the principles and practice of the Communist Party, to defend my honor, my convictions, the whole meaning of my life," Dennis said. "And therefore, sir, I believe that I can best defend my interests and the interests of my party by acting as my own attorney." Medina told Dennis to focus on defending himself, not his party. "You are here as an individual, and the defense of yourself of the crime that is charged here, I think that is the one thing that should be your primary concern," Medina said.

McGohey also raised the concern that with Dennis acting as his own attorney, he would be able to make statements in his opening remarks, objections and questions to witnesses, and his summation, subtly introducing themes and details without taking the stand himself, where he would be subject to cross-examination. It was a fair reading—Dennis had implied he intended to do just that. Medina said he would deal with those issues as they arose and gave Dennis permission to defend himself. The tall, gray-haired party leader quietly moved his seat from the rail to the table, joining the lawyers and leaving his comrades in the back row.

As a strategy, Dennis's move made sense for the defendants, who intended to rebut anything the prosecution witnesses might have to say about party doctrine and teachings. The rest of the lawyers could focus on raising legal objections and tap into their finely honed cross-examination skills. And McCabe, though no longer representing Dennis, was still part of the case as attorney for Henry Winston. All Dennis need do to protect his own rights was join in on any objections the lawyers might raise. So the net effect was to add an expert on party policy and propaganda to the defense team, giving the defendants a direct voice to the jury.

Dennis's journey to the lawyers' table, even if he was a strategic interloper, was long and circuitous, his life one of deprivation for the cause that exacted deep personal costs—including his oldest son. And it's a remarkable story.

———————

Dennis was born Francis X. Waldron Jr. (he assumed different names several times during his life) on August 10, 1905, in Seattle,

Washington, the son of an Irish American railroad worker from New Jersey and a Minnesota farm girl. His father spent his life pursuing get-rich-quick ventures from Alaska to Shanghai, which meant the young family moved often, changing economic classes, in effect, with every scant success or, more often, failure (they remained in Seattle as the father traveled). The father eventually gave up and "resigned himself early to the loser's life on the shabby edges of respectable, lower-class Seattle." Dennis's mother died when he was eleven, an event Dennis's longtime partner, Peggy, later came to believe shattered the young boy's Catholic faith. "I stopped believing in the power of prayer when she died," he once said.[11]

As the teenaged son of a dissolute father, Dennis sold newspapers on street corners, worked in a grocer's horse stable, and delivered goods after school driving a horse and wagon. He migrated to Washington's network of lumber camps, where he crossed paths with Industrial Workers of the World organizers—the Wobblies. He became infatuated with their war stories of beatings and arrests, police showdowns in 1916 in Everett and Centralia, Washington, and their fights for free speech all while trying to organize workers to seek better wages and working conditions. Dennis embraced the current of idealism and romance weaving through the stories, and once back in Seattle began hanging around the American Federation of Labor halls. He was also drawn to street agitators on their soapboxes—particularly the socialists arguing that there was a better way than capitalism. Dennis hit the library and found his own personal light by reading tracts by Lenin, who had recently led the Russian Bolsheviks in their revolution. His kinship with the Wobblies faded and he fell in with the communists, joining the party just after his twenty-first birthday.

Peggy Dennis also was a person of many names. She was born Regina Karasick in New York City, the second daughter of Jewish political activists; the mother fled Russia after being ordered to Siberia as a dangerous radical. As the 1905 Russian revolt erupted, before Peggy Dennis was born, the family contemplated returning to join the fight. But the uprising was squelched and the parents stayed in New York, then moved to Los Angeles in 1912 as a cure for the mother's chronic asthma. Peggy Dennis grew up amid radical schools and movements—she became a communist at age sixteen, married a fellow activist at age eighteen, and moved to San Francisco as part of the leadership of the Young Communist League.

The marriage didn't last. Peggy, still a newlywed, traveled in June 1928 to the Pacific Coast Marxist Summer School in Woodland, California, a few miles north of Davis in the Central Valley. Dennis was also assigned to the camp, leading seminars and discussions on Marxist principles, just a few months after his father had died in Washington. The two quickly fell in love. It was a radical's romance. They never married, and it's unclear whether Peggy divorced her first husband. Over the next few years the couple moved around California as Dennis organized and agitated from the docks of San Pedro to the farm fields of the Imperial Valley. In November 1929 the couple had a child, whom they named Tim, an event that effectively took Peggy out of active participation in the radical movement. Dennis soldiered on, though, and was arrested several times and occasionally beaten by police, who were particularly vicious in the Imperial Valley. One of the arrests stemmed from Dennis's leadership of a March 6, 1930, rally to demand jobs and food that ended in chaos, and under police clubs, at Los Angeles City Hall.

It's interesting to compare accounts of that demonstration. In Peggy Dennis's telling, the participants numbered ten thousand, a peaceful joyous group marching behind banners—until they encountered the police. "Machine guns were targeted on them from roof tops. One thousand police on foot, horseback and in patrol cars clubbed, tear-gassed and horse-bumped them into side streets. Falling, fighting, marching, singing, shouting, the demonstrators inched their way through side streets and over barricades towards their elected city official, Mayor John C. Porter. All they wanted was to present their needs. City Hall was guarded like a medieval fortress. Inside the Mayor hid from his hungry, jobless, constituency. Like many others, Gene and his defense unit had been beaten into unconsciousness and dragged by their feet to a patrol car and to jail. We counted our injured by the hundreds."

The *Los Angeles Times*—and it need be noted that the paper was virulently anti-communist, and thus interested in lessening the march's significance—described the scene much differently. Under the headline "Red March on City Hall Made Fiasco by Police," the *Times* reported: "The widely heralded march on the City Hall by local communists and Red sympathizers failed of its purpose yesterday when the projected demonstration was swallowed up in a throng of five thousand idly curious and nonparticipating spectators, and left the radical leaders grumbling about the lack of unity in their ranks." The story that followed was a gleeful accounting of police using blackjacks to subdue those who resisted arrest.

"A good many of the men arrested received thwackings on their heads when they resisted the officers, but aside from a few scratches and bumps none of them received injuries to display to their 'comrades.' The most obdurate of the radicals were the women, and their men leaders cowered in the crowds for the most part and permitted those 'Bolshevixen' to do the public scratching, kicking and howling. The whole affair was most disheartening to the communists. They had planned a serious mass demonstration and it was smothered completely by the alertness of the officers and the disinclination of the onlookers to join the lawlessness."[12]

Somewhere between the two accounts the truth exists. It's hard to imagine five thousand "idly curious" people just happened by the demonstration, or came to watch it as a spectacle, as the *Times* reported. But it's also hard to believe Peggy Dennis's account of ten thousand people mounting a Bastille-style storming that fell short. In all, the paper said, twenty-six people were arrested, including Dennis. Peggy Dennis reports that he required unspecified surgery two weeks later when a gash on his skull from a police baton became infected.

As the trial from that arrest began in May 1930, Dennis, acting as his own attorney, and his fellow defendants sought to challenge the selection of the jury as unrepresentative, presaging the Foley Square trial nearly two decades later. The challenge failed, and before the trial ended Dennis got word of a pending, separate Imperial Valley indictment on charges of "conspiracy to foment revolution during the cantaloupe season," later amended to "suspicion of criminal syndicalism." The potential sentence was forty-two years in prison, as opposed to the six months he might face in the Los Angeles case. So Dennis went underground, began calling himself Tim Ryan, and moved to New York City—without his wife and son.

Dennis, as Ryan, traveled among America's leading industrial cities—Detroit, Chicago, Pittsburgh—as an organizer for the Trade Union Unity League, a communist offshoot focusing on heavy industries. After seven months Peggy Dennis received a letter from him saying that he was "leaving, reluctantly, for more distant places," a letter that, he told her, had been posted after he left. He had been ordered to Moscow, and in a few weeks Peggy Dennis and the couple's young son followed.

By then the world had fallen into the Great Depression, and conditions in Moscow were even worse than in the United States. Peggy Dennis took the severe deprivations in stride, a function, she believed, of the times and the young communist society's struggles to get on its feet. Harder to take was Dennis's lack of openness. He had known, but hadn't shared with his wife, that he wouldn't be in Moscow long. After some negotiations to keep him out of an office job, which he despised, Dennis began training as an international organizer, and a few weeks after the family had settled into a slice of a Moscow apartment in the winter of 1931 he announced he would soon be going to the Far East, and then South Africa, leaving Peggy and their son behind in Moscow.

In Peggy's account, written decades later, the anger still leaps off the page. She was as much a true believer in communism as he, but she also saw the importance of family. While she balked at the forced separation by party orders, she acceded to them, and she tried to cope with the difficult living conditions. "I invested each unfamiliar personal hardship with an emotionalism about sharing the new, difficult Soviet construction," she wrote of Stalin's "Five Year Plans" to accelerate industrial development. "I took a puritanical pleasure in the very starkness of daily life: the communal kitchens and toilets down long, dark corridors; the cramped one-room with Tim ensconced behind a nook we created by pushing the large wooden wardrobe perpendicular to the wall at the far end of the room; spit-baths in a tin wash basin filled from the tea kettle heated in the communal kitchen; trips to the public bath-house which became a social event; ration cards that produced little else than our daily allotment of bread." She worked as a teacher, then in an office at Profintern—the organization seeking to spread communism through labor unions—where she amassed clippings files from American and British newspapers and gave weekly updates to various committees. Among those she reported to was Irving Potash, who would later join her husband in the dock in Medina's courtroom.

After two years Dennis returned to Moscow briefly, en route to Shanghai, where Mao Zedong's communist insurgents were slowly taking over the countryside. He left on bad terms after accusing Peggy Dennis of trading sex for her advancement in Moscow—an unusual display of petulance for him. But a few months later Peggy Dennis was on the road herself, ordered to travel Europe for a year serving as a liaison among communist groups in different countries. Her son, Tim, age four when she began her travels, was taken in by the Comintern's International Children's Home in Ivanovo, some 140 miles northeast of Moscow. Peggy Dennis doesn't delve into the emotions of leaving her child behind and paints the work itself as uneventful—boring, even—but her description makes it sound as though she was working as a spy courier, posing as a tourist while delivering news and money to people in the underground.

Eventually she joined Dennis in Shanghai for a time; then they both split off on other assignments—he remained in China, it appears, while she skipped among Istanbul, Cairo, Haifa, and Tel Aviv. Returning to Moscow in January 1935, she found Dennis awaiting her with word that after months of requests, the couple was being allowed to return to the United States to work with the party there, in their home country. Dennis believed that the legal charges he had fled would likely not be pursued if they returned (in part because he was no longer Frank Waldron).

But Tim, they were told, would not be allowed to join them. The belief was that if people in the United States knew the couple had traveled the world as underground communist organizers, the Dennises would face severe problems and likely arrest. And Tim, who had effectively been raised in Russia, spoke only Russian, an impossible thing to explain away. So the boy would be sent later, the couple was told. "Back in our room, Gene paced grimly. With a drink in one hand and a chain-lit cigarette in the other, he sought to bring his emotions under control. For once, I remained silent. With back to the wall, I stood hugging my body with crossed arms, keeping it from falling apart." Her options, she thought, were to agree or to stay in Moscow with Tim—and the longer she stayed, the more difficult it would be to get permission for the boy to leave. "I faced the fact the only way to get Tim home was for us to go ahead and pave the way by assimilating ourselves quickly and fully into the home scene."

The United States they arrived in was in much worse shape than when they had left. The couple—adopting now the names Eugene and Peggy Dennis—was deployed to Wisconsin, where they took part in political and organizing campaigns, trying to carve out a piece of the progressive political scene for the communists. When war broke out in Spain they petitioned to go join the fight, and in 1937 received permission, traveling to Paris to await contacts who were to smuggle them across the border. But before they could slip through the Pyrenees, new orders came directing them to Moscow instead, where Dennis was to serve as a U.S. representative to the Comintern—office work he hated. The silver lining for Peggy Dennis—they were reunited with Tim.

They also found old friends had disappeared. When they inquired, they were told not to. It was the time of the Great Purge. Voids marked the dead, and old friends were now fearful strangers, onetime intimates to be distrusted. Less than a year later, they returned to the United States—again without Tim—and Dennis stepped into the top leadership of the American party. They traveled to Moscow again in 1941 and fled home under evacuation orders as the German army marched eastward. They spent the war years in New York City, where their second son, Gene Jr., was born December 7, 1942. Except for occasional visits after Stalin's death in 1953, Tim remained a stranger to them, growing into adulthood in the Soviet Union, then marrying and beginning his own family there.

And Eugene Dennis entered the top leadership circle of the American Communist Party.

McGohey finally got his chance to lay out for the jury what he and his assistants intended to prove: that the eleven men on trial had engaged in a conspiracy to teach and advocate the necessity of overthrowing the U.S. government.

McGohey took his place in front of the jury, looking every bit the prosecutor in his dark suit, clear-rimmed glasses, and silvering, slicked-back hair parted in the middle. He was a slender man, with a slender face and a thin top lip resting on a fleshier lower lip, like the stern headmaster in a private school. The prosecution's argument was simple, if a bit of a reach. McGohey told the jury in his no-nonsense voice that, under Marxist-Leninist theory, a socialist government could be achieved "only by the violent and forceful seizure of power by the proletariat under the leadership of the Communist Party." The mere fact that the defendants were party leaders, and had created schools and other education programs to spread communism, established their guilt under the 1940 Smith Act, which barred advocating revolution.

McGohey found significance in a series of party policy shifts. In 1943, Stalin, Churchill, and Roosevelt met in Tehran and agreed that their three nations would work together to defeat the Nazis. Taking that lead, the American Communist Party met at a convention in 1944 and dissolved itself, then re-formed as the Communist Political Association, reflecting Browder's wartime urging that the American party should stop focusing on creating a socialist America and work with other groups as a show of American unity. Browder took it as an article of faith that after the war the U.S. and the U.S.S.R. would remain allies. "Browder said that the communists wanted to make sure that humanity would be organized for peace for generations to come," McGohey said. And, McGohey took pains to point out, Foster, Dennis, and most of the other indicted men were there, joining in the acclaim.

But as the war was ending, and the fate of Europe hanging in the balance, the international accord between the Soviets and the West began to fray. The Duclos letter, denouncing Browder and the concept of peaceful coexistence, led to a sudden change in the American party during its 1945 convention. Browder was tossed aside in favor of Foster and Dennis, who, with the others, reaffirmed the party's commitment to Marxist-Leninist theory and denounced Browder. The Communist Political Association was folded, and the conventioneers reconstituted themselves as the CPUSA.

That change, McGohey argued, marked the beginning of the conspiracy. The defendants had supported Browder and his call for peace; now they repudiated him as revisionist. "They went back to the old Communist Party organized to establish socialism in the United States according to the Marxist-Leninist teaching," McGohey told the jury. "That teaching is—as we shall show—that socialism can only be established by the violent overthrow and destruction of our constitutional form of government . . . and the setting up of the dictatorship of the proletariat by violent and forceful seizure of power under the leadership of the Communist Party."

The party organized local clubs in communities and in workplaces and required local members to join. These, McGohey argued, "are not just political or social groups. They are in reality and in fact classes for the indoctrination of their members with the theory and practice of Marxist-Leninist principles" aimed at overthrowing the U.S. government. The clubs sponsored classes in which communist theory was taught, using books published by the party itself. Camps were set up to train those who showed leadership potential.

"In each of these schools it is reiterated constantly that the students are being trained as professional revolutionaries," McGohey said. "Marxism, they are taught, is not merely dogma, it is a guide to action. The Russian revolution is studied in detail as a blueprint for the revolution in every other country." He said they were taught that in Russia "50,000 trained revolutionaries" working under the party had, "by skillfully directing the proletariat at the time of national crisis, brought about the overthrow of the government. This is the model for revolution in this country."

McGohey acknowledged that the new party constitution contained sections that "purport to urge support of American democracy." But that was just a ruse, he said, "mere talk" to mask the devotion to violent overthrow. The prosecution, he said, would call on witnesses to back all that up.

McGohey's opening statement was brief, and when he finished, Isserman rose to tell Medina that the defense had several issues it wanted to bring up. Medina sent the jury from the room and the motions flew. Isserman asked for a direct verdict of acquittal. "The activities charged to the defendants, as described by the U.S. attorney, are all activities embracing political activity, political assembly, the right of assembly, the right of petition, and expression of opinion . . . protected by the First Amendment," Isserman argued.

Medina rejected the motion without comment.

"Further, to compel the defendants to stand trial on these facts is an application of the Smith Act, which is unconstitutional, and such a trial denies the defendants due process of law," Isserman argued. Medina rejected that motion without comment, too. Isserman raised two more related motions seeking a mistrial because McGohey, in talking about the history of the party before April 1, 1945—when the indictment alleged the conspiracy began—had introduced aspects that went beyond the scope of the indictment. Medina found no merit in those, either, and called the jury back into the room.

As the jurors settled into their seats, Dennis stood up at the defense lawyers' table and moved toward a "pulpit-like stand" near the jury box. Tall and stocky with a ruddy face and a vertical shock of gray hair, he began his opening statement in a tight, wavering voice—the effect of a bout of tuberculosis when he was a young man.[13]

No, he said, the Communist Party was not bent on revolution. The indictment did not accuse him and his fellow communists of acting against the U.S. government—just with being communists. And being a communist was nothing like what the government said it was. "Our party does not bear the remotest resemblance to the fantastic conspiracy painted in the indictment," Dennis said. "We communist leaders are accused actually only of exercising our right of political association, of teaching and advocating certain political doctrines and, hence, we are on trial for our political beliefs."

Dennis told the jury that he and the Communist Party had worked to support the U.S. government during World War II, and several of the defendants had served in the military. McGohey cut him off with an objection, complaining to Medina that the indictment mentioned nothing of that and that Dennis was bringing in irrelevant details, which Medina upheld.

"I think, your Honor," Dennis said, "and I respectfully submit, that since we are charged with teaching and advocating certain things since April 1, 1945, that it is very relevant and essential that we establish really what we communists taught, advocated and did, and therefore, sir—" Medina jumped in: "Mr. Dennis, I anticipate certain difficulty in inducing you to appreciate the force of my instructions because you are not a lawyer." After a bit more wrangling, Dennis continued his statement, detailing the acts of the party leaders, including working for Roosevelt's reelection in 1944, and later objecting to Truman's policies. He spoke of the party's stances against lynching in the South, its support of unions, its belief that the United Nations needed to take root before Medina cut him off again. "Mr. Dennis, I cannot see how that has a bearing on the case. It is the same old story. The question is whether you were guilty of the conspiracy which is charged. Now the fact that you advocated a lot of other things seems to me quite beside the point."

Dennis countered that his personal political intent was part of the charges against him, and that to defend himself he needed to establish a contrary explanation of what he was doing during the time covered by the indictment—an argument that Sacher and Isserman rose to join in. "You know," Medina said, "it is a funny thing. The other day Mr. Dennis said he wanted to be his own lawyer, that he could plead for himself, and now it seems as though there were a number of assistants." Isserman argued that he was joining because he feared that if Medina shut down Dennis's reasoning in his opening statement, Isserman would be similarly limited.

Medina let Dennis continue—and the party leader's statements quickly drifted further afield, touching on Indonesia, U.S. government support for Chiang Kai-shek in China, and the fate of Israel before McGohey again objected and Medina shut Dennis off. "I will not let that go on any more more," the judge said. "It is so plainly irrelevant. It is just using the courtroom for the purpose of propaganda, and I won't have it." The two argued—in front of the jury—with Medina calling Dennis "obstinate" and accusing him of trying to run the courtroom and of deliberately disobeying court directives. Medina, clearly exasperated, ordered the court to take an early recess for lunch.

It's unclear what Medina did during lunch recess, but when court reconvened at 2:30 P.M., he remained silent as Dennis resumed his statement, a long dissertation on the history and teaching of Marxist-Leninist thought that rambled through Abraham Lincoln and the American Revolution as a source of inspiration for "people striving to free themselves from the despotism of monarchs and feudalism."

Crockett followed and similarly—but more succinctly—strayed far from the focus of the indictment. He also squabbled briefly with Medina after Crockett told the jury he hoped to be able to introduce as evidence a deposition from the ailing Foster—something Medina had ruled against twice before in the early stages of the case, as Foster's health was deteriorating and his ability to take part came into question.

McCabe was next and managed to get through his statement with minimal interruptions—and no squabbles with Medina. The Philadelphia lawyer warned the jurors to weigh carefully the testimony they would hear from "a witness who has testified he has lived a lie," setting the stage for what would become the defense's rebuttal to the expected series of turncoats and undercover spies who would make the government's case.

The defense's opening statements continued the next day, March 22, finishing up with Gladstein, who again sparred a bit with Medina. When Gladstein finished and sat down, Medina turned to the jury and essentially offered a rebuttal, telling them that the indictment charged each of the men individually with being part of a conspiracy that was against the law under the 1940 Smith Act. In essence, he said, the defendants' argument that their activities were protected under the First Amendment was not an issue for the jury to decide, just whether the evidence they would hear proved beyond a reasonable doubt that the individual defendants had conspired to teach or advocate the necessity of overthrowing the U.S. government.

Medina released the jury, and Gladstein lit into the judge over his comments as "nothing less than a rebuttal argument that might have been made by Mr. McGohey. . . . What your Honor did in making those comments to the jury constitutes prejudicial misconduct on the part of the Court, I assign it as such, and I ask the court to declare a mistrial." Gladstein's argument went nowhere. "Well, I won't do it," Medina said. "If you think I am going to sit here like a bump on a log through this trial, you are making a big mistake."

They spent more than an hour arguing about Medina's behavior, including a bizarre debate over whether Medina's scratching of his head during the defense's opening statements was a habit or a signal to the jury, then moved on to fresh motions by the defense that they be allowed to take a deposition from Foster, whom they described as being tried in absentia. Medina held his ground, then abruptly ended the court session, setting the stage for the next morning to hear the first witness testimony about the charges themselves in a trial now in its tenth week.

McGohey planned to start with his biggest gun: the star witness, Louis Budenz.

SEVEN

Deserters
and Spies

By the time Louis Budenz stepped up to the witness stand in Room 110, raised his right hand, and promised to tell the whole truth and nothing but the truth, he was among the best-known former communists in the United States—far better known than when he was managing editor for the *Daily Worker*. With his headline-spawning defection in 1945, Budenz had become a full-fledged cause célèbre, the man whose Catholicism and faith in God overwhelmed whatever it was that drew him to the Communist Party in the first place.

And, to the communists and their supporters, Budenz was among the most loathed people in America.

Budenz, a slender, balding man with arching eyebrows, was born in 1891 into a strongly Roman Catholic family near Indianapolis and as a boy would walk nearly a mile to attend the daily 6:00 A.M. Mass at the local church. As a teenager educated in parochial schools, Budenz took to heart Pope Leo XIII's *Rerum Novarum*—published the year Budenz was born—on "the rights and duties of capital and labor" that, among other things, assured the moral basis for

121

the dignity of work and the rights of laborers to be paid a reasonable wage. After studying at the Indianapolis Law School, he was admitted to the Indiana bar in 1913 and almost immediately joined the United Carpenters and Joiners, then moved to St. Louis to work for the German Catholic Central-Verein, an influential benevolent society in the pre–World War I years. But Budenz, whose Catholicism was a central part of his life, was summarily excommunicated in 1921 for marrying a divorced woman. Cast off from his church, he devoted even more of his life to social and political causes.[1]

In 1920, Budenz left St. Louis for New York City at the behest of Roger Baldwin to work as publicity director for the American Civil Liberties Union and to engage in a movement to wrest control of electric streetcars from private hands and entrust them to public utilities. A short time later he moved on to edit the new radical socialist magazine *Labor Age*, a position he held for more than a decade while simultaneously working as an organizer for the delightfully named Federation for Full-Fashioned Hosiery Workers. Under their banner he became immersed in street-level unionism, traveling from strike to strike, including the Allen-A Hosiery showdown in Kenosha, Wisconsin. "Concentrating especially on getting injunctions and yellow-dog contracts nullified," Budenz wrote in his memoir, "I was arrested twenty-one times and acquitted twenty-one times in the course of these organizational drives."

In Toledo, Ohio, his arrest—along with those of several other labor leaders—during the infamous 1934 Electric Auto-Lite Company strike was one of the events that fed the Battle of Toledo, when full-scale rioting broke out after the Ohio National Guard opened fire on a mob of protesters, killing two of them. But the violence in Toledo was only part of a raucous summer of often radical-inspired strikes, from the Trotyskist-influenced Teamsters in Minneapolis to the 400,000-member walkouts in the East Coast textile trades to the shutdown of West Coast shipping by Harry Bridges's longshoremen. Amid all that, Budenz stood out as a high-profile player within the leftist corner of the labor movement—his name appeared in twenty-nine *New York Times* articles detailing everything from his involvement in strikes to his speeches to an open letter he wrote in 1931 to William Green, president of the the American Federation of Labor, accusing the group of abandoning the interests of workers.[2]

In October 1935, Budenz made the leap from high-profile leftist union organizer to Communist Party member. He was drawn, he wrote in his memoirs, by the American Communist Party's adoption of the United Front merger of pro-worker movements against Hitler and fascism. Budenz had disliked the centralized control exerted by the Comintern, and by Moscow, over the American communists. He thought the United Front was a positive move because it put the party at the vanguard of the kind of work he had been doing for the past fifteen years. So Budenz decided to become a member.

He joined the *Daily Worker*, eventually moving into management and meeting routinely with Browder, Foster, Dennis, and other top party leaders. But as World War II was winding down and the political winds began shifting again, Budenz's old concerns about domination by Moscow rekindled, and he came to believe the party was simply a shell for Soviet political ambitions that ultimately would harm the very workers communism was supposed to help. At the same time, under the secret tutelage of Monsignor Fulton J. Sheen, Budenz had been preparing to return to the Catholic Church (apparently the public relations value of his defection outweighed church concerns over his marriage to a divorcée). Budenz quietly mapped out an exit strategy for leaving the party. He feared that if his comrades got wind of his plans, they would launch a preemptive smear campaign against him, and he wanted whatever publicity his move generated to serve his purposes, not the party's.

On October 10, 1945, Budenz, his wife, and their three daughters met Sheen at Saint Patrick's Cathedral in Manhattan, where the monsignor welcomed them back into the Church in a private ceremony. Budenz issued a press release renouncing communism and its "aims to establish tyranny over the human spirit" and decreed communism "incompatible" with Catholicism. He immediately left for South Bend, Indiana, where he—again with Sheen's help—had lined up a job teaching at Notre Dame (he eventually moved on to Fordham University in New York City).

The news came as a bolt to the party leadership, and they quickly branded Budenz a traitor to the working class. "The form in which Mr. Budenz states his abandonment of the labor and communist movement is no more than a cover to conceal his flight from the ranks of the labor movement and from the democratic cause of our country and the world," Foster said in a statement that blasted Budenz for his "desertion." *The Daily Worker*, in an editorial, tried to rebut Budenz's stated reasons for leaving the party, arguing that the party didn't ask its members what their religious affiliation might be. And it said the party had many Catholic members, particularly in Europe.[3]

Budenz's split made most of the major newspapers—and likely was one of the factors that drove Soviet spy handler Elizabeth Bentley to turn herself and her list of spy contacts in to the FBI. And it launched Budenz on a new career as academic and professional witness against communism, testifying in criminal cases and before Congress and delivering speeches. He published his memoir, *This Is My Story*, in 1947, and wrote a wide range of magazine and newspaper articles (including a syndicated column) denouncing communism and exposing what he saw as the party's desire to take over the United States.

From the beginning of his preparations for the Foley Square case, McGohey had viewed Budenz as his main witness—a former insider with key evidence about the party's intent. But Budenz had become so busy with his public appearances that in September 1948, two months after the Smith Act indictments, he wrote to McGohey to try to wriggle out of testifying in the trial, at the time scheduled to open in October. Budenz told McGohey that he was overextended and exhausted and that his doctors had advised him to lighten his schedule. McGohey demanded a face-to-face meeting, and over lunch at a Fordham faculty dining hall Budenz told the prosecutor that in the previous several months he had testified in cases in Washington State, before the grand jury in Manhattan (investigating Bentley's allegations), at hearings in Washington, D.C., in a trial in Hawaii (Gladstein was one of the defense lawyers), and then at more hearings in Washington, D.C. The schedule had forced him to miss teaching some of his scheduled classes, including proctoring his own final exams in the spring, and the opening of classes just a few weeks earlier for the fall semester. Budenz was just too busy, he told McGohey, to take the stand.

McGohey, eyeing Budenz, didn't think the former editor looked particularly ill or overstressed. He noted that Budenz picked out a hearty lunch—"roast lamb and vegetables, coffee and apple pie." And McGohey wasn't about to give his star witness much leeway. "I told

Mr. Budenz that under no circumstances would I agree to excuse him," McGohey said, indicating that he also played to Budenz's vanity. "I pointed out to him further that if I were to excuse him without a public official record of the reasons I would be subject to the severest criticism for having failed to call the man who is popularly regarded as the outstanding expert on Communist Party activities at the present time." Then McGohey handed Budenz a subpoena. To seal it, on the way out he stopped at the office of Budenz's superiors at Fordham to reiterate how significant Budenz would be to the government's case.[4]

McGohey, to no one's surprise, prevailed. Budenz took the stand on the morning of March 23 and faced a packed house. Over the next two weeks, under (primarily) McGohey's questioning, Budenz detailed his decade as a key insider within the Communist Party, testifying that party leaders had sworn oaths of fealty to Stalin and that they were training for the day when revolution would come. In one of the more perverse turns in the trial, he introduced what he referred to as "Aesopian language"—testifying that the communist leaders used a verbal shorthand to communicate with their followers that was loosely patterned on a tactic Lenin devised in pre-revolutionary Russia.

The historical existence of "Aesopian language" was real enough. Faced with tight tsarist censorship, Lenin and other leaders would use catchphrases in articles in *Pravda*, their newspaper, that their followers understood to refer to current political events without running afoul of bans. For example, publishing the name of the communistic Russian Social-Democratic Labor Party was forbidden; Lenin and his colleagues would refer to the party in print as "the underground." The Bolshevik agenda of an eight-hour workday and confiscation of land in the name of the workers was referred to as the "uncurtailed demands of 1905." The meaning was clear to those in the know—including, it seems, the censors they were trying to evade—but circumvented the bans on what could be written about.[5] "Lenin and others called this legal method the 'Aesopian' one—after Aesop, the legendary ancient Greek author of fables who presented his vinegary appraisal of human foibles under the guise of doings and sayings of sundry beasts. The didactic, pedantic spirit of those fables apparently appealed to Lenin and led him to use the term."[6]

In Budenz's telling, though, the old ruse to avoid censors became a sinister secret code through which words could be twisted to mean anything, undercutting the very premise of language. "Genuine patriotism" cited by American communists meant loyalty to the Soviet Union, not the United States. A phrase in the opening of the party's constitution that declared the American Communist Party to be based "upon the principles of scientific socialism, Marxism-Leninism," actually meant, Budenz testified, that "socialism can only be attained by the violent shattering of the capitalist state, and the setting up of a dictatorship of the proletariat by force and violence in place of that state. In the United States this would mean that the Communist Party of the United States is basically committed to the overthrow of the United States as set up by the U.S. Constitution." And the phrase in the preamble pledging the party to defend the U.S. Constitution against "reactionary enemies who would destroy democracy and popular liberties" referred, Budenz testified, to "those who are opposed to the communist movement in the Soviet Union. . . . In the Soviet Union, Soviet dictatorship is interpreted as the highest stage of democracy."[7]

There was more than word games in play, Budenz insisted. He said Eugene Dennis had twice, both at the beginning and the end of World War II, told fellow members of the American "politburo" to prepare to go underground and to be ready for civil war. And Budenz credited communist agitation with the start of the seventy-six-day Allis-Chalmers strike in March 1941, which for a time derailed efforts to help supply England with war materiel as it fought Nazi Germany, still in its pact with Stalin. Budenz testified that Dennis had reported at a secret party meeting that he had told union leader Harold Christoffel, a communist sympathizer if not a full member, that a strike at the plant was "recommended" by the politburo "to stop the flow of war materials." Dennis reported that Christoffel said "an occasion for such a stoppage could be found."[8]

On the second day of his testimony, Budenz told the jury that the American party in 1945 changed its wartime stance of cooperation with the U.S. government to its postwar opposition after receiving orders from Dmitri Z. Manuilsky, former head of the Comintern, when, as the leader of the Ukraine, he attended an international meeting in San Francisco. And Budenz testified that the entire "United Front" movement teaming the communists with other groups was simply a marking-time maneuver while the communists continued to plan for revolution.

Budenz's testimony was a learning opportunity for Medina, who openly admitted he knew little about the party. During one argument over the admissability of a document that referred to the Communist International, Medina said, "Probably all of you gentlemen know about this. I don't happen to know about it. What is the Communist International?"[9] He also asked Budenz, as the testimony went along, to define such terms as "cadre" and "communist activist."[10]

For the prosecution, Budenz was a crucial witness, even if he had by then developed a reputation as an erratic finger-pointer. "In most of his previous public appearances, Witness Budenz had destroyed much of his value as an expert on communism by going off half-cocked every time the word was mentioned," *Time* magazine pronounced in its coverage of his testimony. "But this time Witness Budenz, directed by the prosecution, testified icily and directly."[11] The scenarios Budenz—a former insider who had repented the error of his ways—painted about shadowy men using intentionally disingenuous language played right into the growing hysteria about the "Reds in our midst." And in true Orwellian fashion, the mere fact that the communists denied their intentions validated, through Budenz's Aesopian interpretation of their message, that they did indeed intend to foment revolution. To deny was to affirm. "Budenz was like the man who came to a psychiatrist complaining that everything he saw reminded him of a nude woman," Green wrote years after the trial. "Everything the party said or did, no matter what, reminded Budenz—and the prosecution—of violent overthrow, their own pet phobia. All else to them was mere camouflage."[12]

Even more chilling was the government's use of Budenz's testimony to cite books as evidence of criminality. On March 30, McGohey handed Medina's bailiff a copy of *The History of the Communist Party* and asked that it be entered into evidence. Isserman leapt to his feet to object: "We are putting a book on trial." But Medina saw it differently. "It is trying those persons who used the book and other means to allegedly commit a crime, and that is part of the paraphernalia of the crime." In effect, the judge said, books were the same as a burglar's tools, and Budenz cited four of them—

M. J. Olgin's *Why Communism, The Program of the Communist International*, Stalin's *The Foundations of Leninism*, and J. Peters's *Manual on Organization*.[13] The prosecution duly read extensive passages from each into the record, seeking to establish through the books the trajectory of Communist Party theory and its reliance on revolution as key to replacing capitalism.

The defense lawyers went at Budenz with unbridled vehemence. Budenz had been vilifed by the party since his very public departure, and the defense team was openly hostile. On the first day of testimony, Sacher offered a predictable objection to a line of questioning after Budenz testified that party leaders had ordered him to Chicago in 1937 to become editor of the *Midwest Daily Record*, a communist newspaper that Budenz led until it closed down in 1940 and he returned to New York. McGohey asked Budenz who had sent him and where the conversation took place. He sought a clarification after Budenz said the first directions were given on the ninth floor of the *Daily Worker* building, when in fact the paper occupied the ninth floor of the Communist Party's building. McGohey got as far as "Do you mean the ninth floor—" before Sacher cut him off.

"I object to that as leading and subjective to this witness, obviously so," Sacher said. Medina replied that he didn't see a problem with the question since "it seems fairly obvious that that is what the witness meant."

"I don't know that anything that can be taken for obvious with this witness," Sacher said, drawing a demand by McGohey that the comment be stricken from the record as Frank Gordon, one of the assistant prosecutors, pointed a finger at Sacher and told him to sit down, a breach of courtroom decorum. Sacher, naturally, objected.

"Your honor, this man, Mr. Gordon, just turned and pointed his finger at me and said, 'Sit down,'" Sacher said, his voice rising. "I want to call that to the Court's attention. I will not permit myself to be terrorized by counsel for the Government."

Medina, unfazed, told him, "I see you are returning to your old role," eliciting another burst of outrage from Sacher, who objected to Medina's comment in front of the jury. "Mr. Sacher," Medina replied, "I dislike shouting and disorder and I will not tolerate it. I don't know what little passage may have occurred here between counsel here but there is no conceivable justification for your carrying on this way."

"Your Honor," Sacher responded, "Mr. Gordon turned around and he faced me and waved his finger at me and said, 'Sit down.'"

"That is not so," Gordon said, eliciting a stiff "You're a liar" from defendant Gates. Medina told Sacher that the defense lawyer was waving his finger "at me and that doesn't bother me. I don't see why you get so excited. . . . Let's let these little incidents evaporate and not occur any more."

"May I respectfully ask," Sacher said, "that you tell the Government to desist from facing defendants' counsel. Their back is supposed to be turned to me and I prefer to see that part of them."[14]

A little later during the same court session, Budenz testified that around December 1941, after he had returned to New York City, Foster and Dennis met with him and told him he was being appointed managing editor of the *Daily Worker*, which drew an objection from Dennis that Budenz's testimony was hearsay. "Now you see," Medina said, "that is one of the troubles about being your own lawyer because this hearsay business is not fully understood by you. . . . In this instance, when the witness says that you, a defendant, told him this and so, your very telling him of the thing is the fact and hence not hearsay."

Part of the defense strategy seemed to be to confuse the jury—and Medina—with a maelstrom of objections that often led to nonsensical exchanges in the courtroom. On March 24, Medina took note of it, and his growing exasperation was clear. As Budenz tried to testify about which defendants were present at a series of meetings, Isserman, Sacher, Crockett, and Gladstein all pushed different objections, mainly spinning back to the dates of the meetings, which occurred before the time period cited in the indictment. Medina had already denied scores of similar objections, and as Gordon prepared to resume questioning Budenz about Davis's presence at one of the meetings, Gladstein broadened his challenge to Medina, arguing that Budenz's testimony lacked proper legal foundation and should be thrown out.[15]

"You know, Mr. Gladstein, with all these objections, such an atmosphere of confusion seems to be arising here that you cannot keep head or tail of anything in your mind," Medina said. "Now I just want to mention that, and pretty soon I am going to have to do something about it. You cannot follow the testimony with any continuity because there is all this wrangling and discussion over points that seem to me . . . matters of absolute triviality. And I hope you will refrain just a little bit so I can follow the proof."

Gladstein held his ground and pressed Medina for a ruling on his objection. Medina promptly denied it, which drew in Isserman. "I would like to object to your Honor's characterization of counsel in respect to objections as being an undue interference with the right and necessity of counsel to represent their clients in court and as tending to prejudice the proper actions of counsel before the jury."

They eventually got back to Budenz's testimony, briefly, before the defense team added a fresh wave of objections. The exchange—all held in front of the jury—bared the relationships among the participants: Medina as a protector of the prosecution and witnesses, and the defense as the enemy. Medina advised Gordon, then questioning Budenz, not to "let Mr. Sacher annoy you with these things." Gordon told the judge, "All right, I won't let him terrorize me."

"He seems kind of greatly pleased that he is irritating you, and it is probably just part of the way we have to see things here," Medina continued. "But just take my advice and pay no attention to it because—" Sacher cut Medina off, asking if he could take exception "to those observations" by the judge.

"I take it, Mr. Sacher, that that is the kind of thing that adds greatly to the confusion here, and you do it so often," Medina said. "I think, possibly, you could refrain a little bit. It gives you great pleasure, you beam and giggle to yourself there and enjoy it, but it is not pleasant to me."

Sacher objected again, arguing that "I must state for the record that your Honor's characterization of me is not only inaccurate but is also prejudicial."

"I know," Medina said.

The proceedings had other comic moments. On March 26, just after the lunch break and in the midst of another round-robin of defense objections that were uniformly denied, Isserman remained seated at the defense table while he objected to one of Budenz's answers "on the ground the witness has not been qualified." Medina admonished him, "Please rise, Mr. Sacher, when you address the court." "I am sorry, your Honor," Sacher replied. "I wanted to save time." Sacher stood up. "Overruled," Medina said.

For most of Budenz's time on the stand, Dennis let the lawyers handle the objections, arguments, and cross-examinations, though he did rise once during a dispute over Budenz's authority to offer an interpretation of the Communist Party's constitution.[16]

"If the court please," Dennis said, standing up at the defense lawyers' table and clearing his voice before starting over. "If the court please, I must object most strenuously to this line of questions and these allegations. This witness cannot speak for any defendant or any communist. He cannot speak any more than a Benedict Arnold—" McGohey quickly tried to cut him off, but Medina, in an unusual turn, let Dennis go on, asking him about the nature of a witness in a conspiracy. Speaking hypothetically, Medina asked Dennis to envision a conspiracy of several people. "Don't you think that a person who worked with them would be a competent witness to testify as to what they understood?"

Dennis veered sharply from the theoretical. "I think it will be established here before very long that some of these definitions—in fact, all of them—which this witness is volunteering here, can be proved to be very identical as to what Goebbels and Himmlers and others, how they interpreted the principles of Marxism and Leninism. No traitor, no traitor, no Judas could interpret principles—"

"What did you say? Medina interrupted, hearing the word "trader." After some back-and-forth and spellings, in which Dennis offered that "no Benedict Arnold would be asked to interpret the Constitution," Medina shut Dennis off. "Oh, I misunderstood. You were just attacking this witness," the judge said. "I thought you were arguing a point of law."

For all their efforts, the defense could do little to shake Budenz. By then he was a practiced witness and easily wore the mantle of expert. They went at him on cross-examination for four days, first Gladstein, then Sacher, asking Budenz when he had married his wife—forcing Budenz, who had worn his Catholicism as a billboard, to acknowledge he and his current wife had lived together while he was still married to his first. They tried to indict him on technicalities, such as whether he had read all of Lenin's works, as he had written in his memoir (he acknowledged he had not). They pressed the point that Budenz couldn't identify the specific building in which he testified that Dennis had spoken to members during a secret meeting about the impact of the Hitler-Stalin pact, and that Budenz himself at one point felt he was conspiring for the day when the U.S. government would be overthrown—points that hardly resonated well in the defendants' favor.

Budenz was a problematic figure through and through, but he made the government's case that the defendants had been involved in creating the current version of the CPUSA, and that Marxism-Leninisn included abstract tenets that said revolution from below would be necessary to usurp capitalism. And whether that was illegal, Medina held, would not be a decision for the jury. Barring jury nullification—jurors acquitting because of a deep disbelief of the legitimacy of a law—conviction was already in the bag.

While McGohey was presenting his case, the public backlash against the defendants—and communists in general—grew around the country. In Pittsburgh, it sparked a riot.[17]

On the evening of April 2, a Saturday, about 250 people gathered in the North Side Carnegie Hall, adjacent to the Carnegie Library (it was, in fact, the first Carnegie Hall). The 8:00 P.M. program was organized by the CRC and the American Slav Congress to raise money for the communists' Foley Square defense—fifty cents admission, and a hat would be passed during the meeting—and as a protest against the trial. Henry Winston, one of the defendants, was the keynote speaker, along with three other local communist and labor activists, and the crowd was mostly political leftists and civil rights advocates.

The hall stands a few blocks north of the Allegheny River, across from the peninsula shaped by the merger with the Monongahela River to form the Ohio River. As the communist supporters filtered into the hall, a large throng of protesters—two hundred fifty or more—gathered on the street and sidewalk. About one hundred fifty of the protesters, many of them war veterans, were members of Local 601 of CIO United Electrical Workers, Radio and Machine Workers (UE), representing 16,500 Westinghouse Electric Corporation employees in what at one time was one of Pittsburgh's most reliably leftist unions. But after the adoption of the Taft-Hartley Act in 1947, which barred National Labor Relations Board protections to any union whose leadership did not

sign affidavits disavowing communism, Local 601 was split by a
deep division between progressive and conservative members. In
a December 1948 union election, the conservatives won, ousting
incumbent president Tom Fitzpatrick and his progressive team,
which had been resisting the Taft-Hartley requirements. The union
then aggressively began purging itself of leaders and members
who even smelled of progressive beliefs. So by the time of the
North Side Carnegie Hall meeting, Local 601 was solidly—and
vocally—anti-communist. They jeered those who ventured to the
hall and sponsored a sound truck that cruised nearby streets, with
Local 601 member Ernest Vida on the microphone urging a boycott
of the meeting that he said was to raise money for the defense of
men "who have said that in the event of war between the U.S. and
Russia they would support Russia."[18] About fifty members of the
new Amvets Post No. 38 showed up, too, marching from their nearby
clubhouse at Avery and Nash streets to the Carnegie Hall steps.
Under the direction of Police Superintendent Harvey J. Scott—the
department chief—some fifty policemen stood guard, with another
fifty out of view in the nearby North Side Police Station.

As the meeting progressed inside, the throng grew outside. One
estimate put the crowd at five thousand people, and it included
small groups from the Catholic War Veterans, the American Legion,
and the Disabled American Veterans, as well as more members
of Local 601. Someone set up a public address system, and the
demonstrators' language grew more bombastic. Fearing violence,
Fr. Charles Owen Rice, a priest active in labor circles, took the
microphone and urged the crowd to calm down. Few paid him any
attention, although Scott, the police superintendent, persuaded the
Amvets protesters to go home, or at least to leave the rally. The
rest continued to picket and parade, chanting and sloganeering
and working themselves up into an excitable mob. John Duffy,
president of electricians Local 613, which left the more radical
UE to affiliate with the United Auto Workers, shouted out that
"the communist chickens had come home to roost." Evidencing
the left-right divide in the house of labor, Fitzpatrick, the ousted
union leader, showed up near the start of the session and was
spotted by his anti-communist brother and fellow Local 601 member,
Mike Fitzpatrick, climbing the steps to enter the hall. Mike
denounced his brother loudly to the picketers, but Tom took it

in stride, stopping at the top of the steps to wave to the jeering crowd before entering the building. Those chants, and others, echoed inside, and the speakers used the tension to try to draw more donations out of the attendees.

The program ended around 10:00 P.M. Scott, who had already called in the extra fifty officers on standby at the North Side Police Station, tried to find a way to separate the protesters from the departing leftists. He set up a cordon at a side entry to the hall, out of sight of the main protest on the east side of the building, and used his officers as a human shield. At 10:10 P.M., he began ushering people out of the building and through Diamond Square, a park southwest of the hall. But scouts from the protest alerted the throng and they quickly swarmed the exodus, overwhelming Scott's detachment, and the melee was on.

Local communist leader William Albertson later condemned police for "shirking their duty" and said Pittsburgh was under a "state of fascism." But reports of the melee indicate no collusion—simply a hundred-strong detachment of officers overwhelmed by a much larger mob (whether the police, seeing the size of the growing crowd, should have deployed more cops is another matter). The mob started swinging fists and sticks as the leftists ran for refuge. Police on motorcycles roared loudly through the crowd in the streets, trying to disperse it. At the corner of Federal and Ohio streets, just west of Carnegie Hall, five people jumped into a cab, but driver Robert Jones refused to carry communists so left the car parked on the street, where members of the mob tried to overturn it until police—including Scott—pushed them away. Three women were chased across the street into the lunchroom at Hite's drugstore, where some of the throng continued to harass them until police intervened. More people sought refuge in passing public trolleys on Federal Street, but the rioters broke out the windows, showering them with glass. Still others jumped into police wagons onsite to take away detainees, and the police drivers ferried them a safe distance away, then let them out.

It took a half hour to quell the riot, and when it was over scores of people were hurt, though none reported life-threatening injuries. At least a half-dozen people were arrested and charged with disorderly conduct, nearly all taken in before the riot began. Notably, despite one hundred police witnesses, only one person—

Richard France, twenty-four—was charged with inciting a riot for his role in trying to overturn the taxi. No one was charged with assault.

The defense finished its mostly ineffectual cross-examination of Budenz on the morning of April 6, and the court took its lunch recess. A small throng of newsmen—mostly wire service and radio reporters looking for a tidbit to freshen their stories for the afternoon—cornered McGohey's assistant Frank Gordon in a marbled hallway and asked who the government would call next. Gordon was evasive, and teasing: "All I can tell you is that it's going to be a man."[19]

A few minutes after 2:00 P.M., the break over, Judge Medina stepped up to his bench, settled into his red leather chair, and directed the prosecution to call its next witness. Waiting in a small hallway behind the courtroom was a handsome, curly-haired advertising man from Melrose, Massachusetts, named Herbert A. Philbrick, thirty-three years old and the father of four young daughters. Philbrick had been involved with communist-related groups since 1940 and a member of the Communist Party since 1944. Living in suburban Boston, he had been part of a secret group of professional-class party members and served as something of an educational director in the region, selecting readings and instructing small groups in Marxist-Leninist theory. He also, for the entire time, had been spying for the FBI.[20]

As Philbrick entered the courtroom, it was unclear whether the defendants immediately recognized him, although a few—such as Stachel, the party's education director—had met him before. But as Gordon went through his list of identifying questions—asking Philbrick his name, where he lived, his occupation, and then his connection with the Communist Party—it became clear that the jury was about to hear not from a repentant like Budenz but from a government spy. The wire service and radio reporters had their fresh lead, and several of them hurried from the court for the nearby news room, with its phone banks to their editors' desks. Isserman immediately objected, arguing—unsuccessfully—that whatever Philbrick had to say fell outside the scope of the indictment. "And," he told Medina, "I would also like to plead surprise in connection with it." "I don't wonder," Gordon said, drawing another protest from Isserman—this one successful, as Medina ordered Gordon's one-liner stricken from the record.[21]

The first reports to fly out over the wires and radio were only that Philbrick had taken the stand and had been a secret communist, which caused a flurry among his circle of friends and fellow communists in Boston. The second wave of updates made it clear that Philbrick had been a spy for the FBI. Philbrick and his wife had been concerned that once his role was made public, he and the family might be targeted for retaliation by more radical party members. They also didn't want to face a horde of news reporters. So under the guise of seeking a diversion while Philbrick was out of town on business, Philbrick's wife had made loose plans to drop two of the couple's daughters off at her parents' house and then hide herself and the other two daughters with a sister-in-law in Lynnfield. Since the couple didn't know exactly when Philbrick would testify—nothing in the trial had followed a predictable timetable—she had to leave the plans murky, just saying that they would drop by one day soon and stay for a few days.

Philbrick got the call on the afternoon of April 5. He'd been faking a cold at work for a few days and announced suddenly after lunch that he was going home to try to recover. Instead, he went to the airport and flew to New York City, where FBI agents hid him under guard in a hotel, expecting him to take the stand the next morning. Eva Philbrick waited anxiously at home for the signal from the FBI that her husband had taken the stand, and when it came the next afternoon she packed up the kids and fled the family's Melrose house, telling her sister-in-law and parents the truth once she arrived. So within fifteen minutes of Philbrick's bombshell, and as the first wire reports were flying out from Foley Square, the Philbricks' house was empty, Eva evading the first reporters by a good ten minutes.[22]

Philbrick was an unlikely informant. He grew up during the Depression about fifty miles north of Boston, in Rye Beach, New Hampshire, the son of a railroad man. He started school in a one-room schoolhouse, but the family later moved to Somerville, just across the Charles River from Boston (and a short distance from Cambridge, home to Harvard University). In high school he contemplated a career as a civil engineer and sold newspapers and magazines to save up money for college, but "two of the three banks in which my cash was placed closed their doors in the depression." After graduating he enrolled in night classes at the Lincoln Technical Institute at Northeastern University to keep his days free for work. He sold soap door-to-door, worked as a plumber's assistant, and signed on with an interior decorator and painted walls, varnished floors, and hung wallpaper. He did some heavy construction and hired himself out as a chauffeur. It was through his Baptist church in Somerville that he began to enjoy public relations work, and he slowly moved into it when, upon graduating in 1938, he couldn't find a job as an engineer. He eventually became a sales representative for a direct-mail advertising firm.

Philbrick viewed himself as a pacifist and a Christian progressive. The Depression had a profound effect on his view of how the world should work, even if he was naive about the concepts of markets and supply chains. "Despite the security of a steady job, no practicing Christian in the spring of 1940 could gloat over his good fortune and turn his back on those less fortunate," Philbrick wrote in his memoir. "I found it difficult to ignore the fact that, out in Kansas, farmers burned the grain they could not sell to take the place of the coal they could not buy. At the same time, in Pennsylvania, coal miners—amid mountains of unmined coal—lined up at welfare soup kitchens to receive bread on dole. In a land of untold wealth of fuel and food, people were both cold and hungry. To a twenty-five-year-old, it didn't make sense."[23]

As war barreled across Europe, Philbrick became increasingly concerned about American involvement. He was repulsed by fascism and Hitler but held a deeper dislike for war. One day while making cold calls for his direct-mail employer, he stumbled across the Boston office of the Massachusetts Youth Council, a clearinghouse for progressive youth organizations, including peace groups. Philbrick signed on to help launch a chapter in Cambridge, where he and his new wife, Eva, were living. He quickly found that Communist Party members were sprinkled throughout the movement, and he believed they had subverted the cause of peace to the cause of spreading communism. Philbrick called the local FBI office and made an appointment, and in short order he was an unpaid spy for the federal government reporting on the workings of the Communist Party in Boston.

Nine years later, Philbrick was, for the prosecution, the affirmation of all that Budenz had talked about. Where Budenz was a former communist anxious to tell the world of the evils (as he saw it) of communism, Philbrick was an of-the-moment party member. And where Budenz's involvement in the party ended around the time the alleged conspiracy began, Philbrick had been a member throughout the time period covered by the indictment. Before the trial began, traveling under an assumed name from Boston to New York City, he met several times in secret with McGohey and, more often, Gordon to go over his background and testimony, the questions culled in part from the years of reports he had filed with the FBI.

Philbrick's testimony filled two needs for the prosecution. He was the embodiment of the secretive nature of the party and could testify that it "organized itself on an underground pattern, and spread its doctrines, not openly, but by planned subterfuge." Since Budenz quit the party in 1945, it would be Philbrick who would detail for the jurors how the Communist Party worked in the postwar years covered by the indictment, the secret group to which he belonged, the fake names and private tutoring sessions in Marxist-Leninist theory. "Second, but of no less importance, I was to contribute my testimony to the weight of evidence regarding what the Communist Party taught and advocated in the meetings I attended."[24] The evidence would include books and pamphlets used in the party's education programs. Gil Green, one of the defendants, would say later that Philbrick's appearance caught the eleven party leaders by surprise: "We called Boston to ask if they knew Philbrick, and they said sure, he was a nice guy. He was always inviting us to use his office mimeograph machine."[25]

Over five days Philbrick testified about his early work with youth groups, his progressive activities with the Young Communist League, and his eventual role within the Communist Party. Philbrick said that in 1945, under Foster's direction, the party embarked on a plan to "colonize" crucial industries, and the word was spread through meetings with party members. "We were told to adopt the policy of colonizing, that is taking jobs in key industries," Philbrick testified. "These included the New England textile plants, the leather industry, which is important in Boston, the Boston & Maine railroad, and the General Electric plant in Lynn producing jet airplane engines." Elsewhere in the country, members were to try to land jobs within the automobile, steel, coal, and maritime industries, among others, in preparation for "mass struggles." Later, after the indictments of Foster and the other defendants, they had been told of preparations for taking the party underground should it be outlawed. In 1947, he said, he became one of about seventy members of a professional group of party members—including lawyers and teachers—who were to keep their ties secret, barred from carrying membership cards or even subscribing to the *Daily Worker*. Philbrick served as "literature" director for the group, steering it toward discussions of Leninist-Marxist theory, including the belief that a proletarian state could only be achieved by the violent overthrow of the capitalist state.[26]

"We were instructed that the revolution will not take place next week or next month or two o'clock Wednesday afternoon, but will take place under two circumstances: In case of heavy oppression, or in case of war, in which case the conflict would be converted into civil war," Philbrick testified. "Under either circumstance, it would result in the overthrow of the capitalist class and the dictatorship of the proletariat." And the "capitalist class," Philbrick said, included the established U.S. government. "The definition of the state taught to me was that of an organized system of oppression which consists of the government, the police, the army and so forth, and this is the thing that must be overthrown. Therefore the complete Government must be smashed. It cannot be taken over as it is, but must be completely destroyed."

The defense lawyers, as they did with Budenz, attacked Philbrick as a turncoat, suggesting he sold out his peace-seeking comrades for money. Whenever Philbrick, at prosecutor Gordon's request, read from a text—he called them "manuals," much to the annoyance of the defense—Sacher or another lawyer would seek to read a contradicting or context-setting part of the same book. During cross-examination, McCabe, often raising his voice, tried to get Philbrick to paint a scene of skullduggery—secret meetings with shadowy federal agents—then sidetracked him with arguments over the details of his answers. At one point, Medina squelched an exchange between McCabe and Philbrick, as McCabe was cutting off Philbrick's answers, with a terse "Give him a chance to answer. Let's not get back to this twitchy business." "I am not twitchy,"

McCabe replied. "Maybe the witness is." That, naturally, drew a complaint from Gordon, seeking to protect his witness and give him a little breathing room. "There, your Honor, he said maybe the witness is twitchy," Gordon said. "He shouts at him and doesn't let him answer a question."[27]

Moments later, McCabe drew from Philbrick an admission that he had reviewed one of his secret reports to the FBI before court that morning. McCabe asked that the report be produced for evidence, but Gordon objected, describing the request as a "fishing expedition." But Gladstein argued that Philbrick was testifying about long-ago meetings and conversations. Looking at his reports to the FBI, Gladstein said, would either corroborate or refute his memory. The defense lost that fight, too. "It is my ruling," Medina said, "that the defense counsel have no right to look through the Government's files and seek out what they may find later to their advantage. It would be a queer state of affairs to have, in a criminal prosecution, the Government suddenly put on trial, and that is not going to happen here."[28]

After McCabe, Crockett had a go at Philbrick, trying to paint him as a bit of cheat, drawing cartoons for YCL publications while at his job as an assistant advertising director for a chain of movie theaters, and using his company's mimeograph machine. Then he went after Philbrick's finances, trying to imply that Philbrick had gained financially by working for the FBI—and rubbing Medina raw in the process after Gordon objected to the finance questions: "The implication that the FBI has set this man up in luxury I think has gone far enough." Gladstein argued that Gordon's objection was out of line and outside the testimony. "Well," Medina said, "what else could that question be asked for?" He and Gladstein wrangled for a bit over whether Gordon had violated Medina's court rule that the lawyers were not to offer arguments during their objections. With the jury sitting nearby, Medina told Gladstein: "You always put your charges in such curious language, nothing is ever done in good faith, there is always some sort of intentional, malicious wrong. . . . I don't think it is up to you to tell me what I should do if Mr. Gordon should add a word or two to his objection. Let me take care of the running of this court."[29]

In the end, the defense did little to shake Philbrick, or to paint him in an unsavory light other than that he volunteered as a spy for the FBI and filed regular reports on meetings he attended, people he met, and speeches and private instructions he gave. He also turned over film of YCL events he took, enabling the government to identify members.

The target of Philbrick's testimony, obviously, was the eleven men on trial. But his testimony also included others he alleged were active in Communist Party circles, incuding Dirk Struik, a math professor at the Massachusetts Institute of Technology, who quickly found himself in the crosshairs of anti-communist activists.

During his third day of testimony, on April 8, Philbrick identified Struik as the speaker at an underground session. He said that the academic cited a recent Marxist revolt in Indonesia as a prime example of how arming workers could help overturn a capitalist system, and that someone else at a later session tied that lesson to the need to arm American workers for eventual revolt. Within minutes journalists were on the telephone to Struik looking for comment and reaction. The lanky, Dutch-born academic described himself as a Marxist scholar but said he was not a member of the Communist Party, though he had spoken at events likely linked with communists. He dismissed as "nonsense" Philbrick's assertion that he had preached revolution. "At none of those meetings, nor at the one to which Philbrick referred, have I ever advocated the violent overthrow of the U.S. Government, which I consider a stupid and silly notion."[30]

Yet Struik was close to the communists, telling reporters he was "in sympathy" with many of their beliefs. He was part of a committee that helped oversee the 1943 launch of the Jefferson School of Social Science (Jack Stachel, one of the defendants, was also on the committee), and in 1941 had helped lead a letter-petition from American-based scientists and mathemeticians to their colleagues in the Soviet Union to show support for their efforts against fascism.[31] He was a regular guest and speaker at Jefferson School functions and a persistent signatory to letters protesting fascism and anti-labor policies by the U.S. government, and promoting progressive causes. He also held leadership or advisory roles in two other organizations the Justice Department deemed communist fronts: the Committee for a Democratic Eastern Policy and the American Youth for Democracy.

But Struik also was a mainstream academic. A member of the American Academy of Arts and Sciences, he authored *Yankee Science in the Making*, published by Little, Brown in 1948 to explore the growth of science and technology in New England between the Revolution and the Civil War, and a social history of mathematics. (He also, in 1971, edited and published *Birth of the Communist Manifesto*, an annotation of early drafts and the full text, through International Publishers, whose catalog remains devoted to the writings of Marx and Lenin.) After his name surfaced in court, Struik found himself the target of a coordinated campaign to get him fired from MIT. The university leadership stood behind him, but in 1951—as the McCarthy fervor crescendoed—he was indicted under a Massachusetts Palmer Raids–era anti-anarchy law based primarily on state grand jury testimony from Philbrick. Massachusetts's anti-anarchy law was eventually tossed out by the Supreme Court. But Struik also eventually lost his tenure.[32]

At the end of each day of court, Medina admonished the jury not to read newspaper or magazine articles about the trial, not to listen to the radio, not to discuss the case with anyone, even fellow jurors. At least one juror didn't take Medina's warning to heart.[33]

Carol Nason, the entertainer who made regular drop-in visits at Broadway producer and author Russell Janney's office, stopped in a day or so after Janney had been picked for the jury—the role he wanted so he could research courtroom scenes for his detective novel. She caught Janney just as he was waking up from a nap, and he picked up a newspaper to show her a front-page story about his being selected for the jury. "Carol, go down there and take a good look at the communists that sit in the back of the courtroom," she said he told her. "Take a good look at them. Would you like people like that to rule the country?" He said most had aliases, and insinuated that there was something sinister about people using false names—an odd line to draw for someone in the theater business, talking with a woman who was known to the entertainment world by an assumed name.

He went on to offer his opinion of Medina. "The judge is very fair," Janney told her. "He stressed that these men are not being tried for being communists, but for the overthrow of the government." Nason responded that she thought the indictment said they were accused of advocating the teaching of Marxism-Leninism. Janney argued, "No, for the overthrow of the government—I know it almost by heart." Nason, who unbeknown to Janney supported the party leaders, tried to draw him out. "But won't this prevent a man from being a communist or voicing communist ideas?" she asked. "No, it will not," Janney said. "They are being charged with plotting to overthrow the government—of course it has yet to be proven." Janney finished up by declaring his impartiality.

Nason was back in Janney's office again on April 2. Janney was alone, but she felt like she was interrupting something. "No, it's just that I'm so busy with the damn trial—going down there every day and listening to all that baloney," he said. "I haven't much time to spend in the office now that I'm a professional juror." And he was becoming irritated by the "melodramatic" behavior of the defense lawyers and the trial's anticipated duration. "They tell us it may last into July—isn't that terrible?"

It was fruitful for him, though. Janney was gong home at night to work on the courtroom scenes for his novel, and then again in the mornings, though he confessed to having trouble adjusting his habitual late hours to the courtroom clock. He told her the short nights made it hard for him to follow the evidence in court, especially as the lawyers read lengthy book excerpts into the record. "You know, I actually catch myself falling asleep," Janney said. "They read chapters and chapters of books in order to introduce one paragraph. It's very hard to listen to that. I tell Mrs. Dial, who sits next to me, 'For heaven's sake, if you see me falling asleep, please be sure and wake me immediately.'"

In late April, Nason stopped in again and saw a stack of newspaper clips about the trial—the very items Janney was not supposed to be reading—on the writer's desk. Cutter, the partner, told her Janney "studies them for legal procedure."

Janney's behavior, still far outside the courtroom, would soon find its way in.

EIGHT

Stool Pigeons and Turncoats

The prosecution's witness list consisted primarily of spies or disaf-fected former communists, some with legitimate connections with the party, others who had ancillary and—for the purposes of the trial—inflated roles. In all, thirteen prosecution witnesses were called. Two were FBI investigators. The rest testified about their experiences in the party but also gave McGohey and his prosecu-tion team a means of introducing sometimes decades-old Marxist and Leninist tracts as evidence of the political philosophy's reliance on violent revolution to effect change. And, it should be noted, the prosecution ultimately did not call Bentley, Chambers, or anyone else who was part of the spy investigations that had begun the pro-cess that culminated in the indictments of Dennis and the others.[1]

McGohey thought carefully about his witness list and the order in which he would call them. Budenz was the expert to tell the jury about the sweep of the communists' trajectory from the 1930s through the end of World War II, when it recommitted itself, in his eyes, to violent revolution. Philbrick picked up the timeline from 1945, when Budenz left the party, and carried it to the day he himself took the stand as a surprise witness. The rest of the witnesses were to start tying in specific defendants to the allegations in the indictment.

The third person called to the stand was Frank S. Meyer, a forty-year-old writer and lecturer whose academic background included studies at Princeton, Oxford, and the London School of Economics. He had been a devoted communist from the 1930s through the war years and taught at various communist schools (he testified, as did the others, about the books and pamphlets used in the classes). He had spent several years as educational director in Illinois and testified about his dealings with Green and with Stachel—who he said delivered the news in 1945 that Browderism was dead and armed revolution was back on the party's agenda. Meyer opposed what he described as the reversion to violence. He was particularly demoralized, he testified, when the *Daily Worker* "suppressed" letters by him and others opposing the shift from war-era cooperation back to what he described as Stalin-ordered embrace of violent revolution, as spelled out in Stalin's *The History of the Communist Party of the Soviet Union (Bolshevik)*, published in 1939. A key tenet was Stalin's take on Marxist-Leninist theory, that communism would not rise without the violent overthrow of capitalism. Dennis and Thompson, he said, brushed off his protests about the muzzling of contradictory opinions, so he quit the party.[2]

Meyer was followed on the stand by two FBI agents from Detroit, Eugene H. Stewart and Fred G. Cook, who testified separately that Winter, the Michigan party leader, had bragged at a meeting that the Communist Party was behind crippling strikes in the automotive, steel, electrical, and meat industries in 1945 and 1946—signaling the end of war-era cooperation. Then William O. Nowell took the stand, an odd addition to the prosecution's case whose only role seemed to have been to play to white fears of black nationalism. Nowell, who was black, had been active in the party since 1929, when he joined while working at Ford Motor Company, in Detroit. Over the next five years he rose to national office and spent more than a year studying in Moscow as a "corrective" to his opposition to the party's call for a segregated black homeland in the Black Belt of the South. The party wanted to "utilize the legitimate grievances of American negroes as a means of mobilizing them and using them as part of the preparation for and as part of a proletarian revolution in the United States," Nowell said. In Moscow, he and other students at the Lenin Institute were taught that a rebellion to create a "Negro homeland" in the South "would aid the Northern industrial workers to bring about the Revolution in the North and throughout the whole country. I expressed myself in classes against this segregation movement, because it would isolate the Negroes in the South and use them merely as a tool to create a revolution in which these unsuspecting people would be sacrificed for a cause in which they had not the least understanding." Stachel, Nowell said, was present at the institute (Williamson, Potash, and Hall also passed through) and "told the Institute meeting that my error should be rejected by the student group and that I should be disciplined by the party." Nowell, who returned to the United States in December 1932, quit the party in 1936 after he was stripped of district-level positions over his unrelenting opposition to this "segregation" policy. He claimed he eventually was fired by Ford after retaliatory smears by his former comrades and had occasional brushes with industrial accidents. "They were attempting to drop things out of cranes on me and push things off stockpiles and all that sort of thing," he said. At the time Nowell testified, he was working as a clerk for the Immigration and Naturalization Service in Washington, D.C., a job he landed after his initial conversations with the Department of Justice over whether he would testify.[3]

Some of the witness testimony bordered on the farcical, or at least the fanciful. Charles Nicodemus, a Textile Workers Union member and former communist from Maryland, testified about a meeting in which attendees were told that the United States was hopelessly capitalistic. Revolution, the speaker said, would not happen without help from the Soviet Red Army, which would follow a path across Siberia, through Canada, and then into the United States—traversing some of the most inhospitable terrain in the world. "They could even destroy Detroit," Nicodemus said the meeting was told. His contention drew smirks from the defense table—and one presumes a few laughs from the gallery—and a rebuke from Medina. "Why," he said, "all of the defendants are smiling broadly." Gates and Potash simultaneously responded, "Certainly we are," aggravating Medina further. "We are getting back to the country club atmosphere again," Medina said, referring to earlier orders he had issued that the defendants and their lawyers not introduce humor as a distraction. "There isn't going to be any country club atmosphere in my court."[4]

Gladstein rose. "When a man hears something that is ludicrous and absurd to the extreme, I suppose he is permitted the human reaction of a smile of contempt." No, in fact, Medina said, he is not. "It may seem very funny to the defendants. They seem to enjoy it, but I don't think it is and their laughter is not going to have any effect." Gladstein said the smiles should be expected given the ludicrous nature of the prosecution's case, angering Medina even more. "I am familiar with the practice in criminal cases of trying to laugh something off, and I am not going to have anything but order in my court. When the defendants get hilarious and start laughing and smiling and that sort of thing, it is going to be stopped. You can put that in your book." You can almost see Gladstein's deadpan response: "I would like the record to show that there is no hilarity on the part of any defendant."

Gates egged Medina on. "Do I understand that you are now forbidding me to smile?" he asked. Medina said no, but Gates continued: "It is bad enough we are not allowed to think. Now you want to forbid us to smile as well." "Well," Medina responded, "you are evidently a very bold man and you get up and have your say. That is all right. I am not ordering you not to smile, but I am going to have order in my courtroom, and I am not going to have testimony laughed off." Crockett then rose to object to Medina's comments and described them as "judicial misconduct by the Court in line with various other personal comments he has made concerning the defendants and their counsel." All of the back-and-forth occurred while the jury was sitting in the box, soaking it in.

All but one of the witnesses were men. The sole woman, Angela Calomiris, became something of a media darling, in part because of her appearance and her demeanor. Petite—she considered herself "plump" when she hit 104 pounds[5]—Calomiris was a Greenwich Village freelance photographer, specializing in animal photography. Like Philbrick, she had been a party member until the moment she took the witness stand, another surprise spy in the party "in a black faille suit and off the face straw hat trimmed in velvet and sprouting a twelve-inch green feather."[6] Calomiris testified that she was apolitical when, for the sake of professional contacts, she joined the Photo League in Manhattan, which was on the attorney general's subversive-groups list. It was first and foremost a professional assocation, with such legends as Ansel Adams and Margaret Bourke-White speaking at its events. But communists were members as well, and eventually Calomiris received an overture to join the Communist Party, which she turned down. Sometime later, she testified, she was visited by FBI agents who asked her to accept if she was invited again and to report back to the agency. In 1942 the second invitation came, and Calomiris accepted that time, eventually becoming the financial secretary for the Hell's Kitchen branch. Like Philbrick, she was still a Communist Party member until the moment she stepped into the witness box.[7]

Also like Philbrick, Calomiris was on the stand to detail the nature of the educational programs run by the Communist Party. Under questioning by assistant prosecutor Edward C. Wallace, she testified that as a party member she had dealt with Davis, Green, Thompson, and Williamson. She said Green had spoken at a training session she attended, telling more than one thousand fresh communist recruits that they would be taught the tenets of Marxism-Leninism. At a later session by other instructors, she said, the recruits were told that change would come not by political evolution but by revolution. As she testified about each man, Wallace asked her to step down from the witness stand, approach the array of defendants, and point out whom she was identifying. Green was first, and Calomiris—the "pert communist," as the *Chicago Daily Tribune* described her—walked over and touched the back of his jacket. "Green pulled away, grimaced and brushed at his coat. Miss Calomiris smiled sweetly and walked back to the stand." She repeated the process with Thompson, Williamson, Gates, and Davis, in each instance testifying that the men had spoken at meetings or signed documents and membership cards.[8]

Calomiris also ran through the transition from wartime Browderism to the postwar re-embrace of class conflict and talked about the secretive nature of the group, including burned membership cards and clandestine meetings—legal acts that the prosecution sought to have the jury interpret as guilty and conspiratorial behavior. Calomiris told the jury that the party had targeted what it considered key industries for organizing, details that were spelled out at a meeting the previous year attended by Davis and Thompson.

One of Calomiris's roles in the party was to help organize dock-workers, she said—an odd duty, if true. Sending a downtown photographer to persuade the rough-edged longshoremen on the Hudson River that communism was in their best interests seems a mission destined for failure. But Calomiris said she was given the task because she was already organizing communists at the Yugoslav Home, a social and political club on West Forty-fifth Street, within her Hell's Kitchen district. So it made sense to expand her portfolio to include Yugoslav dockworkers. Calomiris focused on longshoremen working at river piers between West Forty-fourth and West Forty-eighth streets and at the Railway Express plant on West Forty-second Street and Twelfth Avenue. But there was nothing secret about how she and other organizers went about their work: "We had to distribute copies of the *Daily Worker* and leaflets specially written up to recruit these workers at the 6 A.M. mobilizations at the piers and the Railway Express plant," she said. It was an uphill struggle. "In most cases they were not interested in communists, but we tried to make appointments to visit them at their homes." Calomiris and others also would invite those who expressed some interest out to lunch or dinner and the occasional show, while encouraging potential recruits to read party literature and attend meetings.[9]

In an attempt to paint the Communist Party as an ongoing threat, Calomiris said that at the time of the trial those already active in the party—herself included—were studying for revolu-tion, particularly a growing "professional" class of communists. Sessions were held at the Jefferson School of Social Science, the New York Workers School (at the party headquarters), and the Marxist Institute. "I have a class today," she said during her third day on the stand, "but I don't think I'll go."

As they did with Budenz, the defense team worked in a rotation to try to erode Calomiris's credibility, implying she had worked for the FBI purely for the money. Although it wasn't stated directly in court, Calomiris was a lesbian. Later in life she owned and operated Angels' Landing, a popular lesbian-oriented bed-and-breakfast in Provincetown, Massachusetts. McCabe tried to allude to her sexual orientation, which could have hurt her with jurors

9. Lillian Gates, Edna Winston, and Elizabeth Hall, wives of three of the defendants, as the center of a rally opposing the trial. Library of Congress, Prints & Photographs Division, *New York World-Telegram* Collection, LC-USZ62–111605.

in an era in which homosexuality existed in the shadows and was considered in many quarters to be a form of mental illness. McCabe asked Calomiris whether she was married, and when she said no, he asked if she had any children. Medina moved quickly to shut him down, sustaining an objection by Wallace. "Counsel should be admonished about this line of questioning," Wallace said, with Medina agreeing: "It is the kind of thing I don't like to see. . . . I certainly would never have asked a question like that when I was a lawyer."[10] The exchange must have been confusing to the jurors, presuming they didn't know Calomiris's sexual orientation, but the media coverage left the clear implication of the point the defense was trying to make. And it sparked yet another in an unending series of flashpoints between the men gathered around the defense table and Medina.

Throughout the presentation of the prosecution's case, the defense team had grown increasingly aggressive in both its objections and its open contempt toward Medina. There was a lot to have contempt for: Medina again and again sided with the prosecution, cut short defense objections, refused to hear supporting arguments on legal points, and openly derided the defense lawyers for their behavior—which, in truth, was far from the kind of decorum expected in court. They acted like lawyers presuming they had already lost a rigged case, and their combative attitude couldn't have helped their credibility with the jury. It certainly did nothing to bridge the gap with Medina, who kept the death of Judge Eicher in the Nazi trial close to mind.

On April 26, before Calomiris took the stand, the war of words and wills between Medina and the defense team boiled over. The prosecution had called as a witness Garfield Herron, an Alabama farmer who was living in Chicago and working at a war plant when he was recruited to join the Communist Party. Like so many others, he talked with the FBI first and agreed to sign up and then fill in his handlers on the party's activities in Chicago until he left the party in 1947. As part of his testimony, Herron told the jury that at party training sessions he was told to use Marxist-Leninist tracts as a guide to action in the event of a revolution.[11]

To rebut Herron's testimony, Gladstein sought to enter into the record full texts of the books and pamphlets, beginning with Marx's twenty-one-thousand-word *Value, Price, and Profit*, to show that there was much more to Marxism-Leninism than a few scattered references to revolution. Wallace objected that the lengthy pamphlet was irrelevant to the charges in the case, and Medina tried to split the difference, telling Gladstein he could read excerpts to back up specific points during the cross-examination. Medina feared, he told Gladstein, that the defense would use the texts to draw out the proceedings even further. He urged Gladstein to confer with his fellow defense lawyers and settle on which excerpts to read. Sacher, though, jumped up to demand the entire books be read into the record as an "essential" part of the defense. Medina still refused.[12]

"I have told this jury again and again that this is not a trial of books written a hundred years ago, or five years ago, or any number of years ago, and if you are going to try to persuade them it is you are going to have a hard time with me sitting here because the question is, did the defendants enter into the conspiracy which is charged in the indictment, and if they used these books as paraphernalia and apparatus to serve their purpose as charged—" Sacher cut him off:

"To call these books paraphernalia and apparatus, it seems to me, is to reduce writing and books to the level of the tools of thieves. And I tell you the culture of the world will not long survive with that approach to books."

Medina told Sacher to sit down. Dennis lumbered to his feet and continued the point. Medina told him to stop, but Dennis argued on, telling Medina that the indictment against them was nothing more than an attack on their right to free speech. "I suppose you are just daring me to do something to you now, but I'm not going to do it," Medina said. "You gentlemen may be just as disorderly, disobedient, and disrespectful as you choose to be, but you will not goad me into doing something which may prove only a source of difficulty in the trial. Now I tell you again to stop."

Dennis did not. "The final remark, your Honor, is that we defendants intend, as we are duty-bound to do, to show, really what we have advocated, what—" Now it was Medina's turn to interrupt: "I will take an adjournment of five minutes," he announced, then stood up from his red leather chair and hurried off the bench and out his private door. When he returned, Dennis had given up, but Gladstein rose to ask Medina to correct something the judge had said. Medina, sounding petulant, shut Gladstein down before he could make his point: "You may correct any statement you made, but I think you had better leave me alone for the time being."

Tensions snapped again two days later, after Calomiris took the stand—and not over her sexual orientation. Within minutes of Calomiris being sworn in on April 26, the FBI issued a press release lauding her undercover work and vouching for her character, which could be read as a government attempt to build sympathy for Calomiris in the event her sexual orientation came out during testimony. In court, the defense team complained bitterly to Medina that the government was prosecuting its case in the press. Medina pushed back, accusing the defense of trying "your best to put the government on trial, and to put the FBI on trial, and the office of the U.S. Attorney, and to put me on trial, and to put all of the instrumentalities of justice on trial, including the system of selecting jurors. Now, you are not going to do that." He referred to the defense's earlier condemnations of government witnesses as spies, stool pigeons, and Judases.

Gladstein became agitated as he sought to rebut McGohey's comment to the judge that the issue was a function of the freedom of the press. "If the *New York Times* desires to comment any way it likes, that is its right," Gladstein said, his voice rising. "But the FBI has no right—" Medina cut him down: "Please don't shout, Mr. Gladstein. Perhaps you are just trying to disturb me. It does disturb me. It makes me nervous when you do that."[13]

Medina, who began the trial with a demeanor of calm superiority, was letting the defense team get to him, and "he clearly showed the strain of the incessant fifteen-week attack on his authority and motives."[14] The *Daily Worker* was particularly persistent in publishing scathing opinion pieces and front-page articles savaging Medina and the trial, then sending copies of the newspaper to his apartment, where his wife could read it. The defense team's persistence also overwhelmed him at times, and he seemed bewildered by what to do about it. Medina feared both being goaded into making a reversible error and having the trial affect his health. The stress was taking its toll. "This continued wrangling is wearing me down so that I don't see how I can finish this trial," Medina said in open court. "Something has to be done to stop it." But he had no solution other than to keep notes in his green binder and to bide his time.

In the midst of his squabbles with the defense attorneys, Medina did finally agree to one of their requests. Moments after taking the bench on the morning of April 26, he announced he had changed his mind and granted the defense request to depose the ailing Foster where he was living in doctor-ordered seclusion in his apartment.[15]

———————

Medina was leading nearly as secluded a life as Foster. Judge Learned Hand had advised him before the trial started to check into a hotel, warning that the distractions of family and his regular routines would be problematic during such a long and complicated proceeding (though Hand had no idea exactly how long the trial would go on). Medina demurred, but his wife took Hand's suggestion to heart. "I made up my mind to try to turn this place into a hotel room," she said. They stopped going to movies, sold their season tickets to the opera—even cut out church, attending only Easter services at Saint Mark's Episcopal Church in Westhampton. Once good weather set in, Medina's wife spent most of her time at the mansion at Apaucuck Point, which exacerbated Medina's isolation. The judge stayed at the East Seventy-fifth Street apartment during the week, adhering to a strict routine—up early for the commute down East River Drive to the courthouse, preparation for the day in court, adjournment at 4:30 P.M., a workout at the gym, a stop to get the papers, then head home for the ritualistic preparation of a martini—a "sliver" of vermouth with the gin, and a bit of lemon peel—while Harvey Lo, the family's longtime houseman, prepared dinner. After dinner Medina would call his wife out on Long Island, then be in bed by 9:30 P.M. On Fridays he would drive himself in his convertible—with a state police escort—out to join his wife for the weekends, but they were still spent in isolation. Their children were allowed to stop by for a brief visit over cocktails but not invited for dinner. "His life has been completely revolutionized," an unidentified friend told the *World-Telegram*. "From a sociable guy who likes cocktails and theater parties he has been virtually turned into a recluse, isolated from the world."[16]

Medina's desire for isolation might have made sense to him, but in retrospect one has to wonder whether that exacerbated the stress from the trial. With no distractions of note, all he had to concentrate on was the case. He did allow himself one diversion. On April 4, he confirmed an upcoming appointment to sit for a portrait, an event being arranged by famed etcher John Taylor Arms. "I should have answered at once your most interesting letter of March 24, but the whirlpool here has been a little bit too much for me. I shall follow your suggestions to the letter. You may expect me on hand at the National Academy of Design, 1083 Fifth Ave., New York, N.Y., at 8 P.M. on Thursday of this week, April 7. Unless I hear from you to the contrary, I shall bring Eth along as I know she will want to come."

The event was a public display of the process by Arthur W. Heintzelman, one of the leading portraitists and etchers of the era. Apparently Medina had hoped for a memento of the evening and, ever vain, planned on having a formal etching of himself done by Heintzelman. On April 27, Medina again wrote to Arms, complaining about lack of contact. "I have been a little concerned over not hearing from Arthur W. Heintzelman since he gave his demonstration on the evening of April 7th. It was my understanding that he was going to send me a print of the work he did that evening. Perhaps I misunderstood him. In any event, I am anxious to make some arrangement with him for a dry point portrait, although I suppose this will have to wait until the trial is over."[17]

───────────

If communism has a holiday, it is May 1, and the party and eleven defendants weren't about to let the trial distract them from one of their best promotional moments. Fortunately for them, May Day fell on a weekend, when the courthouse was closed. Since May 1 was Sunday, parade organizers decided to hold the parade the day before, on the Saturday. But they would not have the day, or the city's parade routes, to themselves.

Recognizing the publicity value of a counter-demonstration, groups including the American Legion, Amvets, and unions organized their own parades—alternative Loyalty Day Marches, to be held in Manhattan, Brooklyn, Trenton, Boston, and Los Angeles. The chair of the national parade committee was Truman's secretary of labor Maurice J. Tobin, who was also tapped as grand marshal of the Manhattan celebration; Cardinal Spellman of the Archdiocese of New York agreed to serve as "reviewing officer." "This parade," Secretary Tobin said in a prepared statement, "will serve as an inspiring demonstration of our belief in democracy and will greatly assist in combating communistic tendencies." A reporter asked him what he made of the May Day parades being planned. "If they love Russia so much," Tobin replied, "I think it would be a good investment for America to provide boats for them to go over there."[18]

Both Manhattan parades began at 1:00 P.M. on a sunny spring day. The propaganda battle was won by the Loyalty Day Parade, which staged a massive gathering. German American societies, eager to display their patriotism, sent twenty thousand marchers from different social clubs and related organizations. The New York State Catholic War Veterans had already planned its annual convention for the New Yorker Hotel, near Penn Station, that week, and announced that many of its members would stick around to march in the Loyalty Day Parade, a two-thousand-strong contingent. The National Guard also deployed delegations, as did the Boy Scouts of America, who made a point of sending foreign-born Scouts wearing native costumes from their home countries.

A group from Chinatown came, bringing a dragon with them. More than ten thousand flags were ordered and handed out as paraders gathered in staging areas near Ninety-fifth Street and Fifth Avenue, where the parade began. Some 150,000 spectators lined the route, many standing for the full six hours it took the parade to pass, a boisterous procession of marchers and bands moving south along Fifth Avenue—Central Park to their right—to Sixty-second Street, then east to Third Avenue, the official end point.

The May Day Parade paled in comparison. Its route began at Thirty-ninth Street, then went south along Eighth Avenue, a few blocks from the Hudson River, then east along Seventeenth Street past a reviewing stand at Union Square Park before dispersing over the next few blocks. Floats were decorated with political slogans, some denouncing the Marshall Plan and the North Atlantic Pact, others decrying the Taft-Hartley Act. The trial of the communist leadership received its share of protest signs and banners as well—eight of the defendants (all but Gates, Hall, and Green) marched or rode, and one float carried papier-mâché marionettes of Truman, Attorney General Clark, and Medina manipulated by a puppeteer in a silk hat bearing a dollar sign. At 5:00 P.M., by prearrangement, the entire parade of about fifteen thousand marchers stopped for a rendition of "The Star-Spangled Banner" and then "Taps," followed by a recitation of a loyalty oath against fascism. No reliable estimate of viewers exists, but the media consensus was that the crowd was about half of what it had been the previous year—likely reflecting the increasing mood of anti-communism, the rightward turn of most labor unions, and the competition over on Fifth Avenue.

Although the May Day Parade was dwarfed by the Loyalty Day March, the leftists served as a moving flashpoint for confrontations. A small melee broke out between Twenty-fourth and Twenty-fifth streets, with a storefront window getting shattered as a small group of youths began fighting with spectators. Five of the youths were arrested, and three were treated for minor cuts and bruises. Also at Twenty-fifth Street, a parade watcher hurled three eggs at a policeman. His aim was off, as was his escape route—he was arrested and charged with disorderly conduct. Back up at Thirty-fifth Street, as the tail of the parade was passing by, Louis Weiss apparently took a stick and began smacking two brothers, William and James Lloyd. Weiss was arrested, though the details of what sparked the fight were unclear. Things were more peaceful at Union Square, where a few thousand people listened to speeches by three of the Foley Square defendants—Davis, Winston, and Thompson—as well as Gerhart Eisler, soon to flee to East Germany. Dennis was also on the reviewing stand but did not speak.

The next day, as if to accent the Loyalty Day Parades, some thirty thousand people gathered at the rain-drenched Polo Grounds in Brooklyn to hear Vice President Alben W. Barkley, Cardinal Spellman, and Monsignor Sheen denounce communism and religious repression during a special prayer meeting around a sheltered altar in the middle of the baseball park's outfield. Barkley, a Protestant, made a point of telling the crowd he had thrice been to the Vatican and admired Pope Pius XII.[19]

"Life is worthless without liberty," Barkley said as the rain fell. "The American trinity of virtues—life, liberty, and the pursuit of happiness—is being attacked by an ideology and a concept which is the utter negation of these principles. This concept has been imposed by a totalitarian system and is attempting to make inroads on our own democracy. We will do well today as we enjoy our American liberties, to see to it that this wicked, crawling, creeping economic disease, this alien nostrum, shall not be permitted to get a foothold in the United States of America."

Despite the rhetoric, the Communist Party was already losing its "foothold" in the United States, which, in fact, had been more of a toehold. Party membership nationwide—population in 1940: 132 million—peaked at eighty-five thousand in 1942, the first full year of America's involvement in World War II, and during the communists' embrace of cooperation during the struggle against fascism (it's notable that the American communists' political discussion rarely mentioned the war against Japan in the Pacific; its enemy was Stalin's enemy). But with the end of the war, the ouster of Browder, and the onset of the cold war, members fell away in droves.[20]

In fact, the party was reeling. The Truman administration's Loyalty Oaths and the Taft-Hartley Act, even as it was being fought in the courts, were driving party members and sympathizers out of influential government and union positions. Revelations of spying helped fan the anti-communist flames, particularly Elizabeth Bentley's stories of passing secrets to the Soviets during the war years. And the nation was riveted by the showdown between Whittaker Chambers and Alger Hiss.

When court opened on Monday, May 2, Calomiris was still on the witness stand, where she tried to credit the Communist Party with creating the Progressive Party under which Henry Wallace had run for president the previous year. In the winter of 1947, Calomiris said, she had been at a meeting at the Thomas Jefferson section of the party, at 201 West Seventy-second Street, where Gates urged that the Communist Party engage itself in the upcoming presidential election—the first since 1932 that would not include Roosevelt as a candidate. There was some dissent, Calomiris said, about whether the communists should back a new Progressive Party or throw in with the American Labor Party, which already existed. But the more significant part of her testimony was in detailing the organization's secrecy. Under cross-examination by Gladstein—unfortunately for the defense, the more he pressed, the better she looked—Calomiris testified that during the war years, when the Communist Political Association policy was to cooperate with the U.S. government, meetings had recording secretaries and minutes were taken. But after the communists reorganized into the CPUSA in 1945 and ended their period of cooperation, the meetings became secret sessions, open only to members and with no notes taken. Members used only first names or aliases, all evidence—to the prosecution, anyway—of guilty acts.[21]

As Gladstein tried to shake Calomiris, the defense team increasingly aggravated Medina. Gladstein again tried to bring up Calomiris's sexual orientation, asking if she had been demoted within the party over a "morals" issue, drawing a rebuke from the bench.[22] During another argument with Medina over a line of questioning—Gladstein was trying to force Calomiris to say the FBI had paid fines on her behalf, which she denied—the judge made it clear that he was keeping track of the defense team's transgressions. He accused Gladstein of "distinct impertinence" after the lawyer again accused the judge of favoring the prosecution and not giving the defense's objections and arguments proper weight. "There is an accumulation of things you have been doing here," Medina said. "You're not helping yourself or your clients by doing this."

The prosecution was nearing the end of its case. After Calomiris, McGohey had four more witnesses lined up: Thomas A. Younglove, a cement contractor from St. Louis; William Cummings, a Toledo autoworker; John V. Blanc, a Cleveland autoworker; and Balmes Hidalgo Jr., a bank worker. Each of the first three men testified about the training party members received, reinforcing McGohey's point about the use of Stalin's history of the party and other Marxist-Leninist texts and confirming the focus on secrecy and the plans for the party to go underground—and engage in sabotage—should the United States go to war with the Soviet Union. Each also helped McGohey tie in the eleven individual defendants to letters, policy statements, and talks at meetings. Like Philbrick and Calomiris, three of the men had joined the Communist Party at the behest of the FBI and spied for the government the entire time. The fourth, Blanc, had been a member during the 1930s and rejoined in 1944 at Hall's invitation. A short time later, he said, the FBI visited him and he agreed to spy on the group. The defense tried to paint each of the men as unreliable—happily living a lie and propelled by self-interest, none was trustworthy, they intimated.

Younglove and Cummings both testified that the Communist Party was planning for war. Younglove told the jury that one meeting he attended was warned that the Truman administration would use the atomic bomb on Americans before it let the nation's workers organize politically. And during an October 1946 meeting in St. Louis, he testified, party members were told that an emissary from Stalin had sent word that war was in the offing. When it began they were to go underground and sabotage the capitalist war machine from within. Blanc mainly reinforced the earlier testimony about the secretive nature of the party and its reliance on Marxist-Leninist theory and placed Green, Hall, and Winter at various meetings in which strategies and communist ambitions were discussed.

Cummings, a tall, broad-shouldered black man who worked for the Electric Auto-Lite Company (against which Budenz had helped lead the violent strike in 1934), testified that he had joined the party in 1943 and rose to play a significant role. At the time he stepped into the witness box, he was vice president of the

Toledo chapter and a former state committee member, where he worked with Hall, the state director. He reinforced Nowell's earlier testimony that the party sought to take advantage of the living conditions of blacks—and the oppression of lynchings and Jim Crow laws—as an organizing tool. And he cited lessons taught to members that a Bolshevik-style revolution was necessary in the United States to overturn capitalism. Labor-management coopera-tion, he said, was to be viewed as an effort to co-opt the demands of the working class.

Cummings said that at one meeting George Siskind, then the party's educational director, described American workers as the most backward in the world because they believed negotiations and contracts could settle their problems with factory owners and managers. Siskind urged the members, Cummings said, to use their union membership to spread Marxist-Leninist theory and to prepare their fellow workers for the fight to come.

"The only way the American working class could settle its problems was by socialism, which could come only through the dictatorship of the proletariat and destruction of the capitalist class," Cummings said. Siskind told the party members that "the Army and police force are the tools of the capitalist class, so the working class must be taught to hate them. He said Lenin worked with the most militant workers in Russia, and American communists must learn to work with the most militant workers in the shops of America. He said Lenin worked with workers in Russia who knew how to be mass leaders, to get the most out of slow-downs and strikes, and to throw bombs in machinery if necessary, and other things like that. He said American workers must be taught to prepare for that day because it was nearing in America."[23]

Of the four final witnesses, Hidalgo created the most dramatic moment, telling the jury that he had attended a party meeting just the evening before he took the stand. He was well known to the New York–based defendants, and as he approached the defense table to identify Thompson, the New York chair and war hero warned, "Now you keep your hands off me." Hidalgo touched him on the shoulder anyway and told the court, "Comrade Thompson." "You're no comrade of mine, I assure you, you little rat," Thompson retorted.[24] In his testimony, Hidalgo detailed the party organization in New York City and its focus on disaffected groups—youths and minorities, specifically—as fertile ground for organizing. And it was telling that, as the thirteenth and final witness, he was also the seventh FBI informant to testify, which meant that more than half of the government's case relied on the word of people the government had insinuated into the Communist Party.

In the following decades, the FBI would reprise these tactics and infiltrate hundreds of American organizations ranging from civil rights groups in the 1950s to the anti–Vietnam War movement in the 1960s to the environmental and anti-nuclear groups of the 1970s and 1980s, as well as groups opposing American policies in Central America during the Reagan administration through to anti-war and pro-peace groups that cropped up after the invasions of Afghanistan and Iraq. The FBI also infiltrated groups on the far right, including the Ku Klux Klan and militia movements of the 1980s and 1990s.

Over time, the infiltrations were seen as an unsavory practice, and the release of the Church Committee report in 1976 led to demands that the FBI be curtailed. The report, among other things, found that the FBI had kept files on one million Americans from 1960 to 1974 and investigated about five hundred thousand people suspected of being "subversive."[25] Yet reform was minimal. Internal guidelines won out over legislative action, and they have done little to stop domestic surveillance, including infiltrating and monitoring anti-war groups.[26]

At the time Philbrick revealed that the FBI had been spying on Americans, there was barely a murmur of opposition. "The Government had reversed, with spectacular success, the old Red tactic of infiltration," crowed *Time* magazine. "The defense had nothing on Philbrick, and he gave no ground under the nagging cross-examination of bull-roaring, white-haired Louis McCabe. Said one Government official of Philbrick: 'They're going to have a tough time smearing him. He's as clean as a whistle.' There was also another disturbing fact for the defendants to consider: communists anywhere in the U.S. could no longer be sure who among them was a communist."[27]

The defense sought to mitigate the damage from these last four witnesses by again introducing evidence of the party's good works—such as its stance against lynching, and its support for labor—and by countering Marxist-Leninist theory that referred to revolution with other excerpts that talked of less violent change. But the biggest drama was the escalation of the battle between the defense team and Medina.

On May 5, with Younglove on the stand, the government sought to introduce into evidence Stalin's *The History of the Communist Party of the Soviet Union*, drawing renewed objections from the defense lawyers. Before the jury entered the courtroom for the morning, Medina asked for arguments over introducing the book, which had already been cited by several earlier witnesses. The gloves quickly came off.[28]

"Our objection to the introduction of this great classic does not arise, naturally, from any objections to the contents of this book," explained Dennis, taking the opportunity to proselytize his beliefs. "We do object to the introduction of this great classic as material evidence because, by so introducing it or any other book, be it communist or non-communist, what the government, in effect, is endeavoring to do is to place books on trial. . . . We, the defense, have contended and we maintain that no classics nor other books can or should be placed on trial before this or any other jury, and to do so is in violation of the First Amendment of our Constitution."

Medina responded with a hypothetical question that, by extension, revealed his mindset. "Let us suppose, for the purposes of argument, that a group of individuals have decided that they will organize a larger group to overthrow the U.S. government by force and violence and they get some pamphlets and books that were written years ago. But they show just how a violent revolution was brought about, how to do it, how to have persons get uniforms of soldiers and put them on and make out that they are part of the Army and Navy. They show them just how to get in charge of the railroads by violent means and to do all the various other things that will, if the teachings and advocating goes on to its ultimate conclusion, bring about the overthrow of the government by force and violence. Now, how can it be that those books and pamphlets are being tried when the charge is that the individuals used those books and pamphlets and papers of one kind or another as mere instruments for the perpetration of a conspiracy? How can it be a trial of books? I wish you would explain that to me."

Dennis tried to, beginning with "In this connection, it seems to me that any reference to Marxist-Leninist classics—" Medina cut him off: "Suppose it was a book about the French Revolution?" Dennis: "Or the American Revolution?" Medina: "Take any revolution you choose and the book shows just how you can do it when you want to overthrow the government: You take step one, you take step two, and then you have street fighting, and then you have rebellion, and you have civil war, and you do this and that. How is it that the book is being tried?"

"The important thing," Dennis said, "is what interpretations and what conclusions we defendants have placed upon any of the books, any of the material which is offered. What the government is attempting to do is place the books on trial" and use them to "describe . . . things which we haven't taught or advocated." He went on to say that if the prosecution wanted to honestly let the jury see all the books that influenced the thoughts and lessons of the American Communist Party it would also have to refer to the works of Thomas Jefferson and other noncommunists.

"Well," Medina said, "there is the issue in the case, Mr. Dennis. You and the other defendants here say this was all a perfectly innocent thing. We never advocated or taught or intended to teach and advocate the overthrow of the government by force or violence at all. All we wanted was to bring about certain salutary social reforms and do it by a perfectly legitimate party. Now that is the issue in the case. And, as I see it, that goes right to the heart of the matter that is going to be decided."

Medina let the prosecution enter the book into evidence, since witnesses had testified that they had read it as part of their training. He then announced that he would order the jury brought back in. Dennis continued to argue, though, telling Medina to "examine with a grain of salt what these witnesses said, the FBI informers who were sent into our party, with their interpretation, and they are trying to place it in such a way that we the defense will—" Medina cut him off, pointing out that dodgy characters are part of the nature of criminal trials. "Naturally you are not going to find the ordinary citizens walking around the street testify in these cases," he said, adding that credibility of the defense witnesses versus the prosecution witnesses was a key decision for jurors—whom he then ordered back into the room.

Sacher sought to intervene and broaden the argument. Medina tried to get Sacher to stop talking, but Sacher wouldn't, exasperating Medina. "There is no way for me to get you to stop without using a pickaxe. I never saw anything like it. Don't you realize that I have ruled on this thing repeatedly, I have expressed myself not once, not twice, but a dozen times on the issue of whether it is books are being tried . . . why do you do that?" Sacher replied, "Because I have clients to defend." Medina: "Well, go ahead and argue." Sacher sat down: "I have no desire to address a judge who won't listen."

Medina told the defense team that he had asked court officials to review the transcript of the case so far, with an eye toward how much of it had been taken up by defense objections and arguments. "It will make an interesting bit of information when it is all added," he said dryly. Sacher replied with his own touch of sarcasm: "It would be good if it were a trial of the kind" in which defendants were tried, not the lawyers. Medina retorted that he would not "have the lawyers trying me." Sacher said he was willing to pay the court "all the respect that the court is entitled to but—" Medina cut in: "I don't think you are capable of giving any court any respect. I think your temperament is such that you cannot give respect to any court." Sacher responded that he had appeared before many judges, but before he could finish his point Medina cut him off again with a terse threat: "You'll never try another one before me, I'll tell you that." Sacher replied, "I will be deprived of a privilege, but I want to say that we will not be intimidated from doing our duty to our clients as we see it." "Well," Medina replied as the jurors entered the room, "I don't want to be intimidated, either."

On May 11, Medina let the court know the results of the transcript report he had ordered. Of the 8,860 pages of transcript up to that point (including the protracted challenge of the jury system), 1,554 had been taken up by arguments from the defense team. In fact, the defense had been particularly aggressive in disrupting the flow of the prosecution witnesses' testimony, something Medina had underscored on several occasions. And the judge had clearly moved beyond the point of exasperation. He warned the defense attorneys that he was, in effect, taking names, and that there would be penalties for their behavior and their open contempt of the court. Gladstein objected to Medina's comments as "improper" and asked that the jury be instructed to disregard them. "It would have been better," Medina responded, "if you hadn't argued so much." Dennis rose and demanded a mistrial; Medina lectured Dennis on court decorum, reminding him that he had left the bench a few days earlier because Dennis would not stop talking when ordered to do so. He denied the mistrial request.[29]

As freewheeling and argumentative as the defense had been, Medina had no way of knowing that the real fireworks were about to start. On May 20, after Hidalgo finished testifying, the prosecution rested.

NINE

The Defense

McGohey's decision to end his case caught the defense by surprise. A few days earlier, he had told the lawyers, out of court, that he thought it would take about two more weeks for him to finish presenting his evidence. When he announced he had wrapped up his presentation with Hidalgo, and Medina had dismissed the jury for the day, the defense lawyers complained bitterly to the judge, stopping just short of accusing McGohey of sandbagging them. They argued that McGohey's surprise move was cause for a postponement so they could get their arguments and witnesses together. Medina disagreed.

Working off the tops of their heads—Isserman, leading the way, told Medina all his notes were in his office—the lawyers offered a series of arguments and motions urging the judge to quash the indictment or declare a mistrial because of Medina's own conduct from the bench, the government's use of spies, the admission of evidence that was based on the writings of people not on trial or that compromised the defendants' constitutionally protected rights of free speech and assembly, and/or the lack of any "clear and present danger" that the men could actually foment revolution, whatever they might have advocated. Most of the motions were variations on the themes defense lawyers routinely present at the conclusion of a prosecution's case,

166

and Medina dismissed them out of hand. There had indeed been sufficient evidence presented for jurors to consider, he ruled, and he continued to reject accusations of his own bias as nothing more than grandstanding by the defense.

But one argument intrigued Medina. He agreed to listen to a presentation on whether the charges should be dropped because the alleged actions by the eleven men did not reach the "clear and present danger" threshold. "This matter . . . is something that I regard as the one substantial question on which I do want to hear argument," Medina said. "But I don't want to hear this extra-legal emotional stuff. I want to hear legal [arguments] on it, an analysis of the cases and that sort of thing." He told Isserman to be ready with it first thing in the morning.[1]

Isserman and others on the defense team worked most of the night. Isserman had been expecting to make this argument, but not quite so soon, and there was a lot of ground to cover aligning citations of earlier decisions and fine-tuning his reasoning on how they should be applied to the Dennis case. Key was the contention that communism did not inherently call for the overthrow of the U.S. government. And even if it did, the eleven men had done nothing that would lead anyone to conclude they posed a "clear and present danger" of success. That threshold was established by the U.S. Supreme Court in its unanimous 1919 *Schenck v. United States* decision upholding the conviction of an anti-draft activist who had been distributing pamphlets to new military recruits during World War I. In writing the decision, Justice Oliver Wendell Holmes Jr. delineated the criteria under which free speech may be curtailed: "The most stringent protection of free speech would not protect a man in falsely shouting fire in a theatre and causing a panic. It does not even protect a man from an injunction against uttering words that may have all the effect of force. The question in every case is whether the words used are used in such circumstances and are of such a nature as to create a clear and present danger that they will bring about the substantive evils that Congress has a right to prevent. It is a question of proximity and degree."[2] Isserman would argue that under that decision, and later decisions by the Court, the defendants could not be found guilty because there was no evidence that by re-forming the Communist Party they had a "clear and present danger" of success in fomenting revolution.

When court convened in the morning, a Friday, Medina summoned the jurors and immediately dismissed them. He said the morning would likely be consumed by legal arguments, and since he left Friday afternoons open for other court business the jurors might as well go home. He also told them that he would be tied up Monday on an unrelated case, which meant that jurors had a nice long weekend ahead of them.

Once the (presumably happy) jurors cleared the room, Isserman began making his case. First, the defendants were being accused of entering into a conspiracy simply by sharing a political belief, and belonging to an organization that promulgated that belief. Yet holding political beliefs and attending meetings about them was protected activity. "Take these political activities out of the case, your Honor, and there is wholly lacking any proof whatsoever of any conspiracy or common agreement," Isserman said. "It must be conceded that there is no right under the Constitution more precious than the right to engage in political assemblies, the very thing which this government has made an essential and, from its standpoint, a necessary ingredient in this criminal case. . . . The fact that the defendants on many issues are opposed in the most fundamental way to the government is no reason for withdrawing constitutional protection."

Medina accused Isserman of "knocking down a straw man here." No one, he said, was arguing that political speech was not protected. The men had been indicted under a law that proscribed teaching or advocating the violent overthrow of the U.S. government—not engaging in political debates. Isserman told Medina he was wrong. "The very essence of the charge in this case is that the Communist Party . . . was a criminal activity because it based itself on the principles of Marxism and Leninism." Should that action be deemed illegal, free speech and assembly "are being pushed aside."

Medina countered that *Schenck v. U.S.* and other court decisions Isserman cited did not mean that conspiracies to advocate violence were protected. "If they merely got together and formed a party for the purpose of arguing and urging people by peaceful means to change the laws so as to bring about a socialistic society, I would say yes, that was something that was clearly their right to do," Medina said. Isserman countered that Marxist-Leninist theory did not inherently call for the overthrow of the U.S. government, that it was a political theory, and thus was protected.

But even if it didn't have that protection, Isserman said, there was no evidence that the Communist Party leaders posed a threat. "The charge here is simply that the defendants got together and agreed some time in the future to engage in teaching and advocacy," Isserman said. "The charge here is not that any words were used, but that they were going to be used. And if the words were going to be used in the future without any specification as to what they are, then the nature of the words as uttered, as required by the clear and present danger principle, cannot be ascertained. . . . Speech to be made in the future is not subject to and cannot be punished."

Medina said the testimony by the witnesses was not just about words but about the sorts of actions that it would take to make the United States a socialist state. Oddly, Medina asked Isserman what the "substantive evil" would be under the Smith Act. After dancing a bit—Isserman said he couldn't possibly know what was in congressional minds when the act was written—he said he presumed the portion of the Smith Act under which his clients had been indicted was aimed at stopping the overthrow of the government. Medina said that applying Isserman's "clear and present danger" argument to the Smith Act meant "you couldn't punish anybody until the overthrow of the government was about to take place. . . . It seems a little bit absurd to me."

But, Isserman said, "in the period 1945 to 1948, which is the period covered by the indictment, there isn't the slightest suggestion of any imminence whatsoever, whether it be extremely high or extremely low."

"I thought," Medina said, "some of the witnesses testified to a good many conversations, teaching and advocacy, that seemed pretty close."

"The mere fact that your Honor has to say that they testified to conversations indicates that there is no imminence and no danger whatsoever," Isserman countered. "Conversations do not overthrow a government."

In the end, Isserman lost his point. Medina rejected the motions.

When the trial resumed on Tuesday morning, May 23, the defense began its rebuttal with John Gates, the editor of the *Daily Worker*.

Throughout the presentation of the prosecution's case, the defense team had pursued a strategy best described as "disrupt and distract." While it didn't seem to affect the witnesses to any great extent—the lawyers never got much of a rise out of any of them—it did affect Medina. The constant objecting and, to him, insolence of Sacher, Gladstein, Crockett, and the others had left him short-tempered, though ever cognizant of creating a reversible error.

Once the defense began its case, it was McGohey's turn to rise time and again to lodge objections on arcane issues of how foundations were laid for certain questions. But he also argued that many of the questions and answers had little to do with the case. He was generally upheld by Medina, but that didn't mean the testimony was concise. The strategy was to use the defendants and some of their supporters to testify about their lives, the evolution of their beliefs, the patriotism evidenced by their military records, and anything else that would show them as America-loving progressives who believed the country could do a better job of caring for the poor, establishing full citizenship rights for blacks, and ensuring more equitable treatment of female workers. And the defense intended to use the witnesses to directly rebut the testimony of people like Budenz, Philbrick, Calomiris, and Nowell, walking the defendants and their supporters through some of the same local organizations and meetings cited by the prosecution. In the defendants' version of events, talk of revolution was abstract at best. America would be reformed from within, they would argue.

Gates took the stand, and Sacher walked him through his own biography, including watching his father lose the family business—a candy store—during the Depression, and how that sensitized him to the failings of capitalism and fed his evolution as a communist. Over several days Gates read lengthy excerpts from political tracts and party memos and reports to counter those that had been read into the record earlier by prosecution witnesses. Medina wouldn't let him discuss party policies or his actions fighting racism, fascism, or other issues. Sacher tried to ask Gates about his experience fighting against Franco in Spain, but Medina saw that line of questioning as a waste of time and cut him off, angering Gladstein.[3]

"I have always operated on the theory that a man's past state of mind and intention is best illustrated by the things that he did and said and wrote and printed, and his conduct in the past," Gladstein said. "When you accuse him of a certain thing in the year 1949, let us say, the best way of telling exactly what the truth was is to go back and find out what he did before, what he said and what he thought and expressed on the subject at hand. . . . It so happens that one of the issues in this case is the question of the intention of each and every one of the defendants."

Medina stood firm: ""We will not go into the war in Spain." Gladstein wouldn't concede. "My point is this: It is no longer any secret that we are dealing here with a question of ideas, and surely the best evidence of a man's understanding of ideas, be it philosophy, science, economics, or whatever it may be, is to be found in the application of those ideas, in his expression of those ideas."

No, Medina said. In the court, it is a matter of "drawing a line. It is obvious that if I permit these defendants to bring in everything they ever said, everything they ever wrote, all their conduct in all the matters having to do with anti-Semitism, arguing matters for the Negroes, being in support of the Republican government in Spain, being opposed to Chiang Kai-shek, and the Chinese government, and so on, we will be here for an indefinite period, and I have felt that I am drawing the line at the proper place. Now one of those places is that the war in Spain is out."

Gladstein, needling Medina a bit, said that it would indeed take an indefinite period of time to enumerate the defendants' good deeds. Then Thompson stood and started to say that he was "vitally interested in this question of Spain," but Medina warned him against speaking. "Do you think it's wise when you've got a lawyer representing you here, to rise this way and address the court?" Thompson argued that the party's stance on Spain and the defendants' actions there "has very profoundly influenced the position of our party towards many questions, the problem of the state and many other questions, that are vital and essential in any presentation of the development of the line of policies in our party. And that is what you are ruling out when you say you are ruling out the question of Spain."

Medina said his ruling would not limit the defendants' ability to make their case, drawing an objection from Dennis and then Davis, who until then had been quiet. Before Davis could begin speaking, Medina silenced the entire defense table. "Before you say very much I want to make a little observation," Medina said. "You gentlemen have been bobbing up here, saying things and doing things that I did not consider were very proper to do, some of them rather—well, I won't characterize them because we all remember what you and your other defendants have said and done. This is the first time you [Davis] have got up. Now I have determined here that I am going to have a very orderly trial. I don't think in the early stages that any of you gentlemen really thought I meant what I said or that I would succeed."

Gladstein objected, but Medina waved him off and threatened the defendants. "It appears that I have succeeded rather well, and that the proceedings are becoming more regular and orderly every day. I have penalties at my disposal, if the defendants insist upon interrupting the proceedings and holding forth, although they have lawyers to represent them, and I dislike very much doing some of the things that the law places in my power to do. Now, I just want you to remember that."

"It is pretty hard," Davis said, "for the defendants to sit here like a bump on a log, as you say, while a whole lot of rulings are made which are practically cutting the guts out of what our party stands for. This Court claims—"

"I consider that an extremely offensive statement," Medina interjected.

"Well," Davis said, "the whole trial is offensive to me and should have been thrown out a long time ago."

"No defendant gets very much pleasure out of a criminal trial," Medina said.

"Of course," Davis replied. "And I don't see what pleasure the Government should get in bringing this ridiculous and stupid trial in the first place."

"Now, Mr. Davis, do you realize that you may be forcing me to remand you during the remainder of the trial?"

"Well, I cannot help that. All I want to do is to say the truth. That is all."

"Oh you can help it," Medina said. "You can help it."

"And if you wanted the truth," Davis continued, "you would let our party say what it teaches and advocates in Spain and elsewhere."

Medina ignored the last gibe. "If you maintain yourself in an orderly way, you will avoid that [being jailed for contempt]. If you insist upon being disorderly, I shall remand you for the remainder of the trial. Let's get on."

The entire exchange was conducted in full view of the jury.

Gates testified for eleven days, and Sacher, who led the direct examination, was able to get into the record the highlights of Gates's military history—he was a veteran of the Spanish Civil War and was serving as a paratrooper in the Ruhr Valley when World War II ended—as well as his political evolution. Curiously, though perhaps out of ignorance, on cross-examination McGohey did not ask Gates about the dark moments of his experiences in Spain as commissar (a political office) in the 15th Brigade. In August 1938, Gates—a hard disciplinarian—ordered the execution of fellow American Paul White for desertion, despite White's decision to return to his unit. Other American brigade members were appalled by the act, and their outrage led the leaders of the Republican forces to ban further executions. Yet a few days later, faced with an unruly (and unreliable) soldier named Bernard Abramofsky, Gates muttered in front of fellow officers that Abramofsky "ought to be shot," although he ordered him returned to his battalion. Instead, Abramofsky was assassinated by one of the other officers.[4] But the jury heard nothing of those actions.

Gates testified that once he returned from military service he was told that, in absentia, he had been elected to the National Committee of the Communist Party. During cross-examination on June 2, McGohey asked Gates who had told him of his election. It was Dennis, Gates said. McGohey asked Gates what position Dennis held, drawing objections from Sacher and Gladstein, who argued that the information had already been entered into testimony by other witnesses and was included in reports and pamphlets submitted by the prosecution as evidence. Medina said he saw nothing wrong with the question and ordered Gates to answer. After much back-and-forth, and a short recess so the defense could confer, the showdown was defused when McGohey decided not to press the point and demand the answer.

McGohey moved on to ask Gates about his role chairing the party's national Veterans Committee and then asked him who the other members were. Gates balked again as the defense lawyers renewed their objections, adding that the names of other members were irrelevant because they had not been indicted. McGohey countered that he was entitled to the information for establishing the context of Gates's work; Gates accused McGohey of embarking on a fishing expedition. In a break with his usual procedure, Medina didn't issue an immediate ruling. He told the lawyers to prepare written arguments and submit them the next morning, and he would rule then.

Before court convened on June 3, both legal teams and Medina huddled in the judge's chambers. No record exists of what was said, but after a half hour of debate Medina ruled for McGohey and told Sacher that Gates would have to answer the question. Back in court, with the jury in the box and Gates in the witness chair next to Medina, McGohey again asked for the names. Gates told the jury that his codefendants Winston and Thompson were on the committee. McGohey asked who else was a member. Gates dug in.[5]

"It would degrade me in the eyes of my associates and the labor movement, in the eyes of the public, and in the eyes of the jury to act as a common stool pigeon to give you such other information as you desire," Gates said archly. "I don't want to have on my conscience the fact that any human being would lose his means of livelihood, or even his life, because of any such information that I might give you in response to your question. And I invoke my rights under the First and Fifth Amendments to the Constitution not to answer that question any further."

McGohey, surprisingly, said he would accept that answer for the time being. But he then asked Gates who had helped him, when he was the party's director of veterans' affairs, prepare a pamphlet targeting members of the military forces. Gates declined to say. "Those people are people who work in private industry and I will not disclose their names because it would lead to their loss of work, probably, if I did so." Medina ordered Gates to answer. "On the grounds of the First and Fifth Amendments of the Constitution of the United States, I decline to answer that question," Gates said. "And I do so because I would have to bow my head in shame if I gave such information, and I wouldn't be able to raise my head in decent society if I became a stool pigeon under the direction of the court or anybody else."

Medina dismissed the jury, then told Gates the First and Fifth Amendments didn't give him the right to not answer the question.

Dennis rose to Gates's defense, arguing that forcing Gates to answer would open the door for McGohey to learn the names of all communists. "This line of question, among other things, is an un-American effort to infringe on our basic rights and to try and compel the defendants to act as police, as FBI informers," Dennis said. "And I would say that if the court accedes to the request of the prosecution and if it does not sustain our objections that this would be a violation of the traditions embodied in our Bill of Rights. This would be acting in the traditions of Edgar Hoover and Herr Himmler because such rulings could only be conceived and executed in the spirit of a police state inquisition."

Medina tried to cut him off, but Dennis kept going. "I would say in conclusion, your Honor, that no court or no legislative body can kill ideas, political doctrines of the people, such as the communist movement. They can't do that by force or compulsion [and they can't] compel any communist or any reputable working person to bear false testimony and act as an informer against his associates."

Medina had had enough. He told Dennis and the rest of the array that he could not "permit a defendant who has chosen to act as a witness on his own behalf to choose the questions that he will answer and that he will not answer." He turned to Gates, read from the law that gave him the authority to jail witnesses for contempt, and said simply, "You are to be remanded until you have purged yourself of your contempt for a period not to exceed 30 days."

The defense table erupted, with most of the lawyers and defendants jumping to their feet and Hall and Winston stepping toward Medina and the bench as they voiced their outrage.[6] Though the official transcript makes the exchange sound orderly, it was anything but. Court officials quickly sent out a call for help, summoning marshals on duty a few floors above at the Hiss perjury trial.

Winston: "If your Honor please, may I now be heard? More than five thousand Negros have been lynched in this country and the government of the United States should be ashamed for bringing in such monstrosity."

Medina: "Mr. Winston, I hereby direct that you be remanded for the remainder of the trial."

Hall: "It sounds more like a kangaroo court than a court of the United States. I have heard more law and more constitutional rights in kangaroo courts."

Medina: "Now let me see, this is Mr. Hall—"

Hall: "That is right, this is Mr. Hall."

Medina: "Mr. Hall, you are hereby remanded for the remainder of the trial."

The marshals began flooding in, lining up behind the rail and within an arm's reach of the defendants' chairs, and the arguing continued for a few moments before Dennis was able to seize the court's attention. He complained about Medina's "outrageous" decisions but suggested his codefendants sit back down and said he would "urge them not to call for any provocation." They sat, as the *New York Sun* put it, "like a well-disciplined platoon."[7]

———

When Medina sent Gates, Hall, and Winston to jail, he issued an order revoking their $5,000 bail. The defense lawyers asked Medina to suspend his order, which came on a Friday, and to continue bail over the weekend so they could appeal and continue meeting with their clients to prepare their defense. Medina flatly refused, saying he had given the defendants "ample warning" of the potential punishment for their misbehavior. So the defense team appealed that afternoon, in effect, to Medina's boss, Judge Kaufman, who was overseeing the Hiss trial. Kaufman, to no one's surprise, refused to second-guess Medina. So the three defendants were taken to the Federal House of Detention for the weekend.

On Monday, the lawyers appealed the revocation of Gates's bail to the U.S. Court of Appeals and filed writs of habeas corpus to try to free Hall and Winston. Over the next couple of weeks both cases received full hearings, but the appellate judges refused to free any of the men. Gates, they ruled, had waived his Fifth Amendment right when he agreed to testify, and his position was further weakened because the defense had introduced into evidence the pamphlet that Gates then said he didn't want to answer questions about. Separately, the courts ruled that Hall and Winston had been justifiably remanded. By then, Green had joined them in the federal detention center after a June 20 outburst in which, after running arguments about admissibility of evidence and Green's lengthy answers, Green "turned angrily to the judge, and in a sullen, whining, tone" snapped at Medina, "I thought we were going to get a chance to prove our case." Medina found him in contempt and ordered him remanded for the rest of the trial.[8]

While the defense argued that Medina was acting out of prejudice against the defendants, the appeals court ruled that Medina was within his rights to enforce order in his courtroom—and, after reading portions of the transcript, lauded him for his patience. Medina "represented the authority of this Government, which had been defied by enough men acting in concert to make a rather formidable display of opposition, and he saw fit to vindicate this authority by promptly remanding these two appellants. This was quick and appropriate action, well justified by the circumstances."[9]

The jailing of the four men and the shift of the trial from prosecution to defense reinvigorated the protesters in Foley Square Park, across from the courthouse. Hundreds of chanting and parading communist supporters showed up nearly daily, now targeting the Smith Act trial, Medina's decision to remand the four defendants, the arguments being heard and contemplated by the Court of Appeals (also housed at Foley Square), and Hiss's perjury trial. Medina's order also drew criticism from political figures, such as Henry Wallace. "The jail sentences can have the most profound effect on the political and civil liberties of all Americans," Wallace said. "It violates every American concept of fair play, and in my judgment is the use of the power of the court to promote injustice. . . . Let no one make the grave error of believing that because this injustice has been practiced on a communist his own civil rights are not in danger."[10] And the night of Medina's order, June 3, the New York Communist Party hosted a prescheduled fund-raising dinner for the defense committee, charging an estimated nineteen hundred people twenty dollars a ticket for the gathering at the Saint Nicholas Arena at 69 West Sixty-sixth Street. Lillian Gates and Edna Winston, wives of two of the detained men, were among the diners, after spending the earlier part of the day at the Foley Square demonstrations.[11] And they were boisterous, hard-to-ignore demonstrations, drawing as many as five hundred protesters whose chants and shouts could be heard inside the courthouse. When they recognized trial figures entering or leaving the building, they became even louder, saving the most venomous comments for Medina. "Hitler never died, he's sitting at Medina's side," they chanted as the judge descended the granite steps during one lunch break. The June 5 Foley Square protest was led by the wives of Gates and Winston, with several other wives—Mae Williamson,

Peggy Dennis, Gita Potash, and Bertha Stachel—in the crowd. That evening, Davis spoke at a rally at the corner of 126th Street and Lenox Avenue in Harlem, defending his colleagues.

The June 5 rally drew a fair number of counterdemonstrators, though estimates from the time vary widely. One of them, William Crowley, a twenty-nine-year-old army veteran from Brooklyn, was standing with a counterdemonstration of longshoremen when he snapped. With the union men urging him on, Crowley waded into the communist supporters with his fists flying, screaming, "You dirty communist bums!" Police rushed into the thicket to try to stop him as the longshoremen moved closer to the throng, the scene edging closer to full riot. But the police managed to collar Crowley and drag him out of the crowd (he kept screaming "I hate communists!") and move the longshoremen back, defusing the moment. Crowley was hauled off on disorderly conduct charges and appeared at night court that evening, where the judge ordered the charges dropped—and lectured the arresting officer. "What's wrong with defending this country, right here?" the judge said. "During the war they sent us across the ocean to fight those who were trying to destroy America." Crowley, who told reporters he had spent nearly five years with the U.S. Army 186th Field Artillery, said he snapped under communist provocation.

"I watched this bunch romping up and down the sidewalk making slurring remarks about this country, casting aspersions on American justice, and in general making out that Russia was a paradise and America just an undesirable place," he said. "I saw police around and saw they were unable to do anything about the matter. I couldn't take it any more so I just walked over and let one of them have it. I would have got more of them but the cops pulled me off."[12]

The detention center itself was picketed as well, with the children of some of the incarcerated men joining the lines and carrying signs that read, "My daddy is no tattletale, let our daddies out of jail" and "My daddy isn't free, there is danger to democracy."[13] And on June 8, some twenty-five hundred people gathered in Union Square Park to hear speakers denounce Medina and his jailing of the three men. Thompson and Williamson made it in time, after their day in court, and spoke to the crowd, as did Howard Fast, the author, and several other prominent communists and progressive activists.

The effects of the trial were reverberating in other ways in other parts of the country. In Chicago, the testimony in the Smith Act trial cost at least one man his job. Herron, one of the prosecution witnesses, had testified that in 1946, when he went to work at the sprawling Stewart-Warner plant in Chicago, he attended a Communist Party meeting at the home of John S. Kelliher, who at the time of the trial was president of UE Local 1154. On June 8, the company fired Kelliher, who worked at the plant as an assembler. Kelliher was already under suspension for insubordination after having left his spot on the assembly line to join a picket at another factory under strike.[14]

It was hard to avoid the hysteria. Colleges were looking at their faculty with skeptical eyes and firing some teachers over their past or current communist connections. The newspapers and radio were filled with news from the Smith Act trial, as well as the Hiss perjury trial. In Washington, the HUAC won its court fight to find Dalton Trumbo and John Howard Lawson—the first of what would become known as the Hollywood Ten—in contempt of Congress for refusing to tell the HUAC whether they had been members of the Communist Party. On June 30, Justice Department political analyst Judith Coplon was convicted of spying for the Soviets by taking secret FBI files to her lover, Soviet agent Valentin Gubitchev, in New York City. And the behavior of defense lawyers in those cases was coming under fire, with a special federal grand jury urging disbarment for any member of the bar who refused to answer questions on the witness stand or before Congress.[15]

President Truman, who bore some of the responsibility for fanning the flames, recognized the growing anti-communist mood as a national hysteria but predicted the nation would survive it. In a question-and-answer session with White House news reporters, Truman drew parallels with the early years of the country when, fearing war with France, Congress adopted the Alien and Sedition Acts of 1798. He also invoked the political rise of the Ku Klux Klan in the years after World War I and dismissed as "headline hunting" those who were trying to ferret out communists in the administration. He seemed to blame Hoover and the FBI for the current mood, stopping short, when asked about a current rumor of Hoover's resignation, of telling the media that Hoover had his full support.[16]

Some, though, fought against the hysteria. Paul Robeson, the outsized singer and political activist, announced in mid-June that he would end a four-month European tour and return to the United States to testify as a character witness for the defense in the Smith Act trial. "If war-mongers and reactionaries are not stopped they might turn next on the twelve million negroes in the South," he told reporters. He had recently been in Moscow for celebrations marking the sesquicentennial of Russian poet Alexander Pushkin, and Robeson fanned the anti-communist—and racist—flames by declaring the Soviet Union as the country "which I love more than any other." He said his success, like that of such other black Americans as opera singer Marian Anderson, boxer Joe Louis, and Dr. Ralph Bunche, was an anomaly—and they were among the few blacks safe from lynching in America. He said he would have stayed in Russia but felt compelled "to return to my people to be with them to struggle for their liberty."[17]

Robeson would pay a price for his outspokenness.

———————————

In Medina's court, the trial continued at its slow, languorous pace. After Gates finished testifying, the defense called Green and then Davis. Both were led through their early years and their conversions to communism, and Green testified at length—and at times evasively—about what he and the party believed would be required for the United States to embrace socialism. Medina tried repeatedly to get Green to define what the Communist Party considered to be a democracy, and Green and Gates conflicted over the relationship between the *Daily Worker* and the party. Gates, the editor, said the paper was independent from but editorially sympathetic to the cause, while Green said (somewhat inscrutably) that the paper was not a party organ but that the party supported it because of its editorial support for communist principles. The difference might seem minor, but McGohey was arguing that the *Daily Worker* was part of the alleged conspiracy.

Green treated his time on the stand as an opportunity to detail exactly what the American Communist Party stood for. Before he took the stand he wrote on May 30 to his wife that "before me is the most important, the biggest task I've ever faced. I have to defend everything that my life has meant to me, everything that communism stands for. Whether we are convicted or not is not half as important as that we defend our party with honor, without weaseling, without dodging, while indicting those who are the enemies of this nation." The letter was an apology to Lil and their children for apparently failing to return to Chicago for a promised visit (presumably over the long Memorial Day weekend) and is written in the tone of a husband who has received an accusatory letter from his wife about putting his work ahead of his family. "Please, Lil, understand and forgive my failure to keep a promise. You should know by this time that my desire to see you and the kids is certainly as great as is yours and the kids to see me. If you don't know this after all these years then you certainly don't know me."[18]

Given the pressure Green felt to "defend everything that my life has meant," he quickly became exasperated with Medina's decisions to cut short portions of his testimony—which led to the exchange that landed him in jail for the duration of the trial. He came across as a sincere if at times evasive witness. He denied Budenz's description of "Aesopian language," saying the party's Constitution and policy statements were transparent and meant exactly what they said. But under cross-examination, Green admitted that he had at times advocated violence—though only, as he said in a radio speech during his mayoral campaign in 1947, if "heaven forbid, America becomes the victim of a fascist dictatorship and change became impossible by orderly, majority and above all, democratic means." Media accounts of Green's testimony painted that as an admission that he had advocated violence, the reporters missing the key point that the party would fight only if the democracy had already been usurped by fascism.

But McGohey did get both Gates and Green to admit that, fearing repercussions, they had lied on passport applications and other forms in the past to hide their party affiliations. Green, for instance, had been fired from the post office over his political work, then reapplied under a false name. Green also traveled several times to Russia but didn't list the destination on his passport applications, and listed his occupation as "metal worker" and "writer" when he was in fact a paid party functionary.

Against the backdrop of discursive social and political analyses and recaps of communist philosophy, the sharply drawn details of the lies stood out. As it was, the defendants were barred from presenting as much communist theory as they had hoped. Medina ruled that the evidence they presented must address the particulars of the indictment. Yet the prosecution had been given wide latitude to introduce evidence, including books, that predated the time frame covered by the indictment. Medina's demeanor toward the defense lawyers—and the lawyers' toward him—likely hurt their credibility with the jurors. And the defendants' proselytizing during their answers couldn't have earned them many fans in the jury box.

But the biggest problem confronting them was Budenz's testimony about the party's use of Aesopian language. He told the jury, in effect, that any denial by the communist leaders could be read as an admission, impeaching their credibility before they even took the stand. Budenz had his own credibility issues, but by the time of the trial he had become practiced at delivering his specifics, and the party leaders, unaccustomed to brevity, seemed to add legitimacy to the Aesopian-language argument. Denials became affirmations, and long-winded answers decrying capitalism and the failures of the modern state to defend the poor and minorities reinforced McGohey's argument that the men were dangerous radicals bent on sowing the seeds of revolution.

The most compelling testimony from the party leaders came from Davis, who, like Gates and Green, was walked through his personal evolution to communism. Davis talked about growing up as a black man in the South, his career as a lawyer, his defense of Angelo Herndon and how that brought him in close contact with American communists. "This case was the turning point of my whole life," Davis testified. "The judge referred to me and my client as 'niggers' and 'darkies,' and threatened many times to jail me along with my client. I was treated in such a way that I could see before me the whole treatment of the Negro people in the South. The fact that I had been luckier than most people in education and income did not shield me from what all Negroes suffered. So I felt that if there was anything I could do to fight against this and identify myself fully with my own people and strike a blow against the lynch system, I was determined to do it." He said that his defense of Herndon meant he had to understand the nature of communism, and the books drew him to the movement. "They made sense to me. As I read them I thought of them in terms of my father and the Ku Klux Klan crosses burned in his front yard when he became a member of the Republican National Committee, and of my mother, who died early because of that kind of thing."[19]

Over six days, Davis detailed the party's stance on racial issues and his belief that the Communist Party was the best way to end racism in America. The *New York Times* noted that he "conducted himself with courtesy and dignity on the stand, in sharp contrast to the contempt of court that led to the jailing of previous defense witnesses" Gates and Green. Davis also served a different function on the witness stand than Gates and, particularly, Green, who had spent days laying out the party's evolving stance toward the U.S. government. The first two defendants' testimony was aimed at rebutting the prosecution's witnesses—particularly people such as Budenz, Philbrick, and Calomiris—and their contentions that they had been taught in party classes and training sessions that Marxism-Leninism was committed to the violent overthrow of capitalism. When the time came in America, they had testified, the Soviet Union would be there to help them, and if domestic repression increased they would all become part of an underground movement, engaging in sabotage if a shooting war erupted between the United States and the Soviet Union. Gates and Green argued that that was not the case, that the party did not presume a violent overthrow of the government would be necessary to achieve socialism.

Davis's role was to counter the testimony of Nowell and others that the party intended to take advantage of the "second-class citizen" status of African Americans and to foment rebellion that would lead to a separate nation for blacks in the American South. Davis denied that this was part of the party's agenda and also denied that the party was committed to violent overthrow, an accusation he described as "Hitlerian." Davis, who was still a sitting member of the New York City Council, said that he had campaigned about the need to adopt socialism to fight against Jim Crow laws, anti-Semitism, and lynching, but not to overthrow the government with violence.

"I pointed out the perpetrators of this system of force and violence by legal and extra-legal means were never brought to justice, and the system had not been eliminated," he said. "I pledged myself to introduce legislation in the City Council against this force and violence." Medina asked him if he had ever addressed "the charge

10. Benjamin Davis Jr. entering the federal courthouse. He was a member of the New York City Council at the time of the trial. WPA Film Library. Image courtesy of MPI Home Video.

that the Communist Party advocates the overthrow of the Government by force and violence." Davis said he had. "I said that it was pure slander, a Hitlerian distortion of the position of our party in this country. I said it was a strange thing to talk to me as a Negro about force and violence as a communist when all my life I'd been hounded as a Negro and a communist. I said this charge usually comes from Fascist sources to hide the real sources of force and violence, such as the Ku Klux Klan lynchers and police brutes."[20]

But McGohey, on cross-examination, established (or at least raised the likelihood) that Davis, too, had lied in the past. He also forced Davis to change some of his testimony, including where he lived at various times. In a key moment, McGohey went after Davis's contention that he had been the victim of racial epithets by the Georgia judge during the Herndon case because no mention of the verbal abuse appeared in the appeal Davis filed, nor in the transcript; Davis argued that the transcript was likely scrubbed. Trying to further undermine Davis's credibility, McGohey established that Davis swore when he applied for admission to the Georgia bar that he had lived in the state for the previous ten years when, in fact, he had also lived in other states during that time as he was earning his academic degrees. Davis maintained that he considered Georgia home, much as college students keep their parents' home as a legal address while living temporarily out of state.

Individually, the points McGohey was trying to make seem like minor details, forgetfulness, or conflicting interpretations. But on the heels of McGohey's cross-examinations of Gates and Green, Davis's minor admissions echoed the theme that the Communist Party leaders were prone to lying—reinforcing Budenz's testimony that, in their case, a no could mean a yes.

For the jurors, it had to be a frustrating case to follow: witnesses and lawyers taking turns reading long, hard-to-fathom policy and theory statements; the extended answers, especially by Green; the squabbling between the defense lawyers and Medina, punctuated by shouts and sarcastic taunts. The jurors had been warned when they were selected in mid-March that the case would last several weeks—and here it was mid-July, four months later, with no end in sight and, from their perspective, the defense to blame.

The defendants had gone into the trial presuming they would not get a fair hearing and the deck was stacked against them. But it also became clear as the trial progressed they were doing little to help their own cause. Any sliver of hope for acquittals disappeared in the summer heat.

By late July, Gates had served his thirty-day sentence for contempt of court and was released—without naming the names McGohey wanted. But Hall, Winston, and Green had been ordered remanded until the end of the trial. So when court adjourned each day the three men were shackled together and ferried under guard in a nondescript van from the courthouse to the West Street Federal House of Detention, a dank facility among the wharves and storage buildings on the far side of the West Village. Often a handful of supporters would wait at the driveway's edge until the van left, and there were regular protests outside the detention center itself.

Lil Green had decided to move temporarily to New York, leaving the children with friends and family in Chicago. Ralph, the youngest, eventually joined her in New York for the summer, and they stayed in an apartment in Far Rockaway, a long train ride from the courthouse in lower Manhattan. The available records don't indicate when she arrived, but it likely was just before or just after Green was ordered remanded. The indictment, arrest, and trial had heaped stress on the marriage; Green's incarceration only added to it, leading to some sort of emotional rupture between the couple and an outburst by Lil during one of the trial recesses. What happened doesn't show up in detail anywhere, but Green tried to reassure his wife afterward. "Look kid, you must relax and take things in stride," he wrote from jail in a letter that began, "What occurred at recess time has disturbed me considerably. . . . This trial won't go on forever. Even if the worst happens and I do not get out before the trial is over—something which can still be altered—I will be out when the trial is over, whether convicted or not." Green believed that the underlying constitutional issues meant the Supreme Court would ultimately have to weigh in on the legitimacy of the Smith Act proscriptions against political speech and advocacy. "Of course, if the war danger became acute in the next weeks, things could change for the worse, but I do not believe that development is likely." He waxed romantic about the time they would spend together once he was released, just them and the kids off somewhere unspecified. "We will take them out [of school] for a few weeks and take our chances on their making up for lost time," he wrote. "In the meantime, please, relax. This hypertension is no good—for you, the kids, or myself. It certainly is going to reflect itself in a feeling of insecurity on the part of Ralphy. As for me, it's not going to make this business any easier. I know that in many ways you have the tougher end of the assignment but there is no sense worrying about what cannot be changed."[21]

In a later letter, he refers to the difficulty the families of the defendants faced navigating the jail bureaucracy to see the incarcerated men. "Needless to say, I was most keenly [disappointed] in not being able to spend some time with you. . . . The petty bastards will do anything to harass, to pin-prick, to show their 'power.' I was especially disturbed because I did want to have a long talk with you. Ever since your emotional display on Tuesday, I have worried about you. Therefore this recent refusal to permit you to see me is particularly cruel."

Green alluded to an arrangement made by Gladstein with jail officials that apparently hadn't been followed. "It is possible that

the marshals were taking petty revenge for the outside demonstrations." Green tried to paint his life with Lil as more exciting than
that of the average couple "who see each other every day for decade
after decade and finally get so bored with one another that they
each seek escape in one direction or another. In our case, every time
I'm away for a period, when I return it is like meeting you for the
first time. . . . And boy, when I get out of here I'm really going to
go after my wife with a special passion and fervor. Nor will I for a
long long time to come shout at any of the kids or find fault with
them. All of you are just perfect—I even love the dust on the top
of the refrigerator that used to get my goat before."[22]

Green, Hall, and Winston were housed with the general population in the detention center, assigned to a cell with twelve bunks.
The food was passable, "starchy, but wholesome." They spent two
one-hour sessions each day exercising on the detention center's
roof. After some wrangling with jail officials, Green was able to
obtain a copy of Marx's *Das Kapital* and embarked on a systematic
study of it, and with Hall and Winston started studying Spanish.
"The worst thing about a joint of this kind is the idle time on
our hands. If this time can be organized, if you can find things to
concentrate on, then you can keep from rotting away," he wrote his
wife. But his time in jail was also making Green reassess himself
in some ways. In another undated letter near the end of the trial
he told Lil, "Never again will I ever read a paper or book when
[they children] want me to play with them. And as for my wife, I
want to renew my acquaintance with her in every way imaginable.
She still is my favorite wife and I still feel young enough to love
her with relish."[23]

By August, the couple was trying to figure out whether Lil should
stay in New York or return to Chicago and rent an apartment near
Green's brother Ben on the North Side. The uncertainty over when
the trial would end complicated matters. Green wrote that he
had talked with Dennis and that the party leader told him they
would likely want him to remain in New York after the trial, which
would mean moving the family again from Chicago. "I don't know
ultimately what will be decided," Green wrote, and advised her
"arrangements should be made for an apartment here, preferably
furnished, until the trial is over and we know what's what." If the
party ultimately sent Green to Chicago, the family could then move
back (though it's hard to see how either decision would lessen the

disruption). But Green also said that the final decision on where to live in the interim was hers to make.[24]

Around Labor Day, with the trial still expected to last a few more weeks, Lil Green moved back to Chicago so the children could start school on time. Green sought to keep up contact through letters, mostly to Lil, occasionally to their children. Referring to Winston's receiving a visitor—possibly his daughter—Green wrote to his own children that "I certainly felt lonesome without my own family." In a separate letter to his wife, he weighed in on a domestic problem—daughter Josie being afflicted with "worms" (probably head lice), a recurring problem that went away when the family was living in New York for the summer. "The fact that she didn't have them all summer and got them again as soon as she returned home leads me to one of two conclusions: Either the worms come from school or from her bed. I would definitely change everything in regard to her bed—have the blankets dry cleaned; shift mattresses with the other bed and put on no clothes she wore last Spring that have not also been thoroughly washed or cleaned."

His letters contain no phrases such as "if we are convicted" but refer to the likelihood of getting bail while the convictions were being appealed. In some places, though, Green was open about his expectation: Conviction was "ninety-nine chances out of one hundred, a week or more delay for sentencing, then the chance to post bail and eventually return to Chicago while the appeals are waged." And if the expected happened, he said, Medina would offer no leniency. "You must begin to prepare yourself and the rest of the family for the shock of a guilty verdict as well as a big sentence. This judge will not give us light sentences, that is definite, especially those of us with no war army service records and with long records in the movement."[25]

TEN

The Peekskill Riots

Since the early days of the trial, Carole Nathanson, the actress using the stage name Carol Nason, had been making regular visits to juror—and Broadway producer—Russell Janney's office, and keeping a diary of the conversations. She noted that he had said disparaging things about the defendants and communism, complained about the length of the trial, and maintained clippings—against Medina's orders—that his assistant told her were research for the mystery novel he was writing. It's unclear whether Janney's comments to Nason were volunteered or drawn out by the actress, who was a party supporter, or whether the details were embellished in her diary. In any event, combined with the press clippings from Janney's speeches in Macon, Georgia, early in the year, before he was selected for the jury, Nason's allegations made a pretty compelling case that Janney was not the objective truth-seeker he made himself out to be during jury selection.

On August 23, the *Daily Compass* published an article that did not name Nason but that included the details of her meetings with Janney. The defense team asked Medina for a two-day delay while it investigated the charges in the article, a request Medina denied. But it was clear the lawyers were already well aware of Nason. The next day, August 24, the defense team filed a nearly one-hundred-page motion demanding a mistrial, or at the very least to have Janney thrown off the jury. The motion included the affidavit from Nason, eighty-seven pages of her handwritten notes, and the newspaper clippings of the Macon speeches.

Medina had become accustomed to the defense's endless motions for mistrials, which he routinely rejected out of hand—usually without even letting the defense team argue its point. Medina had long ago run out of patience with the defense attorneys, at one point directing his marshals physically to put Gladstein and Isserman in their seats when they wouldn't stop arguing. One bailiff went so far as to put his hand on Isserman's shoulder and order him to sit—in front of the full jury. Several times in July and August Medina had told the defense lawyers he found them in contempt of court, with punishments to be meted out at the conclusion of the trial. In June, on a day when the temperature reached ninety-one degrees, Medina became so exasperated by Dennis's refusal to stop talking that he abruptly walked off the bench and went to his chambers to lie down, overwhelmed by stress and exhaustion. "Whether I'd ever get back in that courtroom I did not know," Medina said later. "The heat was excessive, and there was almost constant bickering. . . . All the defense lawyers were not in court together. It seemed to me that some were out resting, so that they worked on me in relays."[1] Medina also had ordered a speed-up in the testimony, limiting defense witnesses to thirty minutes on the stand and regularly cutting short long-winded answers that he perceived to be intentional delaying tactics. It's hard to imagine a judge and a battery of lawyers on worse terms, or a tougher courtroom in which to try to get a favorable ruling from the judge.

But this time, Medina listened to the complaint about Janney.

Sacher announced the motion as soon as court convened that morning, and Medina took the lawyers into his chambers to hear Sacher's full argument—that he wanted the trial postponed for twenty-four to forty-eight hours so the defense team could investigate the details of the *Daily Compass* story and prepare a motion to have Janney removed from the jury. McGohey objected, arguing that the article was not sufficient cause to prompt a delay and that the defense team had had ample time to prepare a motion without postponing testimony. Medina agreed, and the trial resumed—after Medina reread to the jury his trial-opening statement that they were not to discuss the case with anyone, including fellow jurors.

The next morning, August 24, Crockett rose as soon as Medina opened court and said he had a motion to make "of such a nature that I am sure your Honor will agree with me it should be made in the absence of the jury." "What is the character of it?" Medina asked. "Something of the nature I did discuss with counsel yesterday?" Crockett told him it was, and Medina dismissed the jury and told the lawyers he would hear full arguments in his chambers. The defense objected, insisting that the discussion be held in open court, and after a short meeting in chambers, Medina agreed. He reconvened court, without the jury present, and Crockett presented the defense argument asking Medina to bounce Janney and launch an investigation into whether his bias had spread to other jurors through illicit conversations about the trial. Medina summoned the jury back in, told them he was dealing with a legal issue, and sent them home for the day with the standard warning not to read or listen to radio broadcasts about the trial or discuss it with anyone. McGohey asked for a recess so he could digest the details of the motion, and Medina granted it, saying he wanted a chance to look over the papers as well. He then adjourned court for the day.[2]

A larger than usual throng gathered across from the courthouse the next morning, many of them waving new signs denouncing Janney in addition to the usual array of anti-Medina signs—signs that, naturally, were being waved in full view of the jurors reporting for court. If there was any hope among the defendants' supporters that they might actually win a legal point in the trial, it was dashed when Medina took the bench. He immediately denied the motion for a mistrial or Janney's dismissal and then said an investigation would be undertaken, but not into Janney. Medina ordered that none of the papers in the defense motion—which consisted primarily of Nason's handwritten notes—be removed without his permission, saying that he wanted to determine if Nason's conversations with Janney amounted to jury tampering.[3]

Medina also revealed that he had received "several thousand" telegrams and other communications since the start of the trial, many of them apparently part of organized attempts by defense supporters to intimidate him. He linked them with the demonstrations outside, whose loud chants often permeated the thick walls of the courthouse. Part of the onslaught was spurred by the *Daily Worker*, which in a front-page editorial the previous day had urged Americans to flood Medina with telegrams demanding a mistrial over the Janney affair. Medina, speaking to the American public as much as to the court, dismissed those efforts and said they wouldn't sway him. "It is utterly wrong and improper for others, whoever they may be, and by any means, to seek to influence the judge's decision, whether it is by picketing outside the court house, or whether it is by communications of one kind or another which seek to influence the Court or bring pressure to bear upon him," Medina said. "I will not be intimidated, and it seems to me that those things are wrong and should be stopped."

Dennis rose and accused Medina of trying to silence criticism of the court, which he framed as a basic American right. Medina rejected the accusation. "Nothing I have said can be understood to mean, nor do I mean, that those who feel the judge has been wrong should be silenced," Medina said. "But I do say that this new notion of bringing pressure on the judge is essentially wrong. I think if that sort of thing takes root it will be a serious menace to the administration of justice."

Dennis then asked for a postponement while the defense pressed the case that the trial should be removed from Medina's court. He also requested that impeachment proceedings be begun against McGohey for "covering up" Janney's unsuitability to be a juror. Medina rejected both without comment and ordered the jury brought back in, the flash of excitement over in what had become a tedious parade of mostly low-level party functionaries on the witness stand.

Medina's admonitions about pressuring the court did nothing to end the parade of pickets outside. In fact, the next afternoon about one hundred people gathered on the traffic island across from the front steps of the courthouse, chanting, "Jail juror Janney; free the three" and "We demand a mistrial." Janney left the court and stopped at the top of the steps as he saw the pickets, then turned south and walked behind the pillars to skirt the scene. Medina departed a little later. McGohey, his deputy Irving Shapiro, and a handful of FBI agents watched it all from the top of the steps. One suspects they were trying to determine whether they could find cause to file jury-tampering or other charges to try to quell the protests and give the judge and jury some relief, but no one was ever charged.[4] In Washington, the House of Representatives passed legislation banning picketing outside federal courthouses, but the Senate never took the bill up, and it died.

Throughout the trial, the CRC—which was shouldering most of the defense costs—had been hosting speeches, rallies, and fund-raisers like the April gathering in Pittsburgh that had led to the mini riot. In August, the CRC decided to hold a concert near Peekskill, in the Hudson Valley north of New York City, and made the arrangements through People's Artists Inc., a radical group recently formed out of the People's Songs booking agency, which had promoted Woody Guthrie, Pete Seeger, and other leftist folk singers. The director of the new group, Irwin Silber, had also been executive director of People's Songs and was in charge of the Music Section of the Communist Party's Cultural Division.[5] Proceeds from the concert, it was announced, would go to the CRC's Harlem chapter—Davis's home branch—and the star attraction would be singer Paul Robeson.

Robeson had sung in the Peekskill area three times before without issue, including a 1948 fund-raising concert for the Wallace presidential campaign at Peekskill Stadium. But the national atmosphere had changed, and the legendary baritone was becoming as well known for his radical politics as for his singing and acting. Long a champion of equal rights and a campaigner against lynching and Jim Crow laws, Robeson saw in the Communist Party a collection of people willing to treat blacks as legal and social equals. It's unclear whether he was a formal party member, but that's an irrelevancy. Robeson openly supported communism and the Soviet Union, which he saw as more progressive in its attitudes toward blacks than his home country.

In April, while the trial was under way in Manhattan, Robeson attended the Congress of the World Partisans of Peace in Paris, an international gathering of communist peace advocates that also drew such notables as W.E.B. Du Bois, Pablo Picasso, jazz bandleader Artie Shaw, and labor leader Harry Bridges. The event was organized by French communist leader (and Nobel laureate in chemistry) Frédéric Joliot-Curie, and the tone was unabashedly pro Soviet Union communism and anti American capitalism. In Washington, the HUAC declared the conference a communist ruse. Referring to the fallout from the Gouzenko defection, which by then had led to at least eight spying-related convictions in Canada and Great Britain, the committee said the communists "would like nothing better" than to entice American researchers to divulge atomic secrets. "Such is the main purpose of this international movement, which is headed by Frederick Joliot-Curie, French communist and atomic scientist who has attacked the United States for keeping the atomic bomb secret, a tactic he called 'dangerous.' "[6]

At the conference, which drew two thousand delegates, Robeson was among scores who spoke passionately about living conditions around the world and the desire for peace. But Robeson's words—particularly some he apparently never spoke—would echo farther than the messages of the others. Robeson told the throng that America's riches grew from the labor of "millions of blacks" and that "we shall not put up with any hysterical raving that encourages us to make war on anyone. Our will to fight for peace is strong. We shall not make war on anyone. We shall not make war on the Soviet Union." By the time the Associated Press reporter and the *New York Times*'s Lansing Warren finished writing it up, though, Robeson's words were much more strident: "We colonial peoples have contributed to the building of the United States and are determined to share in its wealth. We denounce the policy of the U.S. government, which is similar to that of Hitler and Goebbels. We want peace and liberty and will combat for them along with the Soviet Union, the democracies of Eastern Europe, China and Indonesia. . . . It is unthinkable that American Negroes would go to war in behalf of those who have oppressed us for generations against a country which in one generation has raised our people to the full dignity of mankind."[7]

The inflated reports of Robeson's comments inflamed anti-communists, and he was booed during a concert the next night in Stockholm. But Robeson didn't repudiate the comments attributed to him. He told reporters a couple of days later that while he expected to eventually be jailed for it, he was forgoing concert performances in favor of political speeches. "I will give my life for the colored people's right to live. I see clearly the idea behind the dictatorship of the proletariat. In America dark people are not free; in the U.S.S.R. they are free. My son is going to study atomic energy in the U.S.S.R. This is impossible for him in America, I think."[8] The NAACP quickly issued a statement that Robeson did not speak for the majority of black Americans, a stance echoed by congressman and pastor Adam Clayton Powell during a Sunday sermon a couple of days later. In Connecticut, where Robeson maintained a home, a local politician tried to have him barred from the state.

Robeson spent a week in Russia as part of the June celebrations of the Pushkin sesquicentennial, where he continued to extol the Soviet Union even as he was learning privately of Stalin's purges and the deaths of longtime friends. One visitor to his hotel used hand gestures to signal the room was bugged, and through other gestures and scribbled notes while they made unrelated small talk, the man told Robeson about the fates of others and said that he expected to be executed soon himself. Two days later, he was.[9] How Robeson rationalized his continued support for the Soviet Union is a subject for another place. In any event, by midsummer Robeson was back in the United States, and in mid-July the HUAC began hearing testimony by African Americans on communist influences, which was in essence a tag-team denunciation of Robeson by everyone from a disabled black veteran to color-barrier-breaking baseball player Jackie Robinson. So by the time People's Artists Inc. announced that Robeson would perform at the CRC fund-raiser at Lakeland Acres, a bucolic creek-side picnic grounds three miles northeast of Peekskill, Robeson had become a very large red flag for anti-communist bulls.

The concert was scheduled for August 27, and it drew an outpouring of public denouncements by local residents and political figures. The region was already divided between permanent—and more conservative—year-round residents and New York City liberals and progressives who maintained summer homes. The area also was home to several "red" summer camps, places where Communist Party members and friends could rent cottages or tent space by the week, and traditional sleepaway camps for kids that also included lessons in Marxist-Leninist ideology.

Shortly after the concert was announced, the Peekskill chapter of the American Legion and other members of the Joint Veterans Council, as well as two local chambers of commerce, called for powerful demonstrations, and the local *Peekskill Evening Star* fanned the flames with such headlines as "Robeson Concert Here Aids 'Subversive' Unit." The Thursday before the Saturday evening concert, the leaders of the Joint Veterans Council—representing the American Legion, Veterans of Foreign Wars, Catholic War Veterans, and Jewish War Veterans—met in the office of an assistant Westchester County district attorney, Leland Rubenfeld, to plan their demonstration. Local passions ran so high that the property owner, Willis Jamison, announced that he hadn't been aware of the nature of the booking, and once he learned it involved Robeson and the CRC he checked with his lawyer, who advised him to honor the contract. He was in effect apologizing to his neighbors while rationalizing why he didn't cancel the lease.[10]

On concert day, about two hundred volunteers and stagehands arrived hours before the 8:00 P.M. start time to set up the temporary wooden stage and arrange rows of benches and wooden folding chairs for the audience, which was expected to begin arriving in late afternoon for preshow picnics. Virginia Hirsch, a young union activist from New York, was part of the volunteer work crew, and around 4:00 P.M. she agreed to drive into the nearby village of Shrub Oak to buy sodas for the other six volunteers in her work detail. She noticed "some activity" as she drove out Highland Avenue, the narrow roadway to the picnic grounds, and when she returned a large crowd had formed, "many wearing VFW and American Legion hats, lots drinking beer, and they surrounded my car, began to rock it and were shouting things like 'commie Jew bitch,' 'nigger lover,' and other [epithets]. I was really terrified." Hirsch inched her car, a 1938 Oldsmobile, forward, but "an obese middle-aged man stepped in front." The man was wearing a badge but was not a police officer, and he yelled to Hirsch, "You might get in, but you won't get out." She finally broke free of the crowd and made it to the picnic grounds. Over the next few hours, a few more people filtered in—mostly young supporters from nearby camps who walked through the woods—but the expected throng of early picnickers never arrived. Or at least they never made it to the campground.[11]

One of the last people to drive through was the author Howard Fast, who had rented a house in nearby Croton-on-Hudson for a month's vacation for his family. Fast had agreed to emcee the concert and arrived early for a planned 7:00 P.M. meeting with the organizers to go over the program. He found the roadway lined with "an already unruly crowd of men. . . . They didn't try to stop me, but only jeered and thumbed their noses at me as I turned left into the picnic grounds." One more car made the turn after Fast before the mob sealed off the entrance.

The Joint Veterans Council had arranged for a parade as the anchor for a demonstration, and at 6:00 P.M. about five hundred veterans, many in uniform and wearing their Legion or VFW hats, appeared carrying banners, flags, and posters. The VFW sent along a small fife-and-drum corps, and the military music echoed down the tree-lined dirt roadway. The parade quickly grew, and by dusk some five thousand jeering and cheering people were packed along Highland Avenue, making it impossible for concert-goers to get through and causing a two-mile backup. Despite the advance warning of the demonstration—and the organizational meeting held in the office of a local prosecutor—there were only four Westchester County sheriff's deputies on hand for crowd control. Cars were vandalized, and people seeking to evade the blockade by walking through the woods were beaten by sentries and turned away.[12]

Before the sun set around 7:40 P.M., a young man came running down the roadway to where Fast and some of the others were waiting near the stage. (Fast's meeting never occurred; the organizers couldn't get through.) Breathless, the young man told Fast and the others that there was trouble up on the roadway. Fast and about thirty other people—mostly men and teen-aged boys, a large percentage of them black and Jewish—jogged back up the roadway. It's unclear whether the messenger was one of the volunteers or had been sent in by the mob, but Fast and the others had jogged their way into the middle of a trap. "As we appeared they poured down on us from the road, at least three hundred of them, with billies and brass knuckles and rocks in clenched fists. . . . Such fights don't last long; there were three or four minutes of this, and because the roadway was narrow we were able to beat them back," Fast would recall. But there were hundreds more on the roadway stretching back to the barricade behind—a VFW truck parked sideways and a pile of rocks and tree sections. During the lull, three sheriff's deputies shouldered their way through the mob and talked with Fast and the others, asking why they were causing trouble. As peacekeepers—if that was even their intent—they were worthless. Behind the mob, the demonstration organizers, including John Zimmer of the VFW and Robert J. Field, the Westchester County clerk (and a World War I veteran), climbed on the VFW truck bed, announced the demonstration was over, and urged the crowd to go home, saying their goal of stopping the concert was a success. A few took the victory and left, but most stayed on—now a mob unleashed, its organizers disavowing any connection with what was about to happen.

The volunteers took a count—42 men and about 150 women and children. They directed the women and children to stay below on the picnic grounds, and most of the men arrayed themselves in three lines, hoping to stave off the mob. As dusk settled, and a portable generator was turned on to bathe the venue in light, some of the vigilantes ignited a large wooden cross on one of the hillsides framing the meadow. Hirsch and another worker slipped through the woods to a nearby house and persuaded the resident to let them use the phone to call the New York State Police, but no troopers showed up.

The mob pressed forward two more times, each attack more violent and longer than the previous, until, eventually, they broke through. One of the vigilantes—William Secor, twenty-four, of Shrub Oak—was stabbed, and rumors swirled that he had died. Other vigilantes streamed into the venue, many of them running through the forest to get around Fast and the volunteers, who by then had blocked the roadway on their end with their own truck to give their backs some protection. Between the second and third waves, Fast noticed reporters along the edge of the road, jotting down notes, and the white flash of news cameras. "For the first time, I understood clearly the temper of that gang out there, and for the first time I realized that it was very likely that all of us would die there that evening. Our lines leaned against the truck, half of us bleeding, all of us sobbing, our clothes torn, our scalps open, our faces scarred—and already it seemed like the nightmarish battle had gone on forever."[13]

Behind them, the vigilantes reached the generator and shut it off, plunging the site into darkness. The swarm overwhelmed the women and children, beating some as the mob broke up the stage and heaved the lumber into a pile with the chairs and benches and ignited a massive bonfire. As it burned, they tossed in books and pamphlets that were to have been handed out or sold to concert-goers (Fast would find unnerving similarities to the 1933 book-burnings in Germany just a few months after Hitler rose to power). The volunteers frantically sought safety. Some of the women and children climbed into the back of a truck, and the driver improbably drove the gantlet back up the road to safety, skirting the roadblock somehow (with the demonstration leaders formally washing their hands of the event, the veterans could well have driven off in the VFW truck barricading part of the road). Routed, other volunteers piled into cars and drove up the hill where the remaining mob ordered—and sometimes dragged—the volunteers from their cars. Several were beaten as they scurried along the now car-blocked roadway. As they fled, the vigilantes went to work on the abandoned cars, breaking in roofs, slashing tires, and shattering windows and lights. Eight of the vehicles were rocked from side to side until they rolled over.

Around midnight, thirty-one members of the state police finally arrived and slowly dispersed the mob with the help of a sound truck. They fired magnesium flares into the night sky, which drifted eerily to earth under tiny parachutes, looking like slow-moving stars that bathed the meadow in unnatural white light. Hirsch, her skirt stiff with the blood of a young man whose head had been gashed open, stayed in the meadow until dawn, when the state police finally escorted her and the remaining volunteers "to a nearby camp where good people who had heard of the siege took us back to the city. On our way out, I saw that my car had been thrown over the embankment by the entrance bridge." Nearly all of the volunteers were injured, some severely. Heads were gashed, faces bloodied, a few bones were broken. In the end, several dozen people were injured and eight hospitalized with serious wounds, though no one was killed. Even Secor, the vigilante, survived, his stab wound less grievous than first thought—and apparently accidentally inflicted by another vigilante.

Robeson never made it to the grounds. Before he left Manhattan Saturday evening, he used a pay phone at Grand Central Station to call his friends Sam and Helen Rosen, who had a summer place near Peekskill, to ask about rumors he had heard about the demonstration. Sam Rosen clicked on his radio and confirmed the news. Robeson boarded his train and was met at the Peekskill station about 9:00 P.M. by Helen Rosen and her friend Sydney Danis, with a handful of other supporters. They tried to make their way in two cars to the picnic grounds but got caught up in the traffic jam caused by the blockade. Once Rosen realized what was happening in the traffic jam ahead, she told Danis to turn around and take Robeson to the home of yet another friend, where he spent the night.[14]

The next day, Robeson was back in Manhattan, where he held a press conference at the Capitol Hotel, at Fifty-first Street and Eighth Avenue, denouncing the violence and the vigilantes' success in stopping what he said was to have been a peaceful concert. Hirsch, still in her blood-stiffened skirt, was also there, as were Fast and several other survivors, as well as Ben Davis, an old friend of Robeson's. Virginia Muir, of the American Slav Congress, told reporters her car had been stoned, looted, and rolled over several times by the mob. Enraged, Robeson demanded a federal investigation into the attack, which he described as part of a "national campaign of terror" against progressives. "Behind those few Legionnaires are powerful forces," Robeson said. "Those boys were told what to do."

The demonstration organizers took pride in the results, even if they skirted responsibility for the violence. They noted they had ordered the crowd to disband before the heavy violence broke out and intimated that it might have been sparked by "plug-uglies" from the communist movement—thugs sent in to start trouble to try to make the veterans groups look bad. The *Peekskill Evening Star* reported that "the full story of the riot was confused today in the bitter charges of the concert goers and the counts of the demonstrators, but sentiment in this and surrounding communities seemed to be approval of last night's events." The paper quoted Milton Flynt, commander of Peekskill Post 274 of the American Legion, in military terms. "Our objective was to prevent the Paul Robeson concert, and I think our objective was reached," Flynt said. "Anything which happened after the organized demonstration took place was entirely up to the individual citizens and cannot be blamed on the patriotic organizations. Last night's events should serve notice on the pinks that Peekskill and the Town of Cortlandt don't want anything pertaining to Paul Robeson."

But the Rosens and several hundred of their friends disagreed. The Rosens opened their Katonah summer home Sunday evening for a community meeting about how to respond to the blockade and the violence. About three hundred people showed up (some reports put it at fifteen hundred), including Fast and other marquee communists and sympathizers. They collected several thousand dollars for the defense fund and immediately started making plans for another concert the afternoon of September 4, this one to be held at the abandoned Hollow Brook Golf Course, three miles north of Peekskill and about a mile west of the site of the first, aborted concert.

This time the organizers were ready for violence. They massed a small army of twelve hundred volunteers to stand sentry at the perimeter of the concert grounds. The veterans groups also announced they would again hold a parade, and the route would be the same narrow concrete road that the concert-goers would need to get into the show (the *New York Times* even ran a photograph of the planning session). Concert organizers asked a judge to bar the veterans' parade, but he declined. Governor Thomas Dewey, who took a lot of political heat for the state police's failure to intervene the first time around, ordered all state police who "can be made available" to be on hand to help the Westchester County Sheriff's Department—and one thousand temporarily deputized civilians—with crowd control. Buses were chartered in Manhattan to take union members, Communist Party members, and others north for the concert, with the party estimating fifteen thousand people would show up.

Robeson was the main draw again, and the audience began arriving about 10:30 A.M. This time they got through with no trouble and found safety behind the cordon of volunteer sentries, most drawn from militant labor groups, such as Potash's furriers union. Police confiscated three hundred baseball bats with which the men had armed themselves, but the sentries still had a ready reserve of clubs, sticks, and strategically placed caches of glass bottles. If there was going to be violence, it was going to be an ugly street fight. And a few vigilantes did try to breach the lines but were pushed back, some of them trundled off by the police. Two men with high-powered rifles were routed from the tree line, and, fearing snipers, more than a dozen men stood on the flatbed truck from which Robeson would sing to form a human shield. Potash and Davis were in the audience, and with Fast serving as the emcee, the abbreviated concert went off without a hitch.

The trouble began as the crowd left the concert grounds, some aboard chartered buses, others driving out in personal cars, passing through the sentry line and then a cordon of police and temporary deputies. Just south of the golf course, several thousand vigilantes lined a narrow, banked section of the roadway, creating a lengthy gantlet with the full help of state police troopers and the Westchester County sheriff's deputies.

Tom Lloyd, a member of the executive board of Local 64 of the International Fur and Leather Workers Union, was driving one of the first cars to leave and was held up for nearly an hour by police. By then the mob was in place at the junction of Oregon Road and Strawberry Hill Road. "Somebody warned us to close the windows of our car. As I drove out onto the paved highway a state trooper slowed up the speed of our car by hand motions. I saw that the cars in front of us were being attacked by persons on the left side of the road who were throwing rocks and other missiles. The car in front of us swerved almost out of control when hit by rocks and I was forced to almost stop. Then a shower of rocks and pop bottles hit our car and one broke the windshield, showering glass." The man next to Lloyd was cut up. Lloyd said the police were laughing as he finally edged past the last of the throng.[15]

Davis and Potash were also in that first wave of cars to leave, though traveling in separate vehicles. Davis was one of six people in a Hudson, wedged in the middle of the backseat. "As we emerged slowly from the entrance to the golf course at a speed of three or four miles an hour, the car was peltered [sic] with rocks and stones, many of them too large to be hurled with one hand. They shattered the windshield in front of the driver, and the glass on the door panel on the left-hand side of the car immediately beside the driver. Several of the stones came through the windshield and glass door panels." Those inside were showered with glass, and they scrambled to cover their faces with their coats. "One of the stones struck the driver. One of the huge rocks lodged itself in the glass of the door panel." The driver nearly lost control of the car but regained it and "maintained the car on the road although his face and arms were bleeding." The attack continued for about one hundred yards, the car weaving from side to side as the driver reacted to the barrage, first from vigilantes atop a small embankment on the left side of the road, then from people in the tree branches above, and also from those who stood directly in the road. They rained epithets, too: "Get the dirty Jews." "Kill the kikes." "Hang the Robeson niggers with a rope." "Lynch 'em.'" "Send 'em back to Russia." "We're going to kill all of you." Davis said New York State Police were mixed in with the crowd, laughing and talking with the vigilantes. "As the car passed through, one of the cops hit it with a billy club and said, " 'Go ahead, you commies and sheenies asked for it, now you're getting it.' "[16]

Potash and his wife, Gita, were in the front seat of the next car, with several other passengers in the rear, including concert pianist Ray Lev and William Geffner, a member of the furriers union. Davis looked behind and saw their car getting hit with the same barrage. Gita Potash, looking forward, bore similar witness to the attack on Davis's car. She also said the cars had initially been delayed by the police, and once they were allowed to drive out she saw the mob on the side embankment, then more police motioning for the cars to slow down. Potash was driving, and "as soon as my husband had obeyed the police signal [to slow down], our car too was stoned from the same spot. . . . It was right where the policemen were standing." Before the rocks struck Potash yelled for everyone to close their windows "and to get down as low as possible in the car, and to cover up with whatever we had. I tried to put a jacket around my husband and between him and the left door of the car to protect both of us."

Two rocks broke through the windshield, and a third wedged itself into the pane, showering the Potashes and their passengers with glass. Potash got the worst of it because he couldn't cover his face and still drive. Glass splinters and dust filled his eyes, and he called out for help; Geffner leaned over from the backseat and steered the car as Potash kept his foot on the gas pedal, and with the car moving they managed to change drivers on the fly, Geffner sliding behind the wheel as Potash moved closer to his wife. "My husband's shirt was spattered with blood. There was blood on his face and hands and he said he felt glass in his eyes, face, and mouth." They finally stopped at a pay phone and called the hospital in nearby Croton-on-Hudson but were told the facility was swamped. Since they were headed to Manhattan anyway, they were told to continue south and get treatment at Sinai Hospital. They arrived about 7:00 P.M., and a medical crew spent the next few hours meticulously pulling slivers of glass from Potash's eyeballs and his face.[17]

The attacks continued late into the evening and covered about ten square miles. Even the uninvolved were attacked. One unlucky bus of bar-crawlers from the city, enjoying a night in the suburbs, was attacked. After they persuaded the rock-throwers they weren't communists or even there for the concert, the vigilantes stuck a sign and a flag on the windshield giving the bus safe passage.

Throughout the region, the special deputies did little to stop the attacks, though the state police apparently were slightly more diligent—particularly after one of them was felled by a rock, suffering a deep scalp wound. At least 145 people were injured enough to require medical treatment, 4 of them seriously (one woman lost a finger). Twelve people—including the adult son of the Peekskill police chief—were arrested. Fifteen bus drivers walked off the job, saying they refused to drive communists, leaving their buses and passengers stranded until volunteers were able to get the buses moving.[18]

There was, understandably, a massive outcry from the left over the second day of violence, and several investigations. Governor Dewey, under fire for the complicity of his state troopers, blamed the communists for provoking it and lauded the work of the police in keeping anyone from getting killed. The governor then ordered a special grand jury investigation into the causes of the riots. Six people ultimately were indicted, but none ever went to trial.

Potash's injuries achieved something the defense lawyers had been unable to do—persuade Medina to delay the trial. On September 6, he adjourned it for two days until doctors said Potash had recovered sufficiently to resume his place at the defense table. But the defense was nearly done anyway. On September 2, the Friday before the second Robeson concert, Sacher had told Medina that after the long-sought deposition by Foster was read into the record, defendant Henry Winston would be called as the defense's thirty-second and final witness—and the sixth of the eleven defendants to take the stand. After a trial that had stretched for months, he said, it would be a matter of days before they could move on to closing arguments. But like all the other predictions of the trial's pace, this one proved to be wrong, too.

When the trial resumed September 8, Potash, wearing dark sunglasses, was in his chair in the array of defendants. Sacher opened the session by demanding Medina investigate the Peekskill riots and their possible influence on the trial. Separately he moved that Medina declare a mistrial, arguing that the attacks on Potash, Davis, and the other concert-goers were sparked by government statements about the defendants and communists in general. He also said the attacks proved the extent of prejudice against the defendants and their inability to obtain a fair trial. Medina, not

11. War hero Robert Thompson and Benjamin Davis Jr. made regular appearances at rallies and demonstrations during the trial. Library of Congress, Prints & Photographs Division, *New York World-Telegram* Collection, LC-USZ62–111434.

surprisingly, rejected the motions, though he expressed concern over the violence and the health of Potash and Davis. "I definitely think it was an outrage," Medina said. "There is no question about it." But his role, he said, was to conduct the trial, not to investigate the goings-on in Westchester County. "I made up my mind in the beginning that this trial was not going to be disrupted if I could help it," Medina said. "The trial is now going into its ninth month and this is about the tenth time the defense has tried to get me to initiate some investigation. All of this is part and parcel of an endeavor to make a counter-attack on society, instead of meeting the issues of the trial."[19]

Carl Winter, the Michigan chair, resumed the stand and over the next few days offered his version of the testimony already given by others over the evolution of the party from the 1930s through the war to the reconstitution of 1945 and denied that achieving communism in the United States would require violent overthrow of the government, though he acknowledged that the new communist government might have to use force to dissolve class distinctions and against the "repressive" police forces. Unfortunately for the defense, his testimony on the 1940 formation of the Communist Political Association opened the door for McGohey to read into the record part of the founding document that said the change was being made in part so the leadership wouldn't have to register under the 1940 Voorhis Act as agents of a foreign government, something McGohey tried to imply was evidence of the communists' subterfuge.

The friction between Medina and the defense team continued unabated. On August 30, the defense had called to the stand Arthur Schusterman, who worked with Charles Nicodemus, the prosecution witness and FBI spy, in the Celanese plant in Cumberland, Maryland. Gladstein began walking Schusterman through his union affiliations—paralleling the questions McGohey had asked Nicodemus to establish his role—but Medina upheld a prosecution objection, ruling the questions irrelevant. Gladstein reminded Medina that the judge had allowed similar questions by McGohey of the prosecution witness and that the same rules ought to apply. But Medina told Gladstein that the defense had, in effect, worn out his tolerance. "Mr. Gladstein," Medina said, "at the earliest stages of this trial, before I was convinced that it had become an endurance contest, I permitted a great many things that I thought were on the fringe of relevancy, and I found that I could not do that without unduly prolonging the trial." He rejected Gladstein's complaint that he was applying two standards, a lax one for the prosecution and a stringent one for the defense, describing instead an erosion of tolerance. What was once leeway, he said, was now distraction. "I do not consider that as favoring one side as against the other at all."[20]

A few days later, on September 12, Winter refused to answer a question from McGohey about whether his father-in-law, Alfred Wagenknecht, one of the founders of the original American Communist Party, had been present at the 1940 convention that led to the creation of the Communist Political Association. It was a moment of high absurdity—Wagenknecht had been quoted in the *Daily Worker*, making it clear he was there, but Winter declined to answer, echoing Gates's earlier refusal to name others involved in party activities for fear of making them targets of future prosecution. "I must respectfully decline to answer that question on the grounds that to do otherwise would be in violation of my rights under the First Amendment," Winter said, going on to also invoke the Fifth Amendment against self-incrimination. "The naming of persons participating in that convention could lay them and me open to further prosecution."

Medina told him he had no constitutional right to not answer the question. Winter still refused, and Medina ordered him locked up for thirty days, where he would join Green, Hall, and Winston.[21] Winter responded for the duration of his cross-examination by McGohey with a collapse of memory, responding "I don't recall" to such rudimentary questions as under what name was his phone number listed.[22] In an ensuing squabble with the defense lawyers over McGohey's attempts to question Winter over false names, Medina issued contempt citations against Crockett and Sacher. But by then the citations were just extra bullets in the already loaded gun. Medina had already found all six of the defense lawyers—including Dennis, acting as his own lawyer—in contempt and had told them he would hand down penalties once the trial ended.[23]

The last of the major testimony came in a bit of theatrics. Foster, still recovering from his strokes, had been deposed by both the defense and prosecution. In effect, he testified at home. On September 16, with the 394-page deposition transcript in hand,

Gates took the witness stand and, with Sacher reading the questions, responded as though he were Foster. The next day, Wallace read the cross-examination questions to his assistant Shapiro, now in the witness stand as Foster. There were no bombshells—and none expected, at that point. Foster denied there was any conspiracy and said that the prosecution was misinterpreting Marx and Lenin when it argued that Marxist-Leninist theory was a prescription for the overthrow of the U.S. government. Changes in beliefs and theory after Marx and Lenin, mainly developed through the United Front movement against fascism, had rendered the call for violent struggle "obsolete."

"We are convinced it is possible in the United States to elect by legal, democratic, peaceful means a coalition government which will move toward socialism," Foster said. "Once in office, such a coalition government would find itself compelled to die under the attack of capitalism or move toward socialism." A "people's front" would arise to lead the way past capitalism, he said. And individuals who sought the violent overthrow of the U.S. government "would be promptly expelled from our party as provocateurs or stool pigeons."[24]

As the prosecution had with the other party leaders, on cross-examination Wallace drilled into Foster's travel history and use of false names to obtain visas, which Foster sought to explain away as necessary tactics in the face of government repression, including travel bans. And he acknowledged that his loyalty was to class more than country. Wallace tried to get him to equate that allegiance with opposition to the United States by introducing old interviews and testimony Foster had given in other settings. In one instance, when asked to choose between "the red flag" of communism and the American flag, Foster said a true communist would align with the red. "The Red Flag is the flag of the revolutionary class and we are a part of the revolutionary class," he said, adding that they "owe no allegiance" to the flags of capitalist nations. But in the deposition, Foster disavowed those statements, saying they no longer reflected his views or the views of the party. And he joined Green, Gates, and the others in rejecting Budenz's accusation that they used "Aesopian language" to obscure their true positions. "We Communists love our country and we love our people," Foster said. "We spit on those who accuse us of being foreign agents."[25]

When the reenactment of Foster's deposition ended, the defense called Robeson to the stand, hoping his presence—he was a large man and charismatic speaker—and personal story would help humanize the defendants' cause. Crockett led the examination before the packed courtroom but was frustrated at every turn. After some preliminary questions about Robeson's background, Medina interrupted to ask Crockett if he had been called as a character witness. Crockett said no, then launched into a series of questions about whether Robeson had ever heard the defendants' public speeches. He hoped to have Robeson testify that he had never heard the men give voice to dreams of revolution, but McGohey objected that the testimony would do nothing to rebut the allegations that the defendants had written about the need to overturn the U.S. government. Crockett, increasingly frustrated, ended his examination after twenty minutes, and Robeson left the witness stand, effectively neutralized. A moment of potentially high drama had collapsed under McGohey's objections and Medina's rulings—but it also collapsed under yet another misjudgment by the defense team. If Robeson had been called as a character witness, much of what Crockett sought to get into the record likely would have been allowed. Because Robeson had no direct connection with the events alleged in the indictment, however, Medina shut him off.[26]

Winston was the last witness, and the last defendant, to testify. His two days on the stand were an echo of the testimony of the others—blanket denials that he believed the U.S. government should be overthrown and assertions that the indictment was based on misinterpretations or outdated versions of Marxist-Leninist theory. That was followed by the now familiar cross-examination by McGohey attacking Winston's credibility, forcing him to change minor points of testimony that reinforced the recurring prosecution theme that the defendants were evasive and untrustworthy.

Finally, on the morning of September 23, just over nine months after the trial began with the challenge to the jury selection system, the defense rested. It had been a long, arduous road. Since the trial opened in January, court had been in session 158 days. The prosecution offered fifteen witnesses; the defense thirty-five witnesses, six of them defendants. Including the jury challenge at the start, the transcript covered 19,859 pages and an estimated five million words. The pretrial arguments alone took up 4,825 pages. And, between them, the two sides offered more than 750 exhibits, 332 from the government and 420 from the defense, most of them political tracts. It cost the government about one million dollars and the defense about five hundred thousand dollars. In a post-trial tally, *Life* magazine listed Medina's high point as March 31, when he rejected seventy defense motions—a remarkable amount considering a typical court day lasted about five hours.[27]

While the testimony in the case may have ended, the trial was not over. Medina gave both sides a week to prepare their summations and to offer their suggestions for what he would include in his charge to the jurors—his final instructions on what they were to consider as they retired to weigh guilt versus innocence.

ELEVEN

Guilty

The summations were, to state the obvious, a rehash of the main arguments in the trial. McGohey, for the prosecution, was given a full day. The defense team was allotted four days, though Medina rejected a last-minute request by Davis, a lawyer, to fire his attorney and give his own summation to the jury. That prompted objections by the rest of the defense team, which led to yet another acerbic confrontation with Medina. The defense lawyers said Medina's refusal to allow Davis to deliver his own summation was part of a pattern of discrimination by the judge toward the defendants. In rejecting the request, Medina told Davis that during the trial he had exhibited a "lack of good faith," "had displayed a violent disposition," and was part and parcel of the "disorderly and contemptuous conduct" by the defendants. "Why don't they behave themselves?" Medina asked, with the jury out of the room. "That's been the whole trouble."[1] Medina also rejected a raft of defense motions—mostly versions of similar motions that had been filed and rejected before.

Sensing the end was nigh, Medina expanded the court day, ordering sessions to begin at 10:00 A.M. instead of 10:30 A.M. and cutting the lunch break by fifteen minutes, so the jury could retire for deliberations before the end of the week, while the arguments were still fresh in their minds. So a few minutes after 10:00 A.M. on October 7, a Friday, Isserman rose from the defense table to try to persuade the jury that nothing they had heard during the previous nine months suggested that the eleven defendants believed in violent revolution. This was, Isserman argued, a political trial.

"The Communist Party is in the dock with these defendants," he said. "This is a trial of a political party. For the first time since the Alien Sedition Act of 1798 [sic] we find leaders of a political party on trial." Key, he said, was the Constitution's protection of political expression under the First Amendment—regardless of how unpopular the speech might be. "Once the deadly hand of censor- ship clamps down, whether that censorship be exercised by blue pencil, by criminal prosecution or the fear of prosecution, America will have turned its back on its glorious past and traditions."[2]

McCabe was next, and he focused on the government's use of "stool pigeon witnesses. And by stool pigeons I mean not all of the prosecution's witnesses, but those who were paid informers at the time they were members of the Communist Party." He went on to define "informers" as "a word of denunciation" used by most people in close connection with the words "filthy, despicable, dirty. . . . Once a person is identified as an informer, there is nothing further that can be added to it in the eyes of decent people." The government's case, he argued, was built on the words of people who, by the mere fact of their decision to take money to live a lie, were not trustworthy. He went on to pick out the inconsistencies in testimony by Philbrick, Nicodemus, Younglove, and the others.[3]

Gladstein was next, and with his theatrical flair he sought to place the trial against the broader context of the Constitution, the First Amendment, and the American tradition of the free exchange of political ideas. The Smith Act, he argued, was contrary to all of that. Sacher followed and, picking up the argument, told the jury that the prosecution's case was built around a willful misreading of the party's beliefs. All the acts cited by the prosecution and its witnesses were protected exercises of the right to free speech and assembly and to a free press. He argued that the government had not provided any evidence that the 1945 reformulation of the wartime Communist Political Association into the CPUSA was Moscow-directed, nor aimed at advocating revolution. The use by communists of false names and travel documents was necessitated by political persecution, not skullduggery, he said. And, he reiterated, the key testimony for the prosecution came out of the mouths of liars, stool pigeons, and FBI plants.[4]

Sacher mocked the government's case as "dime-novel conspiracies." Where Isserman had started the summations with the tone of an impassioned lecturer, Sacher took the "we all know better" tack, smiling broadly and intimating that he and the jurors could see that the government's case was ludicrous on its face—a delivery that the New York Times's reporter, Russell Porter, noted had little effect. Sacher would ridicule some part of the government's case then pause, chuckling, inviting the jury to laugh with him. "They did not even smile." Most of Sacher's summation skipped past specifics, though, and focused on the broad themes—that the government, big business, and Wall Street were conspiring against the working class for whom the Communist Party was standing up, clearly hoping that at least one of the working-class members of the jury would buy into the argument and force a hung jury. And he said the timing of the prosecution—the indictment coming in the midst of Truman's reelection campaign, and after the Communist Party had thrown in with the Wallace campaign—was proof that it was politically motivated and geared initially toward assuring Truman's reelection. In fact, he said, the case was initiated not by McGohey, the prosecutor, but "by the great white father in Washington," an odd allusion to the president. Sacher also sought to put some distance between the antics of the defense lawyers and the defendants, asking the jurors not to hold the defendants responsible for the defense lawyers' behavior during the trial, which he described as "zealous."

Crockett and Dennis, the last of the six to give summations, were the most emotional. Crockett veered from the line that the defendants were being persecuted for their beliefs to an indictment of the U.S. government and American society over the maltreatment of blacks. Dennis argued that he and the other ten men were on trial simply for their beliefs and that the government's intent was to silence political speech—a clear violation of the First Amendment. His words were forceful, often caustic, contrasting with his clipped voice and halting delivery as he read his summation as though delivering a report.[5]

When they finished, it was McGohey's turn. Tall and silver-haired, he spoke dispassionately about the evolution of the Communist Party, about the teachings of Marxism-Leninism, about the predictions of a violent showdown to install a socialist government. He recapped the highlights of testimony by Budenz, Philbrick, Calomiris, and the others—cutting through the lengthy, discursive books and pamphlets that had been read into the record, the days of evasive cross-examination of the defendants, and the lofty arguments that the trial was political, not criminal. The Smith Act, McGohey said, made it illegal to advocate or teach the necessity of overthrowing the U.S. government. The evidence, he said, showed that that was exactly what the eleven men seated at the edge of the court had been doing.

As the defense had attacked the credibility of Budenz and the other prosecution witnesses, McGohey went after the credibility of the six defendants who had testified. "You heard them on the witness stand," he said. "You heard their answers on direct examination, when they recollected in detail events which occurred years ago. You heard answers which went on for hours. And, you also heard the defendants on cross-examination—when, as though someone had pressed a button, their memories suddenly deteriorated to the point that they couldn't remember events unless we confronted them with irrefutable documents—and even the certified record of his only child's birth could not restore Carl Winter's recollection as to where he lived at the time. Every one of them has been demonstrated to be unworthy of belief. They were shown to have sworn falsely on many prior occasions. John Gates and Gilbert Green, at least, asserted that they considered it proper and right, and justified to lie under oath when it suits their own purposes." McGohey said the evidence clearly showed that the men had taught and advocated for revolution. "They ask you to believe they never taught or advocated any such thing at any time, but their utter lack of credibility makes their denials valueless."

The last words fell to Medina—his charge to the jury. On October 13, he read the lengthy instructions that said, in effect, the jurors were to weigh the evidence to see if it proved beyond a reasonable doubt that the eleven defendants had violated the 1940 Smith Act by advocating or teaching the necessity of overthrowing the U.S. government. In a key point, he told the jurors that books, ideas, and political beliefs were not on trial, negating a key defense argument. He also told the jurors that the right to free speech is not absolute and that there had been a clear and present danger of the overthrow of the U.S. government—essentially telling the jury that the defendants were guilty.[6]

The jury retired about 3:30 P.M. and over the next few hours asked the bailiffs to bring them several exhibits—Stalin's *Problems with Leninism*, the program for the Third International, the draft resolution adopted by the Communist Political Association, and Duclos's letter criticizing Browderism. As the jury worked, the eight defendants free on bail waited with their lawyers and wives in the corridor and turned down requests from reporters for comment—except for Stachel, who offered a benign "I feel very confident in general." Inside, a young volunteer sat at the defense table, his feet propped up as he read a red-covered book opened to the chapter "Proletarian Revolution." Finally, around 10:15 P.M., Thelma Dial, the forewoman, sent a note to Medina that the jury of eight women and four men was tired and wanted to adjourn and go to bed. Medina agreed, and they were bused off to the Knickerbocker Hotel at 120 West Forty-fifth Street to spend the night under the protection of the U.S. marshals.[7]

The next morning, the jurors were bused to a Schrafft's Restaurant, on Broadway near Chambers Street, where they ate breakfast under the watchful eyes of six marshals, then walked "chatting and laughing" the two blocks to the courthouse, where the demonstrators were again in full voice, and full signage. By 9:30 A.M. the jurors had resumed their deliberations, which most expected to drag on for days as they sifted through the nine months of testimony, exhibits, accusations, and denials. Yet at 11:00 A.M., Dial sent word to Medina that the jury was done, after only seven hours of deliberation.

The court came alive as the word went out, and defendants, reporters, and the merely curious flooded into Room 110. Around 11:20 A.M., with the defendants "with their wooden faces" already in their seats and the gallery full to overflowing, the jurors filed in and took their places in the box. The clerk asked Dial if the jury had reached a verdict. Yes, she said, they had. And what was it?

the clerk asked. Speaking in a thin, shaking voice, Dial said, "The jury finds each of the defendants guilty."

There was a rustle in the courtroom but no significant outpouring. Ten marshals moved to stand behind the row of defendants while others eyed the crowd, and the eleven freshly convicted men sat stoically as the clerk polled the individual jurors to make sure that they had indeed found each of the defendants guilty. Some of the defendants were roiling inside, even though they had expected to be convicted. "The words were a shock," Gates wrote later.[8] Medina thanked the jurors, asked them not to grant interviews to the media because their words "would be subject to misinterpretation, subject to repetition and change and do irreparable harm to the administration of justice," and then dismissed them. The eight women and four men gathered up their belongings and filed past the prosecution and defense tables, through the gate and down the central aisle through the gallery, and out the door to the hallway. As they passed, one young man in the crowd hissed, "How could you do this to us?"[9]

Once the jury had left, Medina turned his attention to the defense table, saying he had some "unfinished business" to take care of. Speaking in an even voice, Medina asked the five defense lawyers and Dennis to rise. Reading slowly from a prepared statement, he carefully detailed the accumulated sins that had been committed in his courtroom, citing forty examples of contempt he felt had been shown by Sacher, Gladstein, Crockett, McCabe, Isserman, and, acting as his own attorney, Dennis. He accused them of acting in "a cold and calculating manner" to delay and confuse the trial, provoke incidents to spark a mistrial, and "impair . . . my health so that the trial could not continue." There would be retribution, he had warned during the trial. Now it was time to exact it. One by one, Medina ordered the lawyers to jail: Sacher, Gladstein, and Dennis for six months; Crockett and Isserman for four months; McCabe for thirty days.

The gallery gasped in shock at the first announcement, and by the end the lawyers were enraged, accusing Medina of prejudice against them and of miscarrying justice. Sacher launched into an impassioned defense of the lawyers' conduct and warned Medina that his finding of contempt jeopardized lawyers everywhere engaged in defending justice and freedom, including lawyers "in the South seeking to democratize the jury system there." He told Medina that they were paying the price for liberty, but Medina cut him off with a scolding: "It isn't the price of liberty. It's the price of misbehavior and disorder. You continue in the same brazen manner you used throughout the trial. You try to make it appear as though it was nonexistent and you had never done any of these things." He accused Sacher of a "mealy mouth" approach to legal arguments.

Gladstein weighed in briefly, condemning the finding, as did Crockett, who called being cited for contempt by Medina "a badge of honor . . . for vigorously prosecuting what I believe to be the proper conception of the American Constitution." And he said he would behave the same way again should another such trial arise.

Dennis struck a tone of bitterness. "This trial, and the verdict, is an evil and an illegitimate product of a bipartisan conspiracy, of a conspiracy of men who want to destroy the Bill of Rights and peace, and I think the adjudgment [*sic*] of counsel and the accompanying decision to remand the defendants without bail is in keeping with the sinister and police-state character of this trial." He railed against the contempt sentences and warned—as he had often during the trial—that it signaled a rise of fascism. "As in Nazi Germany, in Mussolini Italy, men also sat in high tribunals, also wore black robes and also handed down pro-fascist decisions. But I would remind the court that the people reversed those verdicts and decisions just as our people will reverse the decisions and verdict in this case, and the people's verdict will be for peace, for democracy, and for social progress."

Medina shrugged off the complaints, ordered the eleven party leaders' bail revoked, set sentencing for the next week, and abruptly adjourned court.[10]

———————

The day of sentencing, October 21, 1949, dawned under a cover of gray clouds, the air raw and tasting of winter. Supporters of the eleven communist leaders, augmented by the merely curious, began filtering into Foley Square Park hours before the courthouse opened. They found a cordon of New York City police already in place. A second bank of policemen on horseback filled the street, a show of force as the crowd grew several hundred strong. Speakers

took turns standing on a box beneath a small tree to rail against
the convictions. Some of the protesters carried signs, and as the
morning progressed they broke out in chants, agitating for the
release of the eleven men.[11]

Afraid of a rush on the courtroom, marshals kept the courthouse
doors locked except for the front entry, where they closely scrutinized all who lined up to pass through. Other marshals entered
Room 110—where the trial had been held, and where Medina
would mete out the sentences—and slowly and methodically
checked under seats and tables, in heating ducts, and under the
judge's bench to ensure no one had snuck in during the night and
planted a bomb.

For much of the trial, spectators were mostly journalists, relatives, and political sympathizers, and they had their choice of
seats. But this final day—judgment day—drew the same kind
of interest that marked the trial's opening nine months earlier.
The regulars found themselves fighting for space amid a throng
of additional media, court officials, and others drawn to see what
sentence Medina would impose. Extra seats were brought in, but
still there weren't enough places to sit, so the standing-room-only
crowd lined the walls at the back and along the sides. Mixed in
were some of the dozens of marshals, FBI men, and city police
detached to keep peace in the courthouse.

The eleven defendants had spent the week since their conviction
in the West Street Federal House of Detention on the far side of the
West Village. It was a jail, not a prison, and the eleven communists
were mixed in with the other inmates. As short-timers, they were
not given duties and so spent the days talking, playing cards and
board games, waiting for meetings with their lawyers, and chatting with visitors.[12] But on sentencing day they were taken early,
handcuffed together, and loaded into a van for the cross-town trip
to the courthouse, where they were unloaded under cover and then
escorted to a detention area near Room 110.

The meticulous Medina, normally precise about time, was unusu-
ally slow in taking the bench that morning. A few minutes before
11:00 A.M., nearly a half hour after the scheduled time, Medina
finally sent word through his bailiff that he was ready, that it was
time to move the defendants into the courtroom. Free now of their
handcuffs and dressed in "ordinary business suits," the men filed

in singly, and in reverse order from the way their names appeared in the indictment. Hall was first, then came Winter, Green, Potash, Gates, Winston, Davis, Thompson, Stachel, Williamson, and, finally, Dennis, his shock of gray-white hair an exclamation point. The men settled into red-backed leather chairs arrayed at a ninety-degree angle to Medina, facing the now empty jury box. Dennis's seat was closest to the judge; Hall sat closest to the gallery. A few of the men smiled and offered self-conscious waves to wives and other familiar faces in the audience, but most sat still and quiet.

Once the defendants were settled, Medina, wearing his traditional black robe, swept in from the side door and mounted the short steps to the bench and his red leather swivel chair. As he had through most of the trial, Medina exuded a sense of calm and control. Folding his hands on the top of his desk, he began by asking whether there were any motions to be considered. To no one's surprise, Gladstein, Crockett, and the other defense attorneys had a list ready, asking Medina to throw out the initial arrests, set aside the jury's verdict, and order a new trial. Speaking deliberately, Medina denied the requests, rejecting the argument that the trial had not been conducted fairly, then invited the defendants to say a few words before he imposed the sentences.[13]

Dennis, who had acted as his own attorney, led the way as the chief defendant. His now familiar clipped, hesitant voice belied the anger in the words he read from a prepared statement. He defiantly pledged the eleven men would "resolutely continue to champion our beliefs, our ideals, the principles of Marxism-Leninism, of scientific socialism. Come what may, we and our party will exercise our inalienable rights. We will defend our legality. We will function and grow as the vanguard party of the working class." He scored the "fascist-like controlled trial," which he described as a "sinister political frame-up that brought in a loaded verdict" by the misguided jury. "I say to your Honor," Dennis concluded, "that it is with a clear conscience, with full confidence in our ultimate vindication and with firm conviction, that ideas and scientific theories can never be imprisoned."

After Dennis sat down, Medina continued down the row of defendants, with Williamson, Stachel, and Thompson saying simply that they subscribed to what Dennis had just said. Davis, though, rose and, in a terse, anger-driven voice, placed the trial against the backdrop of the history of American civil rights. Blacks in the United States existed as second-class citizens, he said, and trials such as the one he and his colleagues had endured threatened to limit all Americans' political rights. He linked the Ku Klux Klan with "the men of Wall Street" as complicit in oppressing not just black people but the working class. And the American people would rise, he warned. "I will not be intimidated," Davis said. "I was not intimidated by the lynchers' court in Georgia, and I will not be intimidated by any court, by any forces of reaction anywhere, and neither will Winston, and neither will my people and my party. We are confident that the American people are going to realize what is happening here and they will realize that their liberties, their peace and their democracy are imperiled. We have all the confidence in them because the future belongs to the people of America, Negro and white."

The last six defendants then followed one by one, telling the judge in a few short phrases that they agreed with what Dennis and Davis had said and had nothing to add. Given the length of the trial, the speeches were surprisingly concise.

McGohey then stood and in a practiced, deliberate voice laid out the defendants' records. They had used false names. They had traveled to the Soviet Union on forged documents. Three of the men were foreign born and the subject of deportation proceedings. McGohey, already nominated to a post as a federal judge, asked for the maximum sentence, ten years per man. "Today, in the atmosphere of the Cold War, the potential danger of these men as leaders of a subversive group is probably incalculable," McGohey said. "We do not say that they would ever succeed in overthrowing the government of the United States, but they would attempt to do so."

The defense attorneys argued for leniency, and one—O. John Rogge, a former assistant U.S. attorney brought in to appear on Davis's behalf—accused Medina of not having a firm grasp of the facts, an argument that fell flat. Medina waved off the defense arguments and, about two hours after the hearing had begun, abruptly asked the defendants whether they were ready to hear the sentences.

All eleven rose and faced the bench, the gallery silent behind them. Medina began by talking about the scope of the activities that led to the convictions and about a recent change in the Smith

Act by Congress reducing the maximum sentence from ten years to five years. Because of that change, he said, he would sentence the men to the current maximum, not the maximum in place at the time they were indicted (which he could have done legally). Starting with Dennis, he went on down the line, sentencing each man separately to five years in prison and a $10,000 fine. The only exception was Thompson. In recognition of his receiving the Distinguished Service Cross for his actions in the U.S. Army during World War II, Medina sentenced him to only three years in prison.

None of the men spoke, and when Medina finished—Hall was the last to be sentenced—the defendants sat quietly, just as they had begun the trial, as their lawyers argued passionately that they should be released on bail while they appealed the verdicts and sentences. McGohey, to no one's surprise, sought to keep the men in jail. If anyone was a flight risk, he said, it was these men, who were part of an international movement. He pointed out that several of them had eluded capture after they were indicted, and several had jumped bail earlier in their lives in other cases.

Medina cleared his throat. If he had any doubt in his mind about the guilt of any of the defendants, he said, he would consider granting bail and letting the appeal courts do their work, but he was convinced of their guilt. Gladstein argued that the Smith Act itself was unconstitutional and that in this case there was no "clear and present danger" to justify abridging the right to free speech and assembly. Again, to no one's surprise, Medina disagreed, saying the defendants had not been convicted merely for their political beliefs or for belonging to the Communist Party. "I made it plain in my charge the jury could not convict for anything like that, but that they had to find there was specific intent to overthrow the government by force and violence and to use words as a rule of action," Medina said. "It seems to me absurd on its face to say, as you do, that there must be a clear and present danger of immediate overthrow to justify prosecution. By any such test, the government would be overthrown before it could protect itself and the very important right of freedom of speech would be gone with all the other freedoms."

Medina denied the bail and, a little before 2:00 P.M., adjourned court, ending his part of the case (though his rulings and actions during the trial would play important roles in the appeals). The eleven men were led back to the holding room, where they were again handcuffed together, then led outside to the waiting van and driven away to the Federal House of Detention as protesters in the park, who had already heard what had transpired, chanted, "We want bail! We want bail!"

Within an hour, the defense attorneys filed the first formal notices of appeal. On November 1, the three-member Circuit Court of Appeals heard arguments on the defendants' demand to be released on bail while their appeal of their convictions worked its way through the federal court system. The prosecution argued against bail but suggested, were it to be granted, that it be set at $100,000 each for Dennis, Green, Hall, Potash, Stachel, Thompson, and Williamson and $75,000 each for Davis, Gates, Winston, and Winter—deemed slightly less likely to flee. The defense sought bail of $10,000 each, arguing that the men had ties to the community and intended to fight the appeals as a matter of principle. Significantly, when pressed by Judge Learned Hand, Shapiro—McGohey had been sworn in as a federal judge a few days earlier—acknowledged that new attorney general J. Howard McGrath—Clark had been elevated to the Supreme Court midway through the trial—recognized the defense had an "arguable" legal point to be decided on appeal: whether the men had been convicted of committing acts protected by the First Amendment. And Shapiro asked that if the defendants were granted bail, the court attach a provision that they could not continue the activities of which they had been convicted—essentially, advocating communism.

Two days later, the court ruled, granting bail of $30,000 each for Dennis, Potash, Stachel, and Williamson and $20,000 for the others. The higher bail was set for the four men because the judges deemed them more likely to flee. Potash, Stachel, and Williamson, in fact, were fighting deportation orders already. But the court did not bar the men from continuing to advocate their political beliefs, signaling that the judges found merit in the possibility that their appeal might succeed.

By evening, the CRC posted bonds to cover the bail and the men were released, greeted outside by about two hundred supporters and then by a smaller gathering at a private reception at the party headquarters, the building festooned with a massive "Welcome Home!" banner. Davis left the party early. He had a rally to attend in Harlem. Despite the trial, and the conviction, Davis was running again for his seat on the New York City Council in elections to be held five days later. The others gave brief speeches to their comrades in the offices, talking of their right to political expression and saying they were confident that the Supreme Court would overturn their convictions based on the First Amendment.[14]

But the leadership of the Communist Party decided to hedge its bets that it could win. Eventually, four of the defendants—Hall, Green, Thompson, and Winston—would obey party orders and do just exactly what the prosecution had warned the court would likely happen. They would disappear.

There were two appeals to be fought—the convictions of the party leaders and the contempt sentences for the lawyers. Neither would succeed, and both would have devastating effects on the Communist Party.

The defense lawyers faced a second tier of trouble as well. Within hours of Medina's sentencing them to jail for contempt, spokesmen for the New York Bar Association began openly discussing disciplinary proceedings against those licensed to practice in New York—Sacher and Isserman. McCabe would face similar challenges in Pennsylvania, Crockett in Michigan, and Gladstein in California. Sacher and Isserman also faced sanctions from the federal courts, curtailing their ability to appear on behalf of clients. They would fight for years, Isserman for more than a decade to get his law license back in New Jersey. But before that came the more significant battle: trying to keep themselves out of prison.

They turned to Paul Ross, a onetime aide to former New York City mayors Fiorello La Guardia and William O'Dwyer, who quickly won them a delay in the initial appeal hearing. He told the U.S. Court of Appeals in New York in early December that he would need more time to prepare; reviewing the twenty-one thousand pages of testimony and exhibits alone would be a herculean undertaking. And Ross warned the appellate judges—Learned Hand, Jerome T. Frank, and Thomas W. Swan—that they, too, might have to read the entire trial transcript to see the context for the contempt citations.

Shapiro, representing the government, argued that there was no need for delay. The issue was simple: the defense lawyers' aggregate behavior over the course of the nine-month trial. But the judges gave Ross and his clients two more months to prepare their case.

The lawyers had their defenders. The CRC feted them with a special dinner in December. And sixteen prominent people signed a public statement expressing their "alarm" at the jailing of lawyers for vigorously defending their clients, fearing it would erode the ability of communists and other political figures to obtain fair trials. The signatories included Albert Einstein, I. F. Stone, and Linus Pauling, as well as Indiana judge Norval K. Harris, who also cochaired with Paul Robeson a committee to defend the eleven party leaders.

In fact, the sentences split the legal community. Even during the trial there were calls for lawyers defending communists—or acting in support of them—to be disbarred. In August, as Truman was contemplating nominating Attorney General Clark to replace the late Frank Murphy on the U.S. Supreme Court, Clark took up the cudgel in an article in *Look* magazine. "Lawyers who are not probably card-carrying communists, but who act like communists or carry out communist missions in offensives against the dignity and order of our courts, should be scrutinized by grievance committees of the bar and the courts," Clark wrote, adding that the Smith Act trial would cost the government about one million dollars. "It is the price we pay to defend ourselves. Communism is on its way out in the country with a one-way ticket."[15]

Legal minds more attuned to the civil rights implications deplored Medina's actions, no matter how out of line the lawyers may have been, as a "grave national danger."[16] The issue swung on perspective—how aggressive should lawyers be in defending their clients before a judge they are convinced is prejudiced against them? For some, latitude should be wide. Others put more weight on decorum. If the lawyers disagreed with decisions they found onerous, they should turn to the appeals courts. But that assessment ignored the practical impact of sending the lawyers to jail: the chilling effect as lawyers weighed whether to take on Communist Party members as clients, effectively barring them access to competent counsel.

In a ninety-page brief filed just before the rescheduled February 4 appeal hearing, U.S. Attorney Irving H. Saypol (he also handled the Hiss and the Julius and Ethel Rosenberg cases) laid out the government's argument that the five lawyers and Dennis had engaged—following Dennis's lead—in a pattern of behaviors designed to interfere with the trial. He described it as standard "Bolshevik conduct" and a "purposeful effort to frustrate the court, and thus to serve the illicit interests of their clients at the expense of the interests of public justice . . . [and] a rejection of the duties inherent in every attorney's oath." The lawyers had aggravated the problem by attacking Medina's integrity while ignoring his orders to stop arguing motions on which he had already ruled (albeit without bothering to hear the grounds for the motions, a practice that infuriated the defense team).

Conversely, the defense team argued it was Medina's behavior that was out of line, complaining that he entered the case biased against the defense, had impugned the defense lawyers' skills and integrity in front of the jury, denied them the opportunity to properly represent their clients, and, as a final shot, denied them a hearing on the charges he compiled against them, appointing himself accuser, jury, and executioner all at once. To uphold Medina's citations and sentences, they argued, "may well become a signal for wholesale disbarment of lawyers who defend communists as well as labor unions and minority groups." They also argued that Medina had no authority, once the trial ended, to impose contempt sentences.[17]

The appellate judges listened to both sides augment their brief with oral arguments, then announced they would reserve decision. It was standard practice, and no one expected an instant ruling. But while the judges were deliberating, American politics took a radical and historic turn beginning with what should have been an uneventful speech by Joseph R. McCarthy, the junior senator from Wisconsin, before a Lincoln Day fund-raising dinner held by fellow Republicans in Wheeling, West Virginia.

TWELVE

In the Wind

All politics might be local, as the adage goes, but political success is a matter of timing and, often, manipulation. Joseph McCarthy used both to his maximum benefit.

McCarthy's story is already familiar: a Wisconsin farm boy turned ambitious lawyer, then politician, who, despite qualifying for a deferment as a circuit court judge, enlisted in the U.S. Marines early in World War II to bolster his political résumé. He left before the war ended, lied about his service to obtain a Distinguished Service Cross, nicknamed himself "Tailgunner Joe," and, after losing his first shot at a U.S. Senate seat in 1944 (while still in uniform), won in 1946 against long-serving progressive Robert La Follette Jr. (son of the famous "Fighting Bob" La Follette) by, in essence, spreading lies that La Follette was a war profiteer.

McCarthy entered the Senate as though moving into a frat house. A regular on the party circuit, he was quick with a joke and a compliment (and even quicker with a drink) and developed a reputation among his fellow senators and the Washington press corps as a legislative lightweight. He never caught on to the relationships that run the Senate, and even though he was joined by many of his colleagues in his virulent anti-communism, he was at heart a spotlight-hungry

226

lone wolf. "From the beginning he displayed only contempt for the traditions of the Senate, defied powerful colleagues, and indulged in debating tactics that other senators sometimes found irresponsible," wrote historian Allen J. Matusow. "McCarthy was, therefore, kept on the fringe of the Senate far away from the centers of real influence and power."[1] But he knew how to make headlines. After he held an inconsequential press conference about the United Mine Workers early in his tenure and saw himself quoted in the *New York Times*, "he realized how easy it was for a senator to generate news stories on his own, and once he mastered the art of shaping public debate by making the headlines, he never looked back," wrote biographer Arthur Herman.[2] He also, in keeping with his fellow Republicans (and quite a few Democrats), saw the rise of communism internationally as a threat to the United States.

By the time the eleven Smith Act defendants argued their appeal, fear of communism was part of the American bloodstream. In the months after the October 1949 convictions, Alger Hiss was convicted of perjury (January 21); former Manhattan Project physicist Klaus Fuchs was arrested in London (February 3) on espionage charges in the case that would eventually lead to the executions of the Rosenbergs (a trail that began with Gouzenko's defection in Canada); and Judith Coplon, a Justice Department employee, and Valentin Gubitchev, a Soviet attaché at the United Nations, went on trial on espionage charges in the same first-floor Foley Square courtroom in which Medina oversaw the Smith Act trial. Coplon had already been convicted the previous June on related spying charges by a federal jury in Washington, D.C. Communism and communist spies were in the air, and the most vituperative of Truman's political foes saw direct links from Stalin to the Oval Office.

On February 6, the leaders of the Republican Party convened in Washington, D.C., to formulate a platform that would unify Republican congressional campaigns for the upcoming November off-year elections. Top among them was opposition to continuing New Deal programs, and, under the slogan "Liberty Against Socialism," the GOP pledged to "advocate a strong policy against the spread of communism or fascism at home and abroad, and that we insist that America's efforts toward this end be directed by those who have no sympathy either with communism or fascism."[3] It's interesting to note that as the country headed into the 2010 off-year congressional elections, the Republicans were similarly looking to rally around the issue of fear and casting Democratic attempts to enact health care reform as an embrace of socialism.[4]

Then, as now, Lincoln's Birthday on February 12 was an annual chance for the party to rally its supporters, and raise money, in the name of the president generally credited as the father of the Republican Party. That weekend Republican Party figures fanned out across the country delivering speeches at local Lincoln dinners. McCarthy drew a short straw: His itinerary would take him from Wheeling, West Virginia, to Salt Lake City, Reno, Las Vegas, and then Huron, North Dakota. The newspapers in Wheeling, writing ahead of his talk there before the Ohio County Women's Republican Club, speculated that McCarthy would discuss policies on the elderly.[5]

When McCarthy landed at the airport in Wheeling, he handed reporters copies of his remarks for that evening. There was nothing in them about aid to the elderly. Rather they included notes from a speech Richard Nixon had given in the House about spies. Later, in delivering his speech based on those notes, McCarthy declared that the United States was in danger of losing the cold war to "communist atheism" because the Department of State was rife with communist agents. McCarthy was described as waving a paper as he declared that he had a list of 205 names of communists or sympathizers working in the State Department, "names that were known to the secretary of state and who nevertheless are still working and shaping the policy of the State Department." It's unclear whether McCarthy used that number or whether reporters picked it up from the prepared speech (in reality, a loose set of notes). McCarthy later adjusted it down to 57, and the number has been the subject of debate ever since—a debate that misses the core issue. How many names McCarthy counted is irrelevant; that McCarthy was calling out names at all was the point.

McCarthy, obviously, wasn't the cause of American anti-communist fervor. That flame that had been ignited by revelations of Soviet spying, the "loss of China" to Mao Zedong's communist forces, and the HUAC and others who sought to roust communists and leftists from government service, union positions, the entertainment industry, and any other place of work or policy that might have public impact. McCarthy, and the campaign of smears and innuendo that he pursued, embodied the wretched excess of those passions, and of the government's blatant disregard of the First Amendment protections of free speech and assembly. But where McCarthy was, in effect, a bully leading a mob bent on destroying careers and families, the Smith Act convictions were in many ways far more onerous. It's one thing to lose a job because of political beliefs; it's something else entirely to lose your freedom because of it. And the Smith Act, if upheld by the courts, would do just that—criminalize political behavior.

On April 5, as McCarthyism began to rage in full, the three-member Court of Appeals upheld most of Medina's findings of contempt by the defense lawyers, voting 2–1. It rejected Medina's finding that the lawyers worked in a conspiracy yet found that the lawyers' behavior merited the sentences Medina imposed. One of the judges, Frank, compared the lawyers' actions to "assaulting the pilot of an airplane in flight, or turning out the lights during a surgical procedure"; or, "to use homelier words, they tried to throw a wrench into the machinery of justice." Yet the justices also said they were not upholding the sentences to retaliate against the lawyers on behalf of Medina's hurt feelings. Rather, they said, they wanted to send a message that such behavior would not be tolerated—a clear warning to other defense attorneys. And the message was received. Over the next few years, scores of Communist Party members and activists charged under the Smith Act would be hard-pressed to find adequate defense counsel.[6]

It took two more years for the Supreme Court to accept the lawyers' appeal, schedule and listen to arguments, review the case file, and issue its ruling. On March 10, 1952, the Court upheld Medina by a 5–3 vote (Justice Clark, who was the attorney general when the Smith Act indictments were handed down, recused himself). On April 24, nearly two and a half years after the jury convicted the eleven defendants, the five lawyers (Dennis was already in prison) turned themselves in at the U.S. Court House at Foley Square, this time entering the third-floor courtroom of Judge John W. Clancy. Shortly after 10:30 A.M. Clancy accepted their appearance, and the men were taken into custody and a couple of hours later transferred in handcuffs by van to the West Street detention center, where their clients had been held.

McCabe, who received a thirty-day sentence, served all his time at the detention center, then quietly resumed his practice in Philadelphia. Gladstein, despite his expressed desire to serve his time near family on the West Coast, was sent to Texarkana, Texas; manacled and in irons, he spent seven weeks being ferried to facilities around the country before finally arriving. After his sentence was served, he returned to San Francisco and resumed his practice—including notable defenses of Harry Bridges.[7]

Sacher and Crockett served their sentences in the federal penitentiary in Ashland, Kentucky. Sacher would eventually survive attempts to disbar him, though it took a Supreme Court decision to do it. He continued to practice law while the disbarment appeals were under way but never regained his pre–Smith Act trial standing as one of the nation's premier litigators. He died in 1963 after, as historian Stanley I. Kutler described it, "having passed his remaining days in relative obscurity and with a diminished practice."[8] Crockett would go on to work in the voting rights campaigns across the South in the 1960s and served as a judge in Detroit before winning election to Congress, where he became a leading figure in trying to force a diplomatic end to apartheid in South Africa. His son, George W. Crockett III, would follow him into the practice of law and to the bench as a judge in Detroit. Isserman paid the biggest price among the lawyers. He served his four months in federal prison in Danbury, Connecticut, and although the others were able to quickly fight their way back into the Bar Association's good graces and resume their legal careers, it took Isserman twelve years to win back the right to practice law.[9]

While the members of the defense team struggled to keep their careers, Medina was welcomed as a hero by an adoring nation. In the weeks after the verdict was announced, newspapers wrote about his next steps as though he were a Hollywood celebrity. Medina needed a break, he told reporters, and he and his wife were contemplating visiting Southern California to take advantage of the warm weather as autumn turned to early winter in Manhattan. Eventually the couple settled on the Bahamas, where they enjoyed the perks of fame—the loan of an admirer's boat, good tables at the best restaurants, a full social calendar to cap Medina's days on the golf course.

Fawning profiles cropped up everywhere. The editors at *Time* magazine placed him in the running for their annual "Man of the Year" cover story—he lost out to Winston Churchill.[10] Fan mail flooded into his chambers. "Congratulations, sir," wrote JD Sutherland of Chicago. "I would like to treat all communists like cockroaches." Frank A. O'Brien, a lawyer from Wheeling, West Virginia, lauded Medina for his treatment of their fellow members of the bar. "The prompt imposition of sentences upon lawyers, who throughout the trial, as reported in the daily press, were guilty of contempt, will have the approval of a nearly unanimous Bar and, as well also, of the public."[11]

Medina clearly reveled in the attention but also struck his familiar self-effacing pose. "The trial was a long and arduous experience," he wrote in response to a letter of congratulations from Jose M. Benitez, in Mexico, from whom Medina had taken Spanish lessons years before in his Riverside Drive apartment. "Sometimes it seemed as though I could not possibly carry on to the end. When it was over, I thought I could at once get away for a nice long rest. Imagine my surprise, when I found myself thrown in the limelight and more or less a national hero for the time being. Fate certainly plays queer tricks with us."[12]

Befitting a trial that lasted nine months and spawned a transcript of more than twenty thousand pages, the defendants' appeal of their convictions was a sprawling argument that elicited a sprawling rebuttal.

On May 2, the team filed a 570-page brief with the appeals court spelling out sixteen different points they believed warranted reversing the convictions, all of them previously raised in motions that Medina had rejected during the trial. Some seemed petulant—complaining about Medina's behavior and the prosecution's use of paid informants and turncoats and arguing that Medina committed judicial error in letting those witnesses testify. But the core appeals arguments were the same points that anchored the defense from the beginning: the challenge of the constitutionality of the jury panel and defendants' ability to receive a fair trial given the nation's political climate (as evidenced, in part, by author and Broadway producer Janney's behavior before and while he was on the jury).

But the key argument mounted by the defense was that the eleven men's individual acts were protected expressions of free speech and assembly under the First Amendment and that any conspiracy allegation based upon those acts was unconstitutional. The Smith Act itself was unconstitutional, they said, because it "frustrated" the First Amendment's essence: "the protection of political expression and activities." They argued that "the myth of a 'communist conspiracy' has been invoked with increasing frequency by reactionary interests to justify attacks upon all groups and theories who challenge the status quo. This case represents a desperate attempt to give new standing to that myth."

Frank Gordon, one of McGohey's assistants during the trial, shouldered the arguments for the government, filing a four-hundred-page brief rebutting the wide range of defense challenges and arguing that ample evidence had been introduced at the trial to prove the defendants' guilt. The CPUSA was in thrall to the Soviet Union, took its marching orders from Moscow, and was preparing for the day when communist revolution came to America. The defendants had lied on passports and other official documents and used "Aesopian language" to mask their true intent. But Gordon's lengthiest argument—115 pages—was spent defending the constitutionality of the Smith Act. Congress, he argued, was within its rights to take actions to preserve the U.S. government against violent overthrow. The Smith Act "is a response to the twin threat of fascism and communism and to the fifth-column activities which the Congress found are invariably associated with those totalitarian movements. The Congressional conclusion that communists present a substantial fifth-column threat is confirmed by indisputable evidence that the communists of the world, including the United States, engage in espionage for the Soviet Union." Of course, there already were laws against espionage, and the Smith Act barred political arguments, not acts of espionage.

A key legal point lay in exactly how serious a threat the American Communist Party posed to the U.S. government. The defense argued that Medina, in his instructions to the jury, erred by declaring that a "clear and present danger" existed that the defendants could succeed. That, the defense argued, was a matter for the jury to decide based on the testimony and evidence—which it believed fell short. Gordon countered for the government that the threshold applied only to the "naïve, impulsive, and hot-headed," not to defendants like the eleven leaders of the Communist Party, who, at the time of the indictment, were part of an international attack on capitalism and, by extension, the U.S. government. "By 1948, it was apparent that in every country in which the Communist Party came within striking distance of power, it brushed aside by force the constitutional forms of government and seized political power," he wrote. "It was demonstrated that in every country in which communists obtained political power, political and personal freedom died. . . . The events between 1940 and 1948 demonstrated again and again that Congress had correctly viewed the Communist Party of the United States as a potential fifth column for the Soviet Union."

The appeal was argued in person over three days in late June in the same courthouse in which the trial was held. Presaging the decision that was to come, the judges explored the two sides' arguments over the constitutionality of the Smith Act. But the key issue was whether the defendants, even if they had advocated the overthrow of the government, were in a position to do so. Sacher argued that without evidence of a plan of action, such as a date for the revolution, then the defendants were guilty only of speech, which is protected. "There is lacking in this case any agreement to commit the substantive crime at all," Sacher said. Gordon, reinforcing the details in the brief he filed, argued that the government was not imagining monsters under the bed. The evidence showed the defendants were part of an international conspiracy, and the American communists' uses of fake names, secret meetings, and "Aesopian language" were the actions of guilty conspirators, not of a political party engaged in legitimate political debate.

The hearing ended on a Friday, and whatever optimistic feelings the defendants and their attorneys might have harbored were likely dashed when they picked up the newspaper Sunday morning to learn that the North Korean army had invaded South Korea, launching a proxy war between the United States and the communist regimes in the Soviet Union and China. Suddenly the abstract became concrete, and fears of the "communist threat" exploded. An article in the *New York Times* speculated that the military move was a "crisis that could contain the seeds of World War Three." The *Chicago Daily Tribune* wondered if the action was part of a Soviet plan to place all of Asia under the red flag. Truman cut short a family vacation in Independence, Missouri, to return to Washington to deal with the crisis as Great Britain and France joined in American denunciations of the North Koreans' aggression—and also announced that the Soviet Union would be held responsible.[13]

By the time the appeals court handed down its unanimous decision six weeks later, American troops were already fighting alongside the South Korean Army in the early days of a massive United Nations military buildup—led by the United States—in South Korea that would end, three years later, in a stalemate. Hand, who wrote the opinion for the appeals court, dismissed all of the defendants' arguments and upheld the eleven convictions, citing, in part, the onset of the war. There was, Judge Hand wrote, sufficient reason in 1940—and in the present—for Congress to fear communism, from the Gouzenko spy revelations to the southward invasion by the North Koreans. The decision was rooted not in law but in the prospect of war, and the potential complicity by American citizens. Thus the court ruled that people could be jailed not for what they did but for what they might wish.

"The Congressional judgment has, indeed, been confirmed, again and again, by events," Hand wrote. "Communism has by forcible overthrow engulfed or attempted to engulf nation after nation, after preparation for the use of force by just such advocacy as this Act forbids. As this is being written, Fifth Column activities are aiding the North Koreans in their war against the United Nations. Again, the President has just now warned all citizens and police officers to be watchful of spies, sabotage, and other subversive activities. The uncovering of a communist spy ring in Canada and the recent conviction of a British atomic scientist on charges of espionage are but further instances of proof, though none be needed, that the Congress was acting wisely, and most reasonably, when it enacted the statute at bar."[14]

Reaction broke along expected lines. Supporters of the party leaders decried it, and anti-communists cheered it. With the developments on the Korean peninsula, the case took on a grim urgency. "The 'clear and present danger' which Judge Hand analyzed in his cogent and eloquent opinion has grown clearer and more grimly present these past weeks and months," the New York Times editorialized on August 3. "The nation can no longer treat with good-humored tolerance groups or individuals whose admitted aim is to defeat the national purpose and aid the national enemies. . . . No one supposed that the American communists are strong enough to carry out open revolution. They are strong enough, however, to sabotage at critical points the effort necessary for national survival of democracy. They are strong enough to make more difficult and more painful the terrible task of the soldiers now fighting in Korea. We are not called upon to give them [the communists] aid and comfort in such an effort."

The editorial concluded with a backhanded mention of those struggling against totalitarianism. "The present plight and future prospects of the eleven communist leaders may be compared and contrasted with the situation of those dissenters behind the Iron Curtain who have dared even so much as to raise their voices against an autocratic government." True, the eleven didn't face exile or execution for opposing their governments, but they did face prison.

The tone of the editorial is telling, treating the First Amendment as a novelty to be tolerated. And while the editorial mentioned sabotage, that particular act was not part of the indictments. The eleven party leaders were convicted of conspiring to talk about the necessity of overthrowing the U.S. government—a political outlook protected by the First Amendment. They had taught a political theory, and it was odd—and a mark of the passions of the era—to see the beacon of the nation's media so cavalierly disregard the First Amendment protections.

From the moment Thelma Dial, the jury foreman, announced the guilty verdict, the Smith Act case was all but certain to have its day before the nation's highest court. In late October, the Supreme Court announced that it would hear an appeal of the conviction but limited it to the crucial issue: the constitutionality of the 1940 Smith Act.

By now the case was named *Dennis v. the United States of America*, and the Supreme Court that would hear the appeal was led by Chief Justice Fred M. Vinson, though few legal scholars would agree with the term "led." In fact, the Vinson Court was among the most dysfunctional in American legal history—primarily because of

Vinson, one of only eight chief justices to earn a "failure" ranking in a survey of past Supreme Court justices. Vinson made it to the nation's top bench because Truman mistakenly thought he would be able to mediate running disputes among some of the sitting justices. It didn't hurt that Vinson was a regular at Truman's poker table.[15]

Vinson was born and raised in Kentucky and arrived in Washington in 1924 as a member of the House of Representatives, where he made tax policy his specialty. A southern conservative Democrat, he became a moderate supporter of Roosevelt's New Deal agenda and struck up a friendship with then-Senator Harry Truman. In 1938, President Roosevelt appointed the nonpracticing lawyer to the U.S. Court of Appeals for the D.C. Circuit, then in 1943 named him as the administration's wartime director of the Office of Economic Stabilization. Vinson was never known for his intellect, but he had the kind of down-home common sense that carried a lot of weight with Truman. He was also a good storyteller, shrewd but likable, and he put a premium on political loyalty. In July 1945, with Roosevelt dead and Truman in the White House, the president tapped his old friend to replace Henry Morgenthau Jr. as secretary of the treasury. Then, after Chief Justice Harlan Fiske Stone died on April 22, 1946, Truman turned to his poker-playing buddy to try to mediate two factions on a Court bitterly divided by personality and political outlook.

One faction was led by Felix Frankfurter, who was generally supported by Justices Stanley Reed, Harold Burton, and Robert Jackson, at the time on leave to head up the prosecution of Nazi war criminals at Nuremburg. The other faction was led by Hugo Black and included William O. Douglas, Wiley B. Rutledge, and Frank Murphy. The Frankfurter faction placed an emphasis on judicial restraint; the Black faction put weight on the rights of the individual, particularly when it came to conflicts over the First Amendment. But there was an undercurrent of personal animus, too, between Jackson and Black stemming from the 1945 *Jewell Ridge Coal Corp. v. Local 6167, United Mine Workers* case. The details of the case are irrelevant to the feud, which grew from Black's decision not to recuse himself even though his former law partner was an attorney for the mine workers. Jackson saw that as a critical ethical lapse, and the bad blood resurfaced with speculation that, after Stone's death, Truman would elevate one of the sitting justices to replace him and appoint a new associate justice.[16] Jackson lobbied for the appointment, arguing that Roosevelt had promised him the top spot on the bench when it came open. Douglas was also considered a contender. As the justices and their supporters jockeyed and lobbied, the dispute was played out in the media, a rare public airing of dirty Supreme Court laundry. Hard lines were drawn. "Matters came to a head," one analyst wrote, "when Douglas and Black reportedly told Truman they'd resign if he elevated Jackson; Felix Frankfurter may have similarly blocked Douglas's candidacy."[17]

Truman, who built one of the worst records of Supreme Court appointments, by selecting judges based on politics over their legal knowledge, felt he needed a peacekeeper on the court more than a constitutional scholar. So he nominated Vinson.[18] The former congressman quickly emerged as something of a royalist. Vinson, seemingly believing in the infallibility of the executive branch, repeatedly gave its claims the benefit of the doubt, eroding individual civil liberties in favor of government institutions. He also proved to be woefully incapable of bringing the battling justices together.[19]

When the Vinson Court convened on the morning of December 4, 1950, to hear the *Dennis* case, eight justices were present; Jackson was back from Germany, but Clark, who had recused himself because he was the attorney general when the party leaders were indicted, was absent. For four hours the Court listened to the defense team—Sacher, Isserman, and Crockett—and the government's lawyers, a team led by Philip B. Perlman, the solicitor general, that included familiar names from the trial—Shapiro, Saypol, Gordon, and Wallace, as well as Assistant Attorney General Lawrence C. Bailey. Justices Douglas, Black, and Frankfurter led the way from the bench, probing both sides on the intricacies of the argument over whether the defendants posed a "clear and present danger" of action—and whether that template even need be applied under the Smith Act. The arguments broke no new ground, though it was clear that the justices were zeroing in on whether the defendants posed a risk of success and whether the "clear and present danger" standard applied. Isserman, somewhat presciently—if hyperbolically—laid out the future if the convictions were upheld. He quoted

Hoover as saying that some "500,000 Americans who . . . do the bidding of the Communist Party" faced persecution. "And it will have an intimidating effect on millions of others who differ from the government in any way. Already men in high places have suffered from McCarthyism and men holding moderate views have been persecuted under pressure of hysteria."[20]

Seven months later, on a cool Monday in June a day after thunderstorms raked and flooded portions of the District of Columbia, the Supreme Court handed down its ruling, a 6–2 vote upholding the convictions and the constitutionality of the 1940 Smith Act. In writing for the majority, Vinson defended Congress's right to enact laws to protect the government.[21]

"Whatever theoretical merit there may be to the argument that there is a 'right' to rebellion against dictatorial governments is without force where the existing structure of the government provides for peaceful and orderly change," Vinson wrote. "We reject any principle of governmental helplessness in the face of preparation for revolution, which principle, carried to its logical conclusion, must lead to anarchy. No one could conceive that it is not within the power of Congress to prohibit acts intended to overthrow the Government by force and violence. The question with which we are concerned here is not whether Congress has such power, but whether the means which it has employed conflict with the First and Fifth Amendments to the Constitution."

And no, Vinson wrote, it did not conflict, because it "is directed at advocacy, not discussion. . . . Congress did not intend to eradicate the free discussion of political theories, to destroy the traditional rights of Americans to discuss and evaluate ideas without fear of governmental sanction. Rather Congress was concerned with the very kind of activity in which the evidence showed these petitioners engaged."

Vinson said the Court did not buy the defendants' argument that they were not ready to act but merely discussing the desirability of a new kind of government. They did indeed present a "clear and present danger" to the U.S. government. "Petitioners intended to overthrow the Government of the United States as speedily as the circumstances would permit. . . . They were properly and constitutionally convicted." And the decision was, in fact, in keeping with earlier decisions (*Gitlow v. New York* in 1925 and *Whitney v.*

California in 1927) in which the Court, though handling unrelated issues, held that it was in the government's interest to limit speech that imperiled the government itself.[22]

Justices Black and Douglas were the lone votes to overturn the conviction, and Black, writing in dissent, was scathing.

"These petitioners were not charged with an attempt to over-throw the Government. They were not charged with overt acts of any kind designed to overthrow the Government. They were not even charged with saying anything or writing anything designed to overthrow the Government. The charge was that they agreed to assemble and to talk and publish certain ideas at a later date: the indictment is that they conspired to organize the Communist Party and to use speech or newspapers and other publications in the future to teach and advocate the forcible overthrow of the Government. No matter how it is worded, this is a virulent form of prior censorship of speech and press, which I believe the First Amendment forbids."

Douglas saw darkness ahead, pointing out that the eleven men were convicted of advocating something allegedly contained in the books they used. "The opinion of the Court does not outlaw these texts nor condemn them to the fire, as the communists do literature offensive to their creed. But if the books themselves are not outlawed, if they can lawfully remain on library shelves, by what reasoning does their use in a classroom become a crime? It would not be a crime under the Act to introduce these books to a class, though that would be teaching what the creed of violent overthrow of the Government is. The Act, as construed, requires the element of intent—that those who teach the creed believe in it. The crime then depends not on what is taught, but on who the teacher is. That is to make freedom of speech turn not on *what is said*, but on the intent with which it is said. Once we start down that road, we enter territory dangerous to the liberties of every citizen." He hoped that a future Court would recognize—and rectify—the error his brethren were committing. "Public opinion being what it now is, few will protest the conviction of these communist petitioners. There is hope, however, that in calmer times, when present pressures, passions and fears subside, this or some later Court will restore the First Amendment liberties to the high preferred place where they belong in a free society."

12. John Gates, editor of the *Daily Worker*, and his wife, Lillian, enter court as Gates turns himself in to serve his sentence. WPA Film Library. Image courtesy of MPI Home Video.

The decision meant Dennis and his ten codefendants were destined for prison. It also, in essence, gave the green light to the FBI and the Department of Justice to begin a roundup of Communist Party members, equating active membership in the party with advocating the overthrow of the U.S. government. The ruling had effectively made membership in the Communist Party a crime.

In the months after the Foley Square convictions, the U.S. attorney's office and the FBI had been preparing cases against what became known as the "second tier" leaders of the party. Twenty-one had been indicted in late June, and by the end of July another dozen had been indicted in a national roundup. After the Supreme Court upheld the *Dennis* decision, federal prosecutors across the country began getting indictments of local party leaders. Eventually, 145 Communist Party members or supporters would be charged, and 108 would be convicted and sentenced to a total of 418 years in prison, though only 28 defendants served postconviction prison time—the 11 men convicted in Medina's court and defendants in related cases in 1952 in New York City and Baltimore.[23]

The defendants and their supporters viewed the decision as further evidence of a fascist turn by the U.S. government, particularly with the escalation of the U.S. involvement in the Korean War. The party leaders talked about whether they should set up a shadow organization, underground, to continue the party operations in the face of what they presumed would be a severe crackdown on overt political activities—their meetings and schools among them. "It was taken as the definitive signal that it was 'five minutes to midnight,' that fascism was on the verge of triumph, and that the only way the party could avoid total destruction was to adopt a form of underground organization modeled on that used by the resistance movements in Nazi-occupied Europe," wrote Dorothy Healey, a California party official who also faced a Smith Act indictment.[24]

The national board was divided, some seeing going underground as necessary, others fearing that it would be taken as proof that the communists, rather than acting as a political party, really were plotting an overthrow. "Our discussions took note of signs of increasing public unease," Green wrote. "Ever more individuals, many of them prominent and esteemed in their fields, were being dragged before the inquisitional committees, in an air of growing unreality. The fog of confusion and intimidation was dense; it would take time to disperse. We had confidence that it would, but for the time being we had to face the realities of intensified repression."[25]

The national fear was intensifying, too, as more American soldiers were deployed to the Koreas. The *Journal-American* led a story with the headline "FBI Ready to Move on 20,000 New York Reds." Emboldened by the Supreme Court decision, congressional supporters of legislation to outlaw the party pressed for action. Green and other communists saw history on the verge of repeating itself—similar moves against radicals during the first Red Scare, after World War I, had decimated the Wobblies.[26]

The ten convicted men—Dennis was already in prison on the contempt of Congress citation—were ordered to appear in Judge Sylvester Ryan's courtroom in the U.S. Court House at Foley Square at 10:30 A.M. on July 2, a Monday. Sacher and Isserman were on hand to represent the men, and Saypol, Gordon, and Wallace were there for the government. Outside, as they had done for the duration of the trial, scores of protesters marched and jeered in Foley Square Park.

The defendants had had the weekend to prepare themselves and to say good-bye to family and friends. As 10:30 neared, they slowly arrived at the courthouse. John Gates and his wife, who was wearing a stylish floppy hat, arrived early, as the protesters were massing, and climbed the granite steps into the courthouse, followed a short time later by Davis, who arrived alone. Dennis

13. Peggy and Eugene Dennis arriving at the courthouse. With Foster's case separated because of his ill health, Dennis became the prime defendant and appellant in *Dennis v. United States* and acted as his own attorney. WPA Film Library. Image courtesy of MPI Home Video.

and his wife, Peggy, took their time climbing the steps, turning to wave and acknowledge the protesters. Winter, Potash, Stachel, and Williamson all followed suit, taking their seats with their families and supporters in the gallery to await the judge, and the start of their prison terms.[27]

Green, Winston, Hall, and Thompson didn't show. They were in the wind.

––––––––––

By the time his six colleagues walked into court for sentencing that morning, Green was already hiding in Chicago, moving from basement to basement of supporters' homes. Hall, Winston, and Thompson had similarly faded into the country, Winston hiding in Brooklyn, just a few miles from the courthouse, and Thompson eventually making his way to California.[28] They were joined by four other Communist Party officials who had been indicted after the initial convictions, forming an eight-man underground that the FBI feared would continue to organize what it saw as treasonous activities.

Some people are better at hiding than others. Hall, the husky former Ohio chairman and the party's future four-time presidential candidate, was the first to be caught—forty pounds lighter and his hair dyed blond—after four months on the run. The party leadership that ordered the men to jump bail had also urged them to flee the country. The California party sent someone to Mexico to scout it as a possible place to hide and reported that "any gringo was going to stick out like a sore thumb." Canada was recommended instead, though apparently that word didn't get passed along.[29] The four Foley Square defendants disagreed with the directive, believing they would be better off hiding with supporters in the United States. Only Hall went along with it, swimming across the Rio Grande on an autumn night to meet supporters on the south bank, who drove him to Mexico City. But the FBI picked up the trail—a member of the support group was suspected of alerting them—and in a dawn raid Hall was nabbed at the hotel by a mixed team of FBI and Mexican federal agents, driven to the border, and then flown from Laredo to Texarkana and imprisoned. The communists—and quite a few Mexicans—argued that Hall had been kidnapped and spirited back to the United States without due process, but the protests didn't get very far. Hall eventually was moved to Leavenworth, in Kansas, and then New York to stand trial on bail-jumping charges. Three years were added to his initial five-year sentence.[30]

It took the FBI two years to catch up with Thompson, the war hero. He was finally tracked down at a cabin near Twain Harte, a small town in the Sierra Nevada foothills northwest of Yosemite National Park in California. Thompson had been there for about three weeks "watching television and playing ping pong" with Sidney Steinberg, another party member who had been indicted in a later wave of Smith Act indictments and fled rather than turn himself in. Four other supporters who had rented the cabin and supplied the men with a car were also arrested. Thompson was taken to Alcatraz before being returned in September to New York to face, like Hall, contempt charges for jumping bail.[31]

While awaiting his hearing, Thompson was held in the general population at the Federal House of Detention on West Street. On October 23, 1953, he was standing in the lunch line with upwards of forty other prisoners when Alexander Pavlovich, a Yugoslav seaman and anti-Tito fascist scheduled for deportation the next morning, slipped in behind him. Pavlovich pulled out a thirty-inch-long, half-inch-wide galvanized iron pipe he had lifted from the prison boiler room and bashed Thompson twice across the back of the head. Guards grabbed him before he could strike again as Thompson crumpled to the floor with a fractured skull. He was rushed to the prison ward at Bellevue Hospital, where doctors performed emergency surgery to repair the crushed part of his skull—one of three such surgeries Thompson would endure.

Party faithful made much of the political overtones in the attack—Pavlovich, a fascist, going after Thompson, a communist. But the attack seemed to have a more personal motive. Pavlovich feared that if he were returned to Yugoslavia he would be killed for his anti-communist actions—including political assassinations—during the war. With fresh assault charges pending against him in the United States, his deportation was postponed. When he was eventually sentenced to serve three years for the assault, Pavlovich thanked the judge for extending his life.[32]

Thompson recovered sufficiently to appear in court in December 1953 to answer the contempt charges for jumping bail. Four years were added to his initial three-year sentence. He appealed, arguing that his maximum exposure for contempt was a one-year sentence, and in June of 1957, after this initial three-year sentence and seventeen months of his contempt sentence had been served, he was released on bail while the appeal worked its way through the federal legal system.[33] On October 16, 1965, age fifty, he died of a heart attack in his sleep in his Riverside Drive apartment in Manhattan. Supporters laid the cause to the beating he suffered at the federal detention center, though that seems unlikely, given the passage of time. After a protracted legal battle by his widow over whether the convicted communist/decorated war hero could be stripped of the right to be buried at Arlington National Cemetery, his ashes were finally interred there on January 17, 1969.

In the weeks before Thompson was caught in California, he, Green, and Hall had been meeting regularly in Brooklyn to discuss strategy. Green had begun writing for party publications under assumed names. He even attended a party conference in Connecticut, traveling from his hiding spot in Chicago and disappearing again before the conference ended. He also worked on a book, *The Enemy Forgotten*, a political history that he hoped might provide some context for all that he and his friends had been through.

The longer Green and Winston—who by now had moved to Chicago as well—remained at large, the more it bothered the FBI. They were tenacious in trying to track the men down, harassing Green's wife, Lil, and the rest of his family, interfering with their ability to work (they would interview potential bosses to make sure they knew of the family connection) and making life as tough as they could to try to force someone to flip on Green. They frightened Green's mother, intimating that Green could be killed. They bugged Lil's apartment and telephone and often sneaked in while she was out to conduct illicit searches—a routine practice that the agents involved knew was illegal, and also knew had been ordered by Hoover.[34]

It became a game of sorts for Lil, who was spending a lot of time with Doris Fine, whose husband, Fred, was among the second-wave of defendants who had disappeared. M. Wesley Swearingen was a rookie FBI agent assigned with a partner to maintain surveillance on Lil. Swearingen had never done surveillance before; his partner, born and raised in Brooklyn, didn't know how to drive. The women, when out running errands, would drive slowly until they figured out which car was following them, then at railroad tracks would time their crossing for just seconds before the gate-arm dropped. They would also spend hours sunbathing, giving the agents an eyeful—and making them roast in their dark suits in the uncomfortable heat.[35]

But it was also a grueling time for her—as it was for Green, who was living in Chicago close to his family but only able to communicate surreptitiously and through intermediaries. By late 1955, with the Korean War over, McCarthy toothless and condemned by his Senate colleagues, and the wave of anti-communist hysteria largely spent, Green and Winston began talking about ending their exile, presumably with permission from the rest of the party leadership. They feared that Winston, who was black, would be beaten, though there was no clear evidence that he was at any more risk than Green. Still, they reasoned that if Green turned himself in first, with maximum publicity, enough attention would be focused on the FBI that Winston could then follow safely.

There were many reasons to be fearful. The national paranoia had faded, but fears of Soviet spying ran rampant, and the arms race was in full swing against both the backdrop of the cold war and a steady stream of anti-communist movies from Hollywood. The Rosenbergs had been executed sixteen months earlier—their fate sealed by the same Supreme Court that backed the Smith Act. Still, there had been enough of a thaw domestically, Green believed, that it was time to go home. "New political winds are blowing," Green wrote in an open letter to newspapers heralding his decision to come in from hiding. "These give hope that the curtain of fear behind which democratic liberties were undermined and destroyed will be lifted. They also give reason for confidence that the day is not far off when the political rights of communists will be restored." Besides, he said, life on the lam was "in many ways harsher than that of imprisonment," and even further from the touch of family and friends. In prison, at least, he could have visitors.

In early February, as they laid their plans, Green moved from Chicago to the home of yet another couple of supporters in New Jersey, just a few miles from Manhattan. Green liked the house, liked the open space behind it with a pond wide enough for ice-skating. On the last Sunday in February of 1956, he strapped on the skates once more and stepped out onto the ice, his jacket open to the unseasonably warm sun as he glided over the bumpy surface, the wind ruffling his curly, thinning hair. The simple act of skating was an expression of freedom, an opportunity seized, and there would not be any more such moments for the next few years. With the step he was about to take, Green knew he would have even less freedom in the near term, but more freedom later, once it was all over—"the long dark tunnel I knew I had to pass through if I was to reach sunlight again."[36]

The newspapers that weekend had carried stories built around Green's letter, saying that after five years on the run, he was going to turn himself in. On Monday morning, February 27, wearing his good blue suit and a red tie beneath a gabardine topcoat, Gil Green tucked a fat envelope under his arm, hugged his New Jersey hosts good-bye, and climbed into a car driven by a man identified only as Sam; Sam's wife, Irma, rode along. The drive from the New Jersey house to the Hudson Tubes station was short. The plan was to drop Green off so he could take the train alone into Manhattan, making it harder for authorities to trace where he had been, and harder to find accomplices to arrest. Green knew that once the FBI had him in custody, Hoover would spare no effort trying to track down those who had helped him stay out of prison for so long—an embarrassment for the agency.

As Sam drove, the three comrades hid their nervousness behind idle chatter. There was a lot to talk about. Earlier that day in Moscow, Nikita S. Khrushchev had been reaffirmed as the leader of the Communist Party, which was still locked in a power struggle following the death of Joseph Stalin three years earlier.[37] In Montgomery, Alabama, blacks and their supporters in the fight for civil rights were nearly three months into a crippling bus boycott that began with the act of a single individual, Rosa Parks. McCarthy was dead, but the blacklists were still consulted, forcing a generation of political leftists from apolitical careers—teaching, nursing, doctoring—because of the stain of communism. A few blocks from the station, Irma reached over the back of the seat to hand Green a memento: a pen that she hoped he'd be able to keep during the personal trials to come.

At the Hudson Tubes stop, Sam pulled up to the curb, and they all got out. Green hugged them both and thanked them for their help, then quickly slipped alone to the underground platform, where he waited nervously for the next train and the short ride under the Hudson River. He emerged in lower Manhattan around 11:30 A.M., just another man in an overcoat on the city streets.

The first step: Find a mailbox for the package, which contained his manuscript for the book on political history. Then Green made his way to Greenwich Village and, at the corner of Seventh Avenue and Barrow Street, hailed a cab, a 1954 Plymouth. Green told driver Sidney Lapidus that he wanted to go to the federal courthouse at Foley Square. As Lapidus maneuvered the busy Manhattan streets, Green told him who he was and asked him to take his time, cruise around a bit if he had to, then let him out precisely at noon at the foot of the courthouse stairs. There would be a big tip if his arrival was timed as he wanted. Lapidus, who later told FBI agents that he had no idea who Green was or what he meant by "turning himself in," did as Green wished and precisely at noon pulled up to the curb, where a throng of some five hundred people had gathered.

As some of the crowd peered in, Green paid the seventy-five-cent fare and gave Lapidus a five-dollar tip, then stepped out into the warm embrace of his wife, Lil, and their three children, who had come in from Chicago along with his brother Benjamin. His other brother, Harry, had flown in from Los Angeles for the occasion. It was an emotional reunion. Green's youngest son, Ralph, was ten, which meant he had been fatherless for half of his life. "Do you recognize me?" Green asked. "I think I do, Dad," the boy answered.[38]

The reporters had their own questions. Where had he been all this time? "I've been in People's Town, U.S.A., at the corner of Constitution Avenue and Bill of Rights Street," Green said, deflecting the question with a jab at federal authorities. The reporters weren't satisfied, but Green wasn't about to give specifics. "Let's just say I've been enjoying a warm winter." Green greeted well-wishers and old friends in the crowd and delivered one more jab. "Now that I've given myself up, the FBI can release a couple of hundred agents and use them to restore order in Alabama." With that, Green and his family climbed the granite steps and entered the courthouse, making their way to the office of U.S. Attorney Paul W. Williams, where Green's lawyer, John J. Abt, was waiting. After a few moments alone with Lil and the kids, Gilbert Green was officially taken into custody, trading one sort of prison for another.

THIRTEEN

Hollow Vindication

In late summer of 1953, Roberta Vinson, the Supreme Court chief justice's wife, had been feeling so poorly that the Vinsons' family physician, Dr. Henry Ecker, was making a series of house calls to tend to her. He was summoned to the couple's Washington, D.C., apartment once again around 1:00 A.M. on September 8, but this time for a different patient—Vinson himself, who had awakened in extreme discomfort. A little more than an hour later, the affable Kentuckian and poker-playing pal of President Truman was dead of a massive heart attack.[1]

Vinson's death—Frankfurter famously pronounced it evidence "that there is a God"—would radically change the Court's legal perspective. His vacancy was the first for new president Dwight D. Eisenhower, who promptly nominated California governor Earl Warren. Warren was a former state attorney general with a law-and-order reputation and in 1948 had been Dewey's running mate against Truman. He had also set aside his own ambitions for the White House in favor of Eisenhower, helping clear the way for the former general to become the Republican Party's nominee in the 1952 election. If the nomination wasn't a straight payoff, it was pretty close. But Eisenhower also thought there was some synchronicity in their views of justice and the role of the Supreme Court. Eisenhower thought he was appointing a moderate Republican like himself, with a deep respect for law and order and a belief in "reasonable" restrictions on individual rights; after all, as California attorney general, Warren had urged and backed the roundup and imprisonment of Japanese Americans during World War II. As chief justice, however, Warren proved to be a disappointment to Eisenhower. Warren reclaimed the sense of California progressivism that was pervasive when he entered politics and displayed an unanticipated—at least by Eisenhower—respect for individual rights and the First Amendment.[2]

And the Warren Court would end the Smith Act roundups.

By the time Warren assumed the top spot on the bench, 145 people had been charged under the Smith Act, and most of the cases were still working their way through the federal court system.[3] The appeals were routinely rejected by the higher courts, who saw them within the framework of the Dennis decision. One case, though, was a little different. Yates v. United States was from Warren's native California and centered on Oleta Yates and thirteen other West Coast leaders of the Communist Party who had been indicted under the Smith Act in August 1951—a month after the Dennis Supreme Court decision. Like the Foley Square defendants, Yates and her codefendants had been convicted. Like the others, they appealed.

The Yates trial, held in Judge William C. Mathes's second-floor courtroom in the Federal Building in Los Angeles, was devoid of the rancor that had coursed through Medina's courtroom (though the anti-communist bias remained in place).[4] But the prosecution's approach was the same. Relying on paid informants and turncoats, U.S. Attorney Walter S. Binns persuaded jurors in the early winter of 1952 that Yates and the other defendants had, like the Foley Square defendants, advocated that communism supplant the U.S. government through violent revolution. There were some subtle differences in the cases. Unlike Medina, Mathes did not tell jurors as they began deliberations that to violate the Smith Act, the defendants had to have used language that could reasonably be expected to incite action. Mathes had also defined "organize" as meaning that the party had been engaged in ongoing efforts to recruit members, which is protected under the First Amendment. The Yates appeal brief contained many more arguments, but those two elements were the only ones that raised significantly unique issues.[5]

The *Yates* appeal reached the new Warren Court at an opportune moment. In the six years since the *Dennis* decision, four of the nine justices, including the chief justice, had changed. The four departures were men who "had taken a deferential approach" to laws curtailing the actions of communists. They were replaced by judges who put more weight on individual liberties than on the privileges of the state. "The difference," wrote legal historian Geoffrey Stone, "was palpable."[6] Meanwhile, Justice Frankfurter had grown increasingly concerned about the legacy of *Dennis*. He came to recognize—despite having written a concurring opinion—that the decision had unleashed the dogs, as it were, on American communists and represented an improper compromise of First Amendment protections of free speech and assembly. While Frankfurter believed the government had a right to limit speech for its own protection, he was appalled by the wave of Smith Act prosecutions. In his concurring opinion he wrote that "history teaches that the independence of the judiciary is jeopardized when the courts become embroiled in the passions of the day and assume primary responsibility in choosing between competing political, economic, and social pressures. Primary responsibility for adjusting the interests which compete in the situation before us of necessity belongs to the Congress." In other words, he argued that it was up to Congress to mediate such issues. But he came to realize that the Court had failed in its responsibility to protect the core principles of the Constitution and the Bill of Rights.[7] Frankfurter directed his clerks to search for appeals cases that the Court could take up that might limit the effects of *Dennis* without resorting to an outright and embarrassing reversal of the earlier opinion. *Yates* fit the bill.[8]

Ultimately, the Court turned to a series of cases. In what has become known as "Red Monday," the Court issued four opinions on June 17, 1957, that effectively ended the communist persecutions and put a legal nail in the coffin of McCarthyism. The cases had no overt links to each other, other than that the laws involved had been used to target politically active communists. In *Watkins v. United States*, the court curtailed the HUAC's ability to compel answers under threat of a contempt citation, finding that it must prove the sought-after information had a legislative purpose—which ended the worst excesses of the congressional witch-hunt. In *Sweezy v. New Hampshire*, the Court ruled that state bodies must meet that same standard, ending parallel witch-hunts at the state level. And in *Service v. Dulles*, the Court ruled in favor of John S. Service, a longtime State Department employee who challenged his dismissal after a McCarthy-inspired Loyalty Review Board hearing concluded there was "reasonable doubt" about his loyalty. The ruling established that innuendo was no longer enough to cost someone a job.

In *Yates v. United States*, the Court seized upon the minor points within the appeal to undermine the Smith Act, establishing a bar of proof so high that it was doubtful that even the initial *Dennis* case would have survived.

The *Yates* decision was written by Justice John Marshall Harlan, who had joined the bench after Jackson's death in October 1954, and who, as an appeals court judge, had written an opinion upholding a different Smith Act conviction. Warren assigned him to write the *Yates* decision, which, as it did for Frankfurter, represented a change of judicial heart for Harlan. The opinion was, as historian Michal Belknap described it, "long, complex, and painfully dull . . . difficult reading even for a lawyer, but it was a model of scholarship and technical precision."[9] A more literary critic, Harry Kalven, described it as "a sort of *Finnegans Wake* of impossibly nice distinctions."[10]

Harlan, who may have been trying to explain away his earlier opinion upholding the Smith Act, wrote that the *Yates* case was problematic because Mathes's definition of "organize" was too broad. Nor was it clear whether the jury had convicted the *Yates* defendants of "teaching and advocating" revolution, upheld as illegal in *Dennis*, or whether they had been convicted of organizing, a more problematic issue under the First Amendment. In the end the Court ruled that intent is not good enough to establish that teaching or advocating revolution violated the Smith Act. The bar was higher; the proof had to show a reasonable expectation of action.

The decision ordered the acquittal of five of the *Yates* defendants and set aside the convictions of nine others, leaving the decision of whether to retry them up to the government. But the ruling effectively gutted the Smith Act, forcing prosecutors to prove that defendants did not just preach a political belief that the government should be overthrown and replaced by communism, but that their advocacy was aimed at achieving that result. Without incitement, there was no crime. And with that, the Supreme Court brought the Smith Act prosecutions to a screeching halt. No new cases were filed; existing cases went away; none of the *Yates* defendants were retried.

Historian Ellen Schrecker has written about the overall effect on American political and social life of the excesses of the anti-communist purge, and it is worth contemplating here. In many ways, trying to quantify the effect is like trying to measure a void. It's a speculative exercise. We know that the overt enrollment in the CPUSA dropped from the size of a small city at its peak to the size of a small village at its ebb. Never strong, it ceased to be a political factor where at one time it had at least been able to win some low-level elected seats—including Davis's position on the New York City Council. The party has yet to recover.

But the "Red scare," which the *Dennis* decision helped propel by giving legal sanction to political persecution, reached far beyond the party itself. What can't be known is how the exile of leftists affected the union movement; how the summary dismissal of teachers and doctors and lawyers warped the course of education policy, medical delivery, and the courts; how the marginalization of progressive politics shifted the electoral mainstream to the right. The purge had a deep effect on the State Department, particularly the Asia desk, where China experts were ousted as suspected communist sympathizers. Would America's involvement in Vietnam have occurred had they remained in place? There clearly would have been different policies and trajectories in all of those scenarios, but how much and to what effect can never be known. What is clear is that the *Dennis* decision was the victory of the mob over the minority.

The *Yates* decision reined in the mob. But the decision focused on process, and it didn't void the convictions of Dennis, Green, Davis, Gates, and the others convicted in Medina's courtroom. In fact, Belknap suggests that given the fervency of their advocacy, those defendants might well have had their convictions upheld under the new standards set in the *Yates* decision. Stone suggests otherwise, since the *Dennis* defendants didn't have a specific course of action. Regardless, by the time the *Yates* decision came down, most of the *Dennis* defendants had already finished serving their time.

Six of them—Dennis, Stachel, Davis, Potash, Williamson, and Gates—had been released in early 1955, after good behavior trimmed their five-year sentences to three years and eight months. Williamson was deported to England, then returned to his native Scotland in May 1955, even though he had lived in the United States since age ten.[11] Potash left the country on his own a few weeks after his release from prison, choosing to move to Poland rather than await a deportation order. He traveled to other parts of the communist bloc, including China, before sneaking back into the United States only to be caught living under an assumed name in Bronxville, New York, on January 4, 1957—while the Supreme Court was deliberating in *Yates*—and sentenced to two years for immigration law violations. After his release the government declined to seek his deportation, in part because there was no place to send him—neither Poland nor the Soviet Union would take him in. Potash remained active in the CPUSA and lived out his years in the Washington Heights section of Manhattan.[12]

But the world into which they emerged was radically different from when they were convicted. Under the terms of their release, they were barred from resuming their political lives until December 1955. Once that had passed, and they began trying to rebuild the party, they were confronted with a deep internal divide, with Foster—somewhat recovered from his strokes—and Hall representing the pro-Soviet wing, and Dennis and Gates part of a faction that wanted to move the party to a more independent status, reacting to and reflecting the realities of American political and economic life. In a sense, it was a resurfacing of the divide that led to Browder's ouster in 1945.

The party, already deeply shattered by the Smith Act indictments and convictions, was about to confront an all but fatal blow. On February 24, Soviet premier Nikita Khrushchev, in a secret speech to the Twentieth Congress of the Soviet party, denounced Stalin as a paranoid killer who compromised the Soviet Union's ability to defend itself against Hitler by ordering the executions of top military leaders. The revelations stunned communists worldwide—even though many already knew of the 1930s purges and the unexplained disappearances of friends and comrades. For the American faithful, the revelations shook them to the core. Peggy Dennis read a copy of the speech brought home by her husband just before it was reported in the *New York Times*.

"I lay in the half-darkness, the typed pages illuminated only by a bedside light," she wrote. "The cold printed words ricocheted like bouncing pellets. . . . The new Soviet leadership was admitting, three years after Stalin's death to what had been a years-long, deliberate extermination by execution and imprisonment of hundreds of thousands of Socialist, party, and non-party cadre—scapegoats for a misfired economic or political policy which could not be admitted to have been wrong." She described it as a "thirty-year life's commitment that lay shattered. I lay sobbing low, hiccupping whimpers." The American party, already severely weakened by the actions of the U.S. government, fell apart. Those who hadn't dropped out in fear now quit because of shattered illusions, exacerbated by Foster's continued alignment of the party with Moscow, which in June reacted with violence to a workers' strike in Poland and in October responded to a reform movement in Hungary with an invasion.

Dennis himself continued on, trying to revive the socialist dream that brought him to the party in the first place, but the internal squabbles took a toll. As Hall, recently freed from prison, sought to assume the top party post at the annual convention in December 1959, Dennis suffered a debilitating stroke. A few months later, he was diagnosed with lung cancer, and he died January 31, 1961. Foster, who became chairman emeritus with Hall's ascension, died in Moscow eight months later. Davis also died of lung cancer, on August 22, 1964. Stachel, who wrote editorials for the *Daily Worker* after his release from prison, died on New Year's Eve in 1966 after battling heart and kidney issues that first surfaced while he was serving his prison sentence in Danbury, Connecticut.[13]

Gates, another of the defendants released from prison early, resumed his work with the party, too, but in the wake of the Khrushchev revelations and the Soviet clampdown in Hungary, he became disillusioned. As the Foster-Hall faction began to dominate the party, and to Gates's mind usurp the wishes of the party rank and file to move away from Moscow control, Gates quit in January 1958. In a gripping televised interview with a young Mike Wallace, Gates said he left because the party "no longer believes in the freedom that it professes to have as its goal." Gates blamed "unshaken faith" in the Moscow line for helping "the Communist Party go down the drain" and said that while "it contributed a great deal in the past twenty-five years to change America, it was unable to change itself and lost touch with American reality. It kept believing in things that it was no longer possible to believe in."[14] Gates went on to work as researcher for the International Ladies' Garment Workers Union and eventually retired to North Miami Beach, where he died of heart disease and a stroke on May 22, 1992.[15]

Henry Winston had no such change of heart, but he endured a series of health troubles. In prison, Winston was diagnosed with a brain tumor that cost him his sight. He underwent surgery in 1960 and was released the next year after President John F. Kennedy commuted his sentence on humanitarian grounds. Winston traveled to Moscow, where he received further treatment that he claimed improved his eyes, although his vision was never restored. He sued the U.S. government, contending that negligence by prison authorities allowed the tumor to grow until he was blinded. After winning a challenge before the Supreme Court in 1963 that affirmed his right to sue the government, Winston dropped the case as a personal distraction, and in 1966 he joined Hall as cochair of the party. In 1976, while he was in Moscow to celebrate his sixty-fifth birthday, the Soviet Union awarded him the Order of the October Revolution to recognize what it described as his efforts on behalf of "peace, democracy, and social progress." Winston was back in Moscow a decade later for more medical treatment and died there after a long but undisclosed illness.[16]

Winter also resumed his party activities, including chairing the Michigan party, and eventually became editor of The Worker and The World, successor papers to the Daily Worker that Gates once edited. At age eighty-five, he was in Manhattan on November 16, 1991, giving a speech at the party headquarters. Moments later he collapsed with a fatal heart attack.[17]

It's fitting that Green, as one of the last of the convicted men to turn himself in, was also the last to leave prison. He had been given an added three-year sentence for jumping bail and served five and a half years altogether before being released from Leavenworth in June of 1961, four years after the Yates decision and ten years after the Supreme Court upheld his own conviction—which meant he had spent a decade removed from his wife and children. In a last bit of legerdemain, federal prison officials transferred Green to New York City five days before his scheduled release, ostensibly so he could be rearrested on fresh charges accusing him of being a party member (all of the defendants faced those charges, but they eventually were dropped). The real reason, he discovered years later after getting copies of his files from the FBI, was the desire of the prison warden to thwart any plans for a demonstration at the prison marking his release.

In a sad turn of fate, Lil, his partner of some thirty-five years, died less than three years later, in 1964. Green also resumed his party activities, first in Chicago, then in New York, writing and channeling his efforts to oppose the war in Vietnam. He eventually left the party in 1991 when it backed the Soviet hard-liners' attempted coup against Mikhail Gorbachev. He died in Ann Arbor, near where his son Daniel lived, on May 3, 1997.[18]

Of the original twelve indicted men, Hall enjoyed the highest continuing profile and went on to lead the party for more than four decades—far longer than any of his Russian comrades had led the Soviet party. Once Hall wrested control of the party from the terminally ill Dennis and pushed the aging Foster aside, he never let go. He backed the Soviet invasion of Czechoslovakia in 1968—Green opposed it—and generally kept the party policy in synch with the hard-liners in Moscow, even after the hard-liners began fading. Hall also became the party's quadrennial candidate for U.S. president, running in 1972, 1976, 1980, and 1984, the last two times with Angela Davis as his running mate. In electoral terms, Hall was an asterisk: His top vote was 58,709 in the 1976 election in which Democrat Jimmy Carter beat Republican Gerald Ford in the wake of the Watergate scandal. The party, a shell of itself, eventually stopped running presidential candidates because of the expense.

Still, Hall hewed to the hard line. With the fall of the Berlin Wall in 1989, and change formenting in Russia, Hall stayed with the old guard and opposed Gorbachev's reforms. After the collapse of the Soviet Union in 1991, Hall continued on as a lone Stalinist voice until he died on October 13, 2000. As the *New York Times* noted in its obituary, when the Soviet Union ceased to exist, Hall turned his vision of the future to the last bastion of Stalin-style communism on the planet. "The world should see what North Korea has done," Hall said at the time. "In some ways it's a miracle. If you want to take a nice vacation, take it in North Korea."[19]

NOTES

ABBREVIATIONS

Newspapers

AP	Associated Press
CSM	*Christian Science Monitor*
DW	*Daily Worker*
LAT	*Los Angeles Times*
NYDN	*New York Daily News*
NYHT	*New York Herald Tribune*
NYT	*New York Times*
NYWT	*New York World-Telegram*
WP	*Washington Post*

Archives and Papers

CPUSA Archives	Communist Party–United States of America Archives, Tamiment Library, New York University, New York City
Green Papers	Gil Green Papers, Tamiment 95, Tamiment Library, New York University, New York
HST	Harry S. Truman Library and Museum, Independence, Missouri
Medina Papers	Harold R. Medina Papers, MC174, Seeley G. Mudd Manuscript Library, Princeton University, Princeton, N.J.
NLG	National Lawyers Guild Collection, BANC MSS 99/280, Bancroft Library, University of California, Berkeley
Silvermaster file	Available online through the Education and Research Institute, http://education-research.org/CSR/Holdings/Silvermaster/Silvermaster.htm

PREFACE

1. See Geoffrey R. Stone, *Perilous Times: Free Speech in Wartime from the Sedition Act of 1798 to the War on Terrorism* (New York: W. W. Norton, 2004).

2. Robert K. Murray, *Red Scare: A Study in National Hysteria, 1919–1920* (New York: McGraw-Hill, 1964), 68–81.

3. For a full exploration of this theme, see Garry Wills's *Bomb Power: The Modern Presidency and the National Security State* (New York: Penguin Press, 2010).

4. "Group's Attack on Justice Dept. Lawyers Divides Conservatives," NYT, March 10, 2010.

ONE. FEAR, AND HOWARD SMITH'S LAW

1. Description drawn from weather reports in NYT, December 25–27, 1940.

2. "Deadline Passes for Alien Listing; Big Late Rush Here," NYT, December 27, 1940.

3. "Alien Registering Opens in Two Weeks," NYT, June 23, 1940.

4. Geoffrey R. Stone, *Perilous Times: Free Speech in Wartime from the Sedition Act of 1798 to the War on Terrorism* (New York: W. W. Norton, 2004), 251.

5. For a full discussion of prewar spying and Roosevelt's response, see Joseph E. Persico, *Roosevelt's Secret War: FDR and World War II Espionage* (New York: Random House, 2001).

6. See Bruce J. Dierenfield's *Keeper of the Rules: Congressman Howard W. Smith of Virginia* (Charlottesville: University Press of Virginia, 1987), from which these biographical details are drawn.

7. Ibid., 9.

8. Ibid., 15–16.

9. "Ex-Rep. Smith Dies at Home in Virginia," NYT, October 4, 1976.

10. "Growing Espionage Met, Says Murphy," NYT, March 24, 1939.

11. "The Report of the President's Temporary Commission on Employee Loyalty," HST, Student Research File (B File), Loyalty Program, Box 1, 5–6.

12. "Many Offer Help in Anti-Spy Drive," NYT, September 25, 1939.

13. Dierenfield, *Keeper of the Rules*, 77.

14. "Alien Bills Held Civil Rights Peril," NYT, May 9, 1939.

15. Dierenfield, *Keeper of the Rules*, 79.

16. "Roosevelt Signs Bill to List Aliens," NYT, June 30, 1940.

Two. From Spies to Speeches

1. The Soviet spying apparatus had several incarnations over the years covered in this book. For the sake of clarity, the modern acronym is used.

2. "Police Asked to Hunt for Woman Radical," NYT, December 19, 1937.

3. Elizabeth Bentley, *Out of Bondage* (1952; New York: Ivy Books, 1988), 61.

4. Details drawn from Lauren Kessler, *Clever Girl: Elizabeth Bentley, the Spy Who Ushered in the McCarthy Era* (New York: HarperCollins, 2003), 121–124; and Kathryn S. Olmsted, *Red Spy Queen: A Biography of Elizabeth Bentley* (Chapel Hill: University of North Carolina Press, 2002), chapter 5.

5. Biographical details, unless otherwise noted, are drawn from Kessler, *Clever Girl*, 14–27.

6. Olmsted, *Red Spy Queen*, 9–18.

7. Kessler, *Clever Girl*, 109.

8. Olmsted, *Red Spy Queen*, 77–79.

9. Bentley, *Out of Bondage*, 198.

10. Igor Gouzenko, *This Was My Choice*, 2nd ed. (Montreal: Palm Publishers, 1968), 219–237.

11. Diary of William Lyon Mackenzie King, private memo, September 6, 1945, Library and Archives of Canada, http://king.collectionscanada.ca/EN/default.asp.

12. Ibid., September 7, 1945.

13. Louis F. Budenz, *This Is My Story* (New York: McGraw-Hill, 1947), 155–163.

14. "Daily Worker Editor Renounces Communism for Catholic Faith," NYT, October 11, 1945.

15. See Silvermaster file, "urgent" New York field report "director and SAC," November 8, 1945, 65-56402-1; memo from Ladd to Hoover, November 9, 1945, 65-56402-8; and "Report of Special Agent Harold V. Kennedy," December 3, 1945, 65-56402-440X.

16. Allen Weinstein and Alexander Vassiliev, *The Haunted Wood: Soviet Espionage in America—The Stalin Era* (New York: Random House, 1999), 103–105.

17. Olmsted, *Red Spy Queen*, 106.

18. "More Canadians Rounded Up as King Implicates Russians," NYT, February 17, 1946.

19. Bert Andrews, *Washington Witch Hunt* (New York: Random House, 1948), 10–11.

20. "Truman Sets Up Board to Study Purge of Reds in U.S. Agencies," NYHT, November 26, 1946. See also "The Report of the President's Temporary

Commission on Employee Loyalty," HST, Student Research File (B File), Loyalty Program, Box 1, and Truman's March 21, 1947, order "Prescribing Procedures for the Administration of an Employees Loyalty Program in the Executive Branch of the Government," available at http://www.h-net.org/~hst203/documents/loyal.html.

21. For a full exploration of this, see Olmsted, *Red Spy Queen*, 114–118.

22. Hoover to Clark, February 12, 1947, Silvermaster file, 65-56402-2001.

23. Tamm to Hoover, January 13, 1947, Silvermaster file, 65-56402-2007.

24. Hoover to Clark, January 27, 1947, Silvermaster file, 65-56402-2012.

25. Ladd to Hoover, March 10, 1947, Silvermaster file, 65-56402-2137.

26. "Hollywood Briefs," NYT, June 8, 1947.

27. Affidavit dated September 28, 1948, in support of motion to quash the indictments, which details the leaks from the grand jury process. CPUSA Archives, Box 39. Also see "Red Spy Ring to Be Broken Soon by U.S.," by Edward Nellor, *New York Sun*, October 16, 1947.

28. "Rogge Says Clark Plans 'Witch Hunt,'" NYT, November 8, 1947; "Washington Calling, by Marquis Childs: Spy Investigation," WP, November 21, 1947.

29. Article, without headline, was part of a motion to dismiss the indictment filed September 28, 1948. Cited article by Howard Rushmore in the *New York Journal-American*, April 2, 1948.

30. H. B. Fletcher to D. M. Ladd, March 31, 1948, Silvermaster file, 65-56402-378.

31. Scheidt to Hoover, April 3, 1948, Silvermaster file, 65-56402-3196.

32. H. B. Fletcher to Attorney General and FBI Director, April 3, 1948, Silvermaster file, 65-56402-3185.

33. Kessler, *Clever Girl*, 158.

34. "Red Curb Outlined by House Member," NYT, April 9, 1947.

35. Michal R. Belknap, "Cold War in the Courtroom," in *American Political Trials*, ed. Michal R. Belknap, revised and expanded ed. (Westport, Conn.: Praeger, 1994), 210–211. Also see McGohey's handwritten summary of communications in the case, McGohey Papers, HST, Box 1, Folder "Correspondence, memoranda, & notes."

36. McGohey Papers, HST, Box 1, Folder "Correspondence, memoranda, & notes."

37. "Dennis Is Cited, Contempt Charged," NYT, April 10, 1947.

38. "Congress in Quandary over U.S. Communists," NYT, March 7, 1948.

39. Appointment calendar in Clark Papers, HST, Box 97.

40. John Earl Haynes, Harvey Klehr, and Alexander Vassiliev, *Spies: The Rise and Fall of the KGB in America* (New Haven: Yale University Press, 2009), 275.

41. McGohey Papers, HST, Box 1, Folder "Correspondence, memoranda, & notes."

42. David McCullough, *Truman* (New York: Simon and Schuster, 1992), 632–633.

THREE. A SUDDEN AND VIOLENT STORM

1. Gil Green, *Cold War Fugitive: A Personal Story of the McCarthy Years* (New York: International Publishers, 1984), 1–5.

2. Ibid., 2.

3. Ibid., 5.

4. McGohey to Clark, July 15, 1948, McGohey Papers, HST, Box 11, Folder "McGohey-Smith Act case file correspondence, etc."

5. "12 U.S. Commie Chiefs Face N.Y. Indictment," *Washington Times-Herald*, July 20, 1948.

6. Ladd to Hoover, July 28, 1949, Green Papers, Box 7.

7. Ladd to Hoover, July 20, 1948, Green Papers, Box 7; "Report on the Communist Party (U.S.A.)," NYT, March 30, 1947.

8. "12 U.S. Communists Indicted in Anti-Government Plot; Foster, Davis, Others Seized," NYT, July 21, 1948; "FBI Arrests 7 C.P. Leaders in Frame-Up," *DW*, July 21, 1948; and Ladd to Hoover, July 20, 1948, Green Papers, Box 7.

9. "7 Communist Heads Out on Bail," *DW*, July 22, 1948.

10. "8 Communist Chiefs at Liberty on Bail; 9th in Court Today," NYT, July 22, 1948.

11. Ibid.

12. "Indicted Reds Get Wallace Support," NYT, July 22, 1948.

13. "9 of 12 Indicted Reds Found," *WP*, July 22, 1948.

14. Statement dated July 20, 1948, Civil Rights Congress Papers, Schomburg Center for Research in Black Culture, New York Public Library, Reel 2, 919–920.

15. "They Depend on Councilman Davis," *DW*, August 15, 1948.

16. Affidavit in NLG, George W. Crockett Files, Smith Act Trial, Carton 2, Folder "Motions, Memorandi, Briefs, Opinions, Part II."

17. Kessler, *Red Spy Queen*, 159–160.

18. Green's memoir, *Cold War Fugitive*, while clearly defending his political beliefs, offers a compelling overview.

19. Green, *Cold War Fugitive*, 7.

20. Ibid., 8.

21. Mari Jo Buhle, Paul Buhle, and Dan Georgakas, eds., *Encyclopedia of the American Left* (New York: Oxford University Press, 1998), 872–873.

22. Green, *Cold War Fugitive*, 22–23.

23. Green Papers, Box 7, FBI files.

24. "U.S. Protests to the Soviet over Reds' Activities Here; Warns of the Consequences," NYT, August 26, 1935.

25. "End Monopoly on Atom Bomb, Red Rally Told," *Chicago Daily Tribune*, May 2, 1946.

26. David Caute, *The Great Fear: The Anti-Communist Purge Under Truman and Eisenhower* (New York: Simon and Schuster, 1978). See chapter 9, "The Communist Party Goes Under"; 187 quoted.

27. "Ex-Red Reports Federal Spy Ring," WP, July 23, 1948.

28. John Chabot Smith, *Alger Hiss: The True Story* (New York: Holt, Rinehart and Winston, 1976), 161.

29. "Red 'Underground' in Federal Posts Alleged by Editor; In New Deal Era," NYT, August 4, 1948.

30. Smith, *Alger Hiss*, 164–165.

31. "President Is Blunt," NYT, August 6, 1948.

32. Smith, *Alger Hiss*, 167.

33. Ibid., 160–161. Whether Hiss was indeed a communist and working for the Soviets remains murky despite recent scholarship built on the Venona project of intercepted Soviet secret cables and the notes Alexander Vassiliev took of secret KGB files that have since been closed.

34. CPUSA Archives, Box 39, and Foster affidavit, NLG, George W. Crockett Files, Smith Act Trial, Carton 2, Folder "Conspiracy Indictment, individual indictment, Part I."

35. "Meetings Planned to Help Radicals," NYT, July 22, 1948.

36. Kaufman would go on to play much higher-profile roles in subsequent Smith Act trials, including (with Sacher) defending Elizabeth Gurley Flynn, the only top party leader not indicted in the case against Foster et al.

37. "Musicians Vote to Oust Sacher," NYT, September 11, 1948.

38. "Harry Sacher, Lawyer, Dead," NYT, May 23, 1963. All the brief profiles of the defense lawyers are drawn from NYT archives.

39. George Marion, *The Communist Trial: An American Crossroads* (New York: Fairplay Publishers, 1949), 182.

40. Judy Kutulas, *The American Civil Liberties Union and the Making of Modern Liberalism, 1930–1960* (Chapel Hill: University of North Carolina Press, 2006), 82–83.

41. An overview of Isserman's career can be found in NLG, Box 68, Records, 1936–1976, Folder, "Transcripts of two different interviews with Isserman."

42. Stanley I. Kutler, *An American Inquisition: Justice and Injustice in the Cold War* (New York: Hill & Wang, 1982), 156. This fine overview of the era devotes chapter 6 to the 1949 trial.

Four. The Judge, and the Mood

1. Hawthorne Daniel, *Judge Medina* (New York: Wilfred Funk, 1952), 217–218.

2. NLG, George W. Crockett Files, Carton 2, Folder "Conspiracy Indictment, individual indictment, Part I."

3. CPUSA Archives, Box 39; "12 Communists Get Short Court Stay," NYT, August 17, 1948; motion to recuse, November 4, 1948, NLG, George W. Crockett Files, Smith Act Trial, Carton 2, Folder "Conspiracy Indictment, individual indictment, Part III."

4. Letter to Richard Medina, August 23, 1948, Medina Papers, General Correspondence, 1948–1950, Box 40, Folder 1948-M.

5. "Potash Set Free on Bail of $5,000," NYT, March 4, 1948.

6. Letter to Ripley Ropes, March 5, 1948, Medina Papers, General Correspondence, 1948–1950, Box 40, Folder 1948-R.

7. Letter from Frankfurter to Judge Learned Hand, April 24, 1951, cited in J. Woodford Howard, "Commentary," *New York University Law Review* 70 (1995).

8. For a taste, see Harold R. Medina, "A New Judge Tries His First Case," *Cornell Law Quarterly* 34 (1948–1949).

9. Ronald L. Davis, *Duke: The Life and Image of John Wayne* (Norman: University of Oklahoma Press, 1998), 118.

10. J. Woodford Howard, "Advocacy in Constitutional Choice: The Cramer Treason Case, 1941–45," *American Bar Foundation Research Journal* 375 (1986): 376–377.

11. Unless otherwise noted, the family history details are from *Autobiography of Elizabeth Fash Medina and Biography of Joaquin Adolfo Medina*, self-published in 1960 by Stanley F. Medina (one of Harold Medina's sons).

12. U.S. Census records for 1920, Brooklyn Assembly District 17, District 1072, record this as happening in 1875, but the family history and Medina's birth date suggest the 1880 date is more likely.

13. Biographical details are from Sidney Fields, "Only Human: The Making of a Judge," *Daily Mirror*, February 6, 1949; "Rigors of Communists Trial Sentence Medina to Solitary Life," NYWT, September 6, 1949; and Daniel, *Judge Medina*, 10–15.

14. See the 1910 U.S. Census, Brooklyn Ward 3, District 606.

15. "Communists' Day in Court: Profile of the Judge," CSM, January 13, 1949.

16. "Push Judiciary Campaign," NYT, October 10, 1926.

17. J. Woodford Howard, "Judge Harold R. Medina: The 'Freshman' Years," *Judicature* 69 (October/November 1985): 127–138.

18. Daniel, *Judge Medina*, 169–170.

19. Letter to William W. Bailey, a lawyer in the Virgin Islands, August 19,

1948, Medina Papers, General Correspondence, 1948–1950, Box 40, Folder 1948-B.

20. Letter to John J. Buchanan, a friend in Pittsburgh, August 17, 1948, Medina Papers, General Correspondence, 1948–1950, Box 40, Folder 1948-B.

21. Unger believed this, and in interviews in the 1970s cited as evidence Marvin Schick's *Learned Hand's Court* (Baltimore: Johns Hopkins Press, 1970). But Schick only talks (66) about Medina's elevation to the Court of Appeals, which came well after the trial, and makes an improbable argument that Truman appointed Medina "to stifle criticism that his administration was soft on communism." By then, Truman was nearing the end of his second term and not overly concerned about perceptions of being soft on communism.

22. CPUSA Archives, Box 39, and opinion dated November 5, 1948, NLG, George W. Crockett Files, Smith Act Trial, Carton 2, Folder "Conspiracy Indictment, individual indictment, Part III."

23. Transcript of interview with J. Woodford Howard, May 22, 1979, NLG, Box 68, Records, 1936–1976, Folder "Transcripts of two different interviews with Isserman."

24. "They Depend on Councilman Davis," *DW*, August 15, 1948.

25. "Robert Thompson, U.S. Communist Leader, Dies," *NYT*, October 17, 1965.

26. "How a Communist Defended America," *DW*, August 15, 1948.

27. "Communist Party Offers Reward of $15,000 for Arrest of Men Who Stabbed Thompson," *NYT*; "$15,000 Reward Posted in Attack on Red Leader," *NYHT*; and "Attempt to Assassinate Bob Thompson: Communist Leader Stabbed, Beaten by Thugs Near Home," *DW*, all September 23, 1948.

28. "Red Rally Scores 'Fascists' Attack," *NYT*, September 24, 1948.

29. Green Papers, Box 8; Aarti Kotak, "Pearl Hart," 2004, Women's Legal History, Stanford University, http://womenslegalhistory.stanford.edu/papers04/HartP-Kotak04.pdf.

30. "Truman Is Urged to 'Clear' 12 Reds," *NYT*, September 23, 1948.

31. "Preventing War Now Places First as Issue in Poll," *NYT*, April 18, 1948.

32. "Dewey Los Angeles Talk Attacking Communism," transcript of the speech, *NYT*, September 25, 1948.

33. "Text of President Truman's Speech in Reply to Republican Charges on the 'Communist Issue,'" *NYT*, September 29, 1948.

34. Other histories and contemporary newspaper coverage refer to Foster's heart troubles, but the medical reports to the judge make it clear that Foster had suffered strokes.

35. The affidavits are in NLG, George W. Crockett Files, Smith Act Trial,

Carton 2, Folder "Conspiracy Indictment, individual indictment, Part IV."

36. Unless otherwise noted, the details and quotes are from Ralph C. James and Estelle James, "The Purge of the Trotskyites from the Teamsters," *Western Political Quarterly* 19, no. 1 (March 1966): 5–15.

37. Michal R. Belknap, *Cold War Political Justice: The Smith Act, the Communist Party, and American Civil Liberties* (Westport, Conn.: Greenwood Press, 1977), 38–39.

38. "Grant Dunne, CIO Boss, Ends Life in Minneapolis," *Chicago Tribune*, October 5, 1941.

39. Belknap, *Cold War Political Justice*, 40–41; "Sedition Case Mistrial Looms After Justice Eicher Dies," *WP*, December 1, 1944.

40. The exchange is in Medina Papers, General Correspondence, 1948–1950, Box 40, Folder 1948-G.

41. "Detective Is Arrested," *NYT*, November 21, 1948; "Guilty in Morals Case," *NYT*, December 28, 1948; "Burke Retrial Ordered," *NYT*, January 7, 1949; "Freed in Thompson Case," *NYT*, January 14, 1949.

FIVE. BATTLE LINES AND BATTLE SCARS

1. Transcript, 818; "400 Police on Duty as Communists Go on Trial Today," *NYT*, January 17, 1949.

2. "New Jury Panel Is Called for Reds' Trial," AP via *Baltimore Sun*, February 1, 1949, CPUSA Archives, Box 78, Folder 5.

3. "The Trial Was Longest, Most Noisy, Most Controversial in U.S. History," *Look*, October 24, 1949, 34; "Verdict Received by Tense Audience," *NYT*, October 15, 1949.

4. The notes are inordinately hard to decipher. They are in Medina Papers, Box 184, Motions, Notes, Communist Trial Materials and Notebooks.

5. Description drawn from news accounts, including illustration in "Sketchbook of the Communists' Trial," *NYT*, June 19, 1949; "Judge Medina Rules From Rocking Chair," *Baltimore News-Post*, January 21, 1949; "Police Stand By as Trial Begins," *NYT*, January 18, 1949; and "Party Line on Trial," *NYT*, March 27, 1949; transcript, 950.

6. Transcript, 822–824.

7. Ibid., 980–990 and 1053.

8. "Communist Plea Goes to High Court," *NYT*, January 8, 1949; "Indicted Reds Lose High Court Appeal," *NYT*, January 10, 1949.

9. Description is from the summary of the Supreme Court decision, *Fay v. People of the State of New York*, 332 U.S. 261 (1947).

10. See the case summary in the United States Court of Appeals, Second

Circuit decision in *United States v. Dennis et al.*, No. 242, Docket 21538. Decided August 1, 1950.

11. Transcript, 1121–1122.

12. Ibid., 1133.

13. Ibid., 1236–1237; "McGohey Tries to Bar Probe of Grand Jury," *DW*, January 20, 1949.

14. Letter to Ropes, January 24, 1949, Medina Papers, General Correspondence, 1948–1950, Box 40, Folder 1949-R.

15. Daniel, *Judge Medina*, 226.

16. Letter to Burrelle's, January 25, 1949, Medina Papers, General Correspondence, 1948–1950, Box 40, Folder 1949-B; letter to George Skouras, who had given Medina passes to his Skouras Theaters, mentions accepting tickets to a Brooklyn Dodgers game at Ebbets Field, October 14, 1949, ibid., Folder 1949-S.

17. "Trade Unionists Express Concern to Judge Medina over Grand Jury Selection," *California Eagle*, February 10, 1949.

18. Daniel, *Judge Medina*, 226–234.

19. Letter from Medina's secretary, E. Gorman, to Ethel Medina, February 4, 1949, Medina Papers, General Correspondence, 1948–1950, Box 40, Folder 1949-M.

20. "Judge Ends 'Delay'; Reproves Defense in Communist Trial," *NYT*, January 28, 1949.

21. Transcript, 2549–2550.

22. "Red Needling Doesn't Upset Gentle-Voiced Judge Medina," AP via *WP*, February 13, 1949.

23. "Liberty and Violence," *CSM*, Feburary 12, 1949.

24. Letter to Ropes, January 24, 1949, Medina Papers, General Correspondence, 1948–1950, Box 40, Folder 1949-R.

25. "Red Trial Expert Confesses Error," *NYT*, February 10, 1949.

26. "Text of Spellman Plea on Mindszenty," *NYT*, February 7, 1949.

27. "Scores Court Picketing," *NYT*, February 3, 1949.

28. "Truman Blasts 'Traitors' for Soviet Pledge," *WP*, March 4, 1949.

29. "Attack U.S. Jury System," *NYT*, March 4, 1949.

30. Lasky to Medina, undated other than "Friday," Medina Papers, General Correspondence, 1948–1950, Box 40, Folder 1949K–L.

SIX. THE TRIAL OPENS

1. Details from this court session are from the trial transcript, unless otherwise noted.

2. "Tentative Jury for Reds' Trial Is Headed by Negro Housewife," *NYHT*, March 10, 1949; AP dispatch from London, carried in several papers.

3. *Macon Telegraph* clipping in CPUSA Archives, Box 39, unnumbered folder.

4. Nathanson affidavit, CPUSA Archives, Box 39, unnumbered folder. This was a supporting affidavit to an August motion for mistrial citing juror misconduct by Janney.

5. "Barred by University, Red Talks in Street," NYT, January 12, 1949; "Hall Speech Canceled," NYT, January 23, 1949.

6. Biographical details, unless otherwise noted, are from Benjamin Davis, *Communist Councilman from Harlem* (New York: International Publishers, 1969), particularly chapter 1, "The World I Was Born Into," and chapter 8, "Death of My Father."

7. Ibid., chapter 4, "The Herndon Case." For a full discussion of the Herndon case, and the racism surrounding it, see Charles H. Martin, *The Angelo Herndon Case and Southern Justice* (Baton Rouge: Louisiana State University Press, 1976).

8. "The Congress: Work Done," *Time*, March 18, 1940.

9. "Communist Trial Echoes in City Council; Davis Loses Move to Censure Police Cordon," NYT, January 19, 1949; "Costello's Dinner Stirs Inquiry Plea," NYT, February 2, 1949.

10. The following details are from the transcript, 956, and "Dennis Discharges McCabe as Lawyer in Trial of 11 Reds," *New York Sun*, March 17, 1949.

11. Details regarding Dennis's life, unless otherwise noted, are from Peggy Dennis, *The Autobiography of an American Communist: A Personal View of a Political Life, 1925–1975* (Westport, Conn.: Lawrence Hill; Berkeley, Calif.: Creative Arts, 1977); quoted: "resigned himself" and "I stopped believing," 27; "Machine guns," 48; "invested," 68.

12. "Red March on City Hall Made Fiasco by Police," *LAT*, March 7, 1930.

13. "McGohey Declares Reds Here Trained Forces for Revolt," NYT, March 22, 1949; Dennis, *Autobiography of an American Communist*, 31.

Seven. Deserters and Spies

1. For details on Budenz's life, see Louis F. Budenz, *This Is My Story* (New York: McGraw-Hill, 1947); Herbert L. Packer, *Ex-Communist Witnesses: Four Studies in Fact Finding* (Stanford, Calif.: Stanford University Press, 1962), chapter 4; and Leon Applebaum, "Turmoil in Kenosha: The Allen-A Hosiery Dispute of 1928–1929," *Wisconsin Magazine of History* 70, no. 4 (Summer 1987): 281–303.

2. "Budenz Scores A.F. of L.," NYT, January 26, 1931.

3. "*Daily Worker* Editor Renounces Communism for Catholic Faith," NYT,

October 11, 1945; "Foster Calls Budenz 'Deserter' from Labor; Sheen Tells How Editor Re-joined Church," NYT, October 12, 1945.

4. "Memorandum for the File," September 30, 1948, McGohey Papers, Box 1, HST. The subpoena was initially for the start of the trial in October 1948, which ultimately was delayed several times.

5. See Whitman Bassow, "The Pre-Revolutionary Pravda and Tsarist Censorship," *American Slavic and East European Review* 13, no. 1 (Feb. 1954): 47–65.

6. Albert Parry, "On 'Aesopian' Language and Borrowings from Russian," *American Speech* 25, no. 3 (October 1950): 190–196.

7. Transcript, 3638, 3648; "Budenz Says Communists Here Plotted Civil War to Aid Russia," NYT, March 30, 1949.

8. Transcript, 3748–3751; "Budenz Describes a U.S. Politburo," NYT, March 31, 1949.

9. Transcript, 3713.

10. Ibid., 3627.

11. "Communists: Evolution or Revolution," *Time*, April 4, 1949.

12. Gil Green, *Cold War Fugitive: A Personal Story of the McCarthy Years* (New York: International Publishers, 1984), 34–35.

13. Transcript, 3382.

14. Ibid., 3360–3362.

15. Ibid., 3488–3491.

16. Ibid., 3656–3658.

17. Details are from several contemporary news accounts, including "Scores of Reds Mauled by Throngs Outside Rally," AP via *Washington Star*, April 2, 1949; "Pickets Jeer Commie Rally on North Side," *Pittsburgh Press*, April 3, 1949; "Pickets Push Reds as Rally Breaks Up in Wild Night," *Pittsburgh Post-Gazette*, April 3, 1949; and "Communist Rally Ends in Northside Riot," *Pittsburgh Post-Gazette*, April 4, 1949.

18. "Pickets Jeer Commie Rally on North Side," *Pittsburgh Press*, April 3, 1949.

19. "Communists: Unfair Surprise," *Time*, April 18, 1949.

20. Philbrick detailed his experiences in *I Led Three Lives* (New York: McGraw-Hill, 1952). See chapters 15 and 16 for details surrounding the trial.

21. Transcript, 4144–4145.

22. Philbrick, *I Led Three Lives*, 280–290.

23. Ibid., 6.

24. Ibid., 286.

25. Victor S. Navasky, *Naming Names* (New York: Viking, 1991), 32.

26. Transcript, 4220, 4251, 4261; "Communist Plot to 'Colonize' Key Industries Told at Trial," NYT, April 8, 1949.

27. Transcript, 4306.

28. Ibid., 4312–4315.

29. Ibid., 4352.
30. "Professor Terms Charge Nonsense," NYT, April 9, 1949.
31. "Art Notes," last item, NYT, February 5, 1944.
32. For Struik's version of the events, see "The Struik Case of 1951—Dirk Struik Treason Trial," Monthly Review, January 1993.
33. Details in this section are drawn from Nathanson affidavit, CPUSA Archives, Box 39, unnumbered folder. This was a supporting affidavit to an August motion for mistrial citing juror misconduct by Janney.

EIGHT. STOOL PIGEONS AND TURNCOATS

1. Victor S. Navasky, Naming Names (New York: Viking, 1991), 31.
2. Transcript, 4528; "Jury Hears Stalin Ordered Violence," NYT, April 14, 1949.
3. Nowell's testimony, while incidental to the trial, offers another explanation of why the Communist Party was so active in civil rights issues. See transcript, 4629, 4664–4665, 4710, and 4721. Nowell also had testified before the Dies Committee in 1939, making him one of the early semi-pro anti-communist witnesses.
4. Transcript, 4803–4805; "Red Invasion Plan Reported at Trial," NYT, April 23, 1949.
5. "Talk with Miss Calomiris," NYT, November 26, 1950.
6. "FBI Agent Tells How She Posed as Red," NYHT, April 29, 1949.
7. Transcript, 5022–5030; "Girl Aide of FBI Testifies of Seven Years as 'Communist,'" NYT, April 27, 1949.
8. Transcript, scattered references beginning 5022; "Girl Official of Party Stuns Reds at Trial," Chicago Daily Tribune, April 27, 1949.
9. Transcript, 5177–5178; "Communist Drive in Industry Bared," NYT, April 29, 1949.
10. Transcript, 5221; "Witness Parries Red Trial Thrusts," NYT, April 30, 1949.
11. "Medina Walks Out in Red Trial Clash," NYT, April 26, 1949.
12. Ibid.; transcript, 4967–4970.
13. Transcript, 5066–5071; "Judge, Lawyers Clash Again in Trial of Reds," St. Louis Post-Dispatch, April 27, 1949.
14. "'Rumpuses' of Reds Scored by Medina," NYT, April 28, 1949.
15. Transcript, 4978–4949.
16. "Rigors of Communists Trial Sentence Medina to Solitary Life," NYWT, September 6, 1949.
17. Letters from Medina to Arms in Medina Papers, General Correspondence, 1948–1950, Box 40, Folder 1949-A; "The Question Mark," Boston Public Library Professional Staff Association 4, no. 2 (March 1949).

18. Drawn from contemporary news coverage. See especially "Loyalty Rallies to Rival May Day March Set in 5 Cities, with 100,000 Likely in Event Here," NYT, April 23, 1949; "May Day March Down 8th Avenue Seen by 20,000," NYHT, May 1, 1949; and "Ship 'Em Out," INS via *Cincinnati Enquirer*, April 30, 1949.

19. "30,000 Catholics Protest on Reds," NYT, May 2, 1949.

20. Mari Jo Buhle, Paul Buhle, and Dan Georgakas, eds., *Encyclopedia of the American Left* (Urbana and Chicago: University of Chicago Press, 1992), 154.

21. Transcript, 5360–5367.

22. Ibid., 5259.

23. "Call to Gory War by Reds Here Cited," NYT, May 11, 1949.

24. Transcript, 6151; "FBI Informant Met Last Night with Red Group," *New York Sun*, May 18, 1949.

25. "History Repeated: The Dangers of Domestic Spying by Federal Law Enforcement," American Civil Liberties Union, May 29, 2007, available at http://www.aclu.org/images/asset_upload_file893_29902.pdf.

26. "FBI Scrutinizes Antiwar Rallies," NYT, November 23, 2003.

27. "Communists: Unfair Surprise," *Time*, April 18, 1949.

28. Transcript, 5528–5540; "Reds Defense Fails to Bar Book," *New York Post*, May 5, 1949; "Revolt Aim Is Basic Issue of Red Trial, Medina Says," NYWT, May 5, 1949; "Stalin War Alert to U.S. Reds Quoted," NYT, May 6, 1949.

29. Transcript, 5791–5795.

NINE. THE DEFENSE

1. Transcript, 6270–6305. Medina also agreed to hear an argument on the legitimacy of the FBI deputizing civilians to spy on the party, but then paid little attention to it.

2. *Schenck v. United States*, 249 U.S. 47 (1919).

3. Transcript, 6548–6596.

4. Gates's role in Spain has been well documented, though he left this incident out of his memoir, an omission that casts further doubt on its reliability. For details, see Peter N. Carroll, *The Odyssey of the Abraham Lincoln Brigade: Americans in the Spanish Civil War* (Stanford, Calif.: Stanford University Press, 1994), 183–187.

5. Transcript, 6808–6849.

6. The official order remanding Hall and Winston said they had moved toward the bench; the defense denied that, saying the men had stood

up but remained at their chairs. Medina refused to change the order. Transcript, 7038–7044.

7. "Medina Jails Three Reds," *New York Sun*, June 3.
8. Transcript, 7456–7457; "Medina Sends 4th Defendant to Jail for Outburst in Trial of 11 Reds," NYT, June 21, 1949.
9. "Medina Is Upheld by Appeals Court," NYT, July 15, 1949.
10. "Wallace Protests Jailing of 3 Reds," NYT, June 5, 1949; "Jailing of 3 Commies Draws Wallace Fire," NYWT, June 4, 1949.
11. "1900 Diners Pay $20 Each for Communists' Defense," NYT, June 4, 1949.
12. "Plowed into Reds to Defend U.S.A.," *New York Journal-American*, June 6, 1949; "500 Protesting Reds Meet 1-Man Protest," NYDN, June 5, 1949; and other contemporary news accounts.
13. "Children Picket for Jailed Reds," AP via *WP*, June 18, 1949.
14. "Company Fires CIO Head Named as Red," *Chicago Tribune*, June 9, 1949. Kelliher was later identified in a HUAC hearing as a party member, which would fit his history as a particularly militant union leader.
15. "Bar Group to Seek Tight Court Rules on Defense Attorneys in Security Trials," NYT, June 20, 1949.
16. "Truman Declares Hysteria over Reds Sweeps Nation," *NYT*, June 17, 1949.
17. "Robeson Flies to Testify Here at Trial of Reds," NYHT, June 16, 1949.
18. Green to Lil Green, May 30, 1949, Green Papers, Box 3, Folder 1.
19. "Davis Joined Reds to 'Aid His People,'" NYT, July 8, 1949.
20. "Davis Denies Reds Advocated Force," NYT, July 9, 1949.
21. Green to Lil Green, n.d., Green Papers, Box 3, Folder 1.
22. Green to Lil Green, July 22, 1949, Green Papers, Box 3, Folder 1.
23. Green to Lil Green, July 26, 1949, and n.d., Green Papers, Box 3, Folder 1.
24. Green to Lil Green, undated letters (likely from early August), Green Papers, Box 3, Folder 1.
25. Green to his family, undated letters, Green Papers, Box 3, Folder 1.

TEN. THE PEEKSKILL RIOTS

1. "Medina Bitter Only Twice at Abuse by Reds," NYHT, October 15, 1949.
2. Transcript, 10577–10581, 10653–10654.
3. Ibid., 10655–10661.
4. "Pickets at Court, Defying Medina," NYT, August 27, 1949.
5. Richard A. Reuss with JoAnne C. Reuss, *American Folk Music and Left-Wing Politics, 1927–1957* (Lanham, Md.: Scarecrow Press, 2000), 223–226.

6. "Paris Parley Held Maneuver by Reds," NYT, April 19, 1949; Martin Bauml Duberman, *Paul Robeson* (New York: Alfred A. Knopf, 1988), 341–343.

7. For details on the controversy over the quote, see Duberman, *Paul Robeson*, 342; also, "Paris 'Peace Congress' Assails U.S. and Atlantic Pact, Upholds Soviet," NYT, April 21, 1949.

8. Untitled news brief, NYT, April 23, 1949.

9. Duberman, *Paul Robeson*, 352–353.

10. These details and the following descriptions, unless otherwise noted, are drawn from a wide range of contemporary newspaper coverage of the riot, particularly NYT and NYWT.

11. Virginia Hirsch, "The First Peekskill 'Riot': August 27, 1949," speech delivered June 25, 1998, archived at Hartford Web Publishing, http://www.hartford-hwp.com/archives/45a/157.html.

12. Howard Fast, *Peekskill, USA: A Personal Experience* (New York: Civil Rights Congress, 1951), 11, 20. Fast's memoir of the events came two years later, and some of the time sequences conflict with contemporary media reports, but in general it is supported by the contemporary accounts and affidavits of others.

13. Ibid., 33.

14. Duberman, *Paul Robeson*, 364–671.

15. Tom Lloyd affidavit, CPUSA Archives, Box 39.

16. Davis affidavit, CPUSA Archives, Box 39.

17. Gita Potash affidavit, CPUSA Archives, Box 39.

18. "48 Hurt in Clashes at Robeson Rally; Buses Are Stoned," NYT, September 5, 1949; "15 Bus Drivers Walk Out as 'Picnic' Erupts," NYT, September 5, 1949.

19. Transcript, 11091–11105; "Peekskill Affair Invoked by Reds," NYT, September 9, 1949.

20. Transcript, 10914–10915.

21. Transcript, 11305–11310; "Fifth Red on Trial Jailed by Medina," NYT, September 13, 1949.

22. Transcript, 11408–11420.

23. Transcript, 11421–11451; "Lawyer for Reds Held in Contempt," NYT, September 15, 1949.

24. Transcript, 11537, 11563; "Foster Says Reds Plot No Violence," NYT, September 17, 1949; "Passports False, Foster Tells Jury," NYT, September 18, 1949.

25. Transcript, 11619, 11638–11640.

26. "Robeson Testifies for 11 Communists," NYT, September 21, 1949.

27. These statistics were carried in most of the stories marking the end of the testimony. For specific citations, see "Both Sides Rest in Trial of

Reds; To Sum Up Oct. 4," *NYHT*, September 24, 1949; "Communist Trial Ends with 11 Guilty," *Life*, October 24, 1949.

ELEVEN. GUILTY

1. Transcript, 12064; "Jury Is Due to Get Red Case on Oct. 13," *NYT*, October 5, 1949.
2. "Red Defense Pleas Dispute U.S. Proof," *NYT*, October 9, 1949.
3. Transcript, 12124–12162.
4. Gladstein's closing argument, transcript, 12162–12210; Sacher's, 12211–12262.
5. See transcript, 12264–12326 for Crockett and 12326–12373 for Dennis.
6. McGohey and Medina, transcript, 12374–12452.
7. "11 Reds Await Jury's Verdict," *Daily News*, October 14, 1949; "Red Trial Jury Locked Up, Resume at 9:30 a.m.," *Daily Mirror*, October 14, 1949.
8. John Gates, *The Story of an American Communist* (New York: Thomas Nelson, 1958), 131.
9. Transcript, 12516–12522; "11 Top Communists Guilty; Face up to 10 Years for Plot," *New York Post*, October 14, 1949; Gates, *Story of an American Communist*, 131.
10. Transcript, 12522–12537.
11. "Law Change Cited," *NYT*, Oct. 22, 1949. The following description is drawn from the *NYT* coverage.
12. Benjamin Davis, *Communist Councilman from Harlem* (New York: International Publishers, 1969), 183.
13. Transcript, 12684–12723.
14. "Million Bail Asked for Red Leaders," *NYT*, November 2, 1949; "Communists Freed in Bail of $260,000 to Press Appeals," *NYT*, November 4, 1949.
15. "Tom Clark Now Turns on Communist Lawyers," *Daily Compass* coverage of *Look* magazine article fallout, August 16, 1949.
16. "Reds' Counsel Defended," *NYT*, February 3, 1950.
17. "Contempt Penalty Backed in Red Case," *NYT*, February 5, 1950; "Counsel for Reds Attack Penalties," *NYT*, February 18, 1950.

TWELVE. IN THE WIND

1. Allen J. Matusow, ed., *Joseph R. McCarthy* (Englewood Cliffs, N.J.: Prentice-Hall, 1970), 15.
2. Arthur Herman, *Joseph McCarthy: Reexamining the Life and Legacy of America's Most Hated Senator* (New York: Simon and Schuster, 2000), 48.
3. "G.O.P. Poses Issue for '50 as Liberty Versus Socialism," *NYT*, February 7, 1950.

4. Ben Smith, "Exclusive: RNC Document Mocks Donors, Plays on 'Fear,'" March 3, 2010, *Politico.com*, http://www.politico.com/news/stories/0310/33866.html.

5. David M. Oshinsky, *A Conspiracy So Immense: The World of Joe McCarthy* (New York: Free Press, 1983), 107–109.

6. "Contempt Conviction Upheld in Appeal of Reds' Counsel," NYT, April 6, 1950; and, among others, Stanley I. Kutler, *An American Inquisition: Justice and Injustice in the Cold War* (New York: Hill & Wang, 1982), and Jerold S. Auerbach, *Unequal Justice: Lawyers and Social Change in Modern America* (New York: Oxford University Press, 1976), excerpted in George S. Grossman, ed., *The Spirit of American Law* (Boulder, Colo.: Westview Press, 2000), 332.

7. See Kutler, *American Inquisition*, chapter 6, "Kill the Lawyers," for a detailed look at the defense teams' fight against the contempt charges and disbarment.

8. Ibid., 168.

9. Details from Isserman interview with Kutler, 1977; my thanks to Isserman's nephew, the historian Maurice Isserman, for sharing his copy of the transcript of that interview.

10. Letter to Medina's son from John F. Dowd of *Time* magazine, December 5, 1949, Medina Papers, General Correspondence, 1948–1950, Box 40, Folder 1949-D..

11. These and other letters are in Medina Papers, Box 76, Correspondence re: Anti-Communist Trial.

12. Letter to Benitez, November 28, 1949, Medina Papers, General Correspondence, 1948–1950, Box 40, Folder 1949-B.

13. "Don't Be Alarmist, Truman Warns Press," NYT, June 26, 1950; "Defenders Launch Counter Attack, Regain Five Miles North of Capital," *Chicago Daily Tribune*, June 26, 1950.

14. United States Court of Appeals, Second Circuit, *United States v. Dennis et al.*, No. 242, Docket 21538. Decided August 1, 1950.

15. Albert P. Blaustein and Roy M. Mersky, *The First One Hundred Justices: Statistical Studies on the Supreme Court of the United States*, (Hamden, Conn.: Archon Books, 1978), 32–51, rating chart on 40. The ranking was based on a 1970 poll of sixty-five experts on the U.S. Supreme Court, so should be viewed as a consensus opinion rather than a statistical rating. Earl Warren, Vinson's successor, was ranked among the twelve greatest justices primarily for doing what Vinson couldn't—bringing the Court together.

16. For a clear and dispassionate look at the hornet's nest into which Vinson stepped, see James E. St. Clair and Linda C. Gugin, *Chief Justice*

Fred M. Vinson of Kentucky (Lexington: University Press of Kentucky, 2002), 156–173.

17. Barry Siegel, *Claim of Privilege: A Mysterious Plane Crash, a Landmark Supreme Court Case, and the Rise of State Secrets* (New York: HarperCollins, 2008), 149; "Truman Gets View of Hughes on Court," NYT, April 30, 1946.

18. Three of his appointees—Vinson, Sherman Minton, and Harold Burton—made the "failures" list in Blaustein and Merskey, *First One Hundred Justices*, 49. Tom Clark, Truman's only other appointee, was ranked "average" (39).

19. For a deep look at the repercussions of one such decision, see Siegel, *Claim of Privilege*, about the U.S. v. Reynolds case that established the government's right to avoid court disclosure by claiming a state-secrets privilege—a case that was based on a government lie.

20. "High Court Hears Appeal of 11 Reds," NYT, December 5, 1950.

21. *Dennis v. United States*, 341 U.S. 494 (1951). Frankfurter and Jackson also wrote lengthy concurring opinions.

22. Geoffrey R. Stone, *Perilous Times: Free Speech in Wartime from the Sedition Act of 1798 to the War on Terrorism* (New York: W. W. Norton, 2004), 541. Those cases hung on the Fourteenth Amendment and whether states could outlaw speech advocating revolution.

23. David Caute, *The Great Fear: The Anti-Communist Purge Under Truman and Eisenhower* (New York: Simon and Schuster, 1978), 208.

24. Dorothy Healey and Maurice Isserman, *Dorothy Healey Remembers: A Life in the American Communist Party* (New York: Oxford University Press, 1990), 123.

25. Gil Green, *Cold War Fugitive: A Personal Story of the McCarthy Years* (New York: International Publishers, 1984), 57.

26. Bud Schultz and Ruth Schultz, eds., *It Did Happen Here: Recollections of Political Repression in America* (Berkeley: University of California Press, 1989), 84.

27. The description is taken from Pathé newsreel coverage of the event, available at http://www.britishpathe.com/record.php?id=61853.

28. Schultz and Schultz, *It Did Happen Here*, 86.

29. Healey, *Dorothy Healey Remembers*, 123.

30. Green, *Cold War Fugitive*, 99–100; "A New Gus Hall Appears in Court," NYT, November 3, 1951; "Three Years More Given to Gus Hall," NYT, December 28, 1951.

31. "FBI Checks Trail of Captured Reds," NYT, August 29, 1953.

32. "Thompson, Red Leader, Is Battered by Yugoslav Sailor in Prison Here," NYT, October 24, 1953; "Red's Assailant Faces Jail in U.S.," NYT, October 25, 1953; "Red's Assailant Jailed," NYT, March 13, 1954.

33. "Release Ordered for Red in Appeal," NYT, June 19, 1957.

34. See Schultz and Schultz, *It Did Happen Here*, 85–89; and M. Wesley Swearingen, *FBI Secrets: An Agent's Exposé* (Boston: South End Press, 1995), particularly chapter 3, "Chicago's 24-Men Burglary Squad."

35. Swearingen, *FBI Secrets*, 22–23.

36. Green, *Cold War Fugitive*, 136–137. Details in this scene were drawn from the memoir, 156–158, and "Bail-Jumping Red Surrenders." *NYHT*, February 28, 1956.

37. In fact, three days earlier Khrushchev had delivered the "Secret Speech" in which he denounced Stalin for the Great Purge and other atrocities, revelations that would eventually shake Green's political world as well.

38. Green, *Cold War Fugitive*, 165.

THIRTEEN. HOLLOW VINDICATION

1. Ironically, Vinson's final official act had been to read from the bench on June 12 the Court's decision not to intervene in the planned execution of convicted Soviet spies Julius and Ethel Rosenberg, who were electro-cuted hours later at Sing Sing Prison in Ossining, New York.

2. See Henry J. Abraham, *Justices and Presidents: A Political History of Appoint-ments to the Supreme Court* (New York: Oxford University Press, 1992), chapter 10, "The Warren Court, from Ike to LBJ, 1953–1969."

3. For a full consideration of the sweep of all the Smith Act cases, see Michal R. Belknap, *Cold War Political Justice: The Smith Act, the Communist Party, and American Civil Liberties* (Westport, Conn.: Greenwood Press, 1977).

4. Arthur J. Sabin, *In Calmer Times: The Supreme Court and Red Monday* (Phila-delphia: University of Pennsylvania Press, 1999), 161–171.

5. Sabin, *In Calmer Times*, chapter 8, "The Red Monday Cases."

6. Geoffrey R. Stone, *Perilous Times: Free Speech in Wartime from the Sedition Act of 1798 to the War on Terrorism* (New York: W. W. Norton, 2004), 413.

7. Felix Frankfurter, dissenting opinion in *Dennis v. United States*, 341 U.S. 494 (1951); James F. Simon, *The Antagonists: Hugo Black, Felix Frankfurter, and Civil Liberties in Modern America* (New York: Simon and Schuster, 1989), 199–201.

8. Sabin, *In Calmer Times*, 164–168.

9. Belknap, *Cold War Political Justice*, 245.

10. Cited in Melvin I. Urofsky, *The Warren Court: Justices, Rulings, and Legacy* (Santa Barbara, Calif.: ABC-CLIO, 2001), 117.

11. "Red Leader Reaches Britain," *NYT*, May 11, 1955.

12. "U.S. Red in Liverpool," *NYT*, March 13, 1955; "Potash Receives Two-Year Jail Term," *NYT*, January 19, 1957; "U.S. Reds Weigh New Command," *NYT*, September 26, 1964.

13. Details from Peggy Dennis, *The Autobiography of an American Communist: A Personal View of a Political Life, 1925–1975* (Westport, Conn.: Lawrence Hill; Berkeley, Calif.: Creative Arts, 1977); Edward P. Johanningsmeier, *Forging American Communism* (Princeton, N.J.: Princeton University Press, 1994); and "Jack Stachel, U.S. Communist and Party Official, Dies at 65," *NYT*, January 2, 1966.

14. A tape of the interview is at the Harry Ransom Center at the University of Texas at Austin and available online at http://www.hrc.utexas.edu/ multimedia/video/2008/wallace/gates_john_t.html.

15. "John Gates, 78, Former Editor of *The Daily Worker*, Is Dead," *NYT*, May 25, 1992.

16. "Henry Winston Dead in Moscow; Top Leader of Communists in U.S.," *NYT*, December 16, 1986.

17. "Carl Winter, Imprisoned by U.S. as Communist Leader, Dies at 85," *NYT*, November 20, 1991.

18. Gil Green, *Cold War Fugitive: A Personal Story of the McCarthy Years* (New York: International Publishers, 1984), 253–254; "Gilbert Green, Communist Party Leader Jailed for Conspiracy," *NYT*, May 8, 1997.

19. "Gus Hall, Unreconstructed American Communist of 7 Decades, Dies at 90," *NYT*, October 17, 2000.

SELECTED BIBLIOGRAPHY

ARCHIVES

Bancroft Library, University of California, Berkeley

Harry S. Truman Library and Museum, Independence, Missouri

Seeley G. Mudd Manuscript Library, Princeton University, Princeton, New Jersey

Tamiment Library & Robert F. Wagner Labor Archive, New York University, New York, New York

BOOKS

Abraham, Henry J. *Justices and Presidents: A Political History of Appointments to the Supreme Court*. New York: Oxford University Press, 1992.

Abt, John J., with Michael Myerson. *Advocate and Activist: Memoirs of an American Communist Lawyer*. Urbana: University of Illinois Press, 1993.

Belfrage, Cedric. *The American Inquisition, 1945–60: A Profile of the "McCarthy Era."* St. Paul: Thunder's Mouth Press, 1989.

Belknap, Michal R. *Cold War Political Justice: The Smith Act, the Communist Party, and American Civil Liberties*. Westport, Conn.: Greenwood Press, 1977.

———, ed. *American Political Trials*. Revised and expanded ed. Westport, Conn.: Praeger, 1994.

Budenz, Louis Francis. *Men Without Faces: The Communist Conspiracy in the U.S.A.* New York: Harper and Brothers, 1948.

———. *This Is My Story*. New York: McGraw-Hill, 1947.

Caute, David. *The Great Fear: The Anti-Communist Purge Under Truman and Eisenhower*. New York: Simon and Schuster, 1978.

Daniel, Hawthorne. *Judge Medina: A Biography*. New York: Wilfrid Funk, 1952.

281

Davis, Benjamin. *Communist Councilman from Harlem*. New York: International Publishers, 1969.

Dennis, Eugene. *Letters from Prison*. New York: International Publishers, 1956.

Dennis, Peggy. *The Autobiography of an American Communist: A Personal View of a Political Life, 1925–1975*. Westport, Conn.: Lawrence Hill; Berkeley, Calif.: Creative Arts, 1977.

Dierenfield, Bruce J. *Keeper of the Rules: Congressman Howard W. Smith of Virginia*. Charlottesville: University Press of Virginia, 1987.

Duberman, Martin Bauml. *Paul Robeson*. New York: Alfred A. Knopf, 1988.

Fast, Howard. *Being Red*. New York: Dell, 1991.

———. *Peekskill, USA: A Personal Experience*. New York: Civil Rights Congress, 1951.

Gates, John. *The Story of an American Communist*. New York: Thomas Nelson, 1958.

Green, Gil. *Cold War Fugitive: A Personal Story of the McCarthy Years*. New York: International Publishers, 1984.

Herman, Arthur. *Joseph McCarthy: Reexamining the Life and Legacy of America's Most Hated Senator*. New York: Simon and Schuster, 2000.

Johanningsmeier, Edward P. *Forging American Communism: The Life of William Z. Foster*. Princeton, N.J.: Princeton University Press, 1994.

Kessler, Lauren. *Clever Girl: Elizabeth Bentley, the Spy Who Ushered In the McCarthy Era*. New York: HarperCollins, 2003.

Klehr, Harvey, John Earl Haynes, and Fridrikh Igorevich Firsov. *The Secret World of American Communism*. Russian documents translated by Timothy D. Sergay. New Haven: Yale University Press, 1995.

Knight, Amy. *How the Cold War Began: The Igor Gouzenko Affair and the Hunt for Soviet Spies*. New York: Carroll & Graf, 2005.

Marion, George. *The Communist Trial: An American Crossroads*. New York: Fairplay Publishers, 1949.

Matusow, Allen J., ed. *Joseph R. McCarthy*. Englewood Cliffs, N.J.: Prentice-Hall, 1970.

McCullough, David. *Truman*. New York: Simon and Schuster, 1992.

Medina, Judge Harold R. *The Anatomy of Freedom*. New York: Henry Holt, 1959.

Montefiore, Simon Sebag. *Stalin: The Court of the Red Tsar*. New York: Alfred A. Knopf, 2004.

Murray, Robert K. *Red Scare: A Study in National Hysteria, 1919–1920*. New York: McGraw-Hill, 1964.

Navasky, Victor S. *Naming Names*. New York: Viking, 1991.

Olmsted, Kathryn S. *Red Spy Queen: A Biography of Elizabeth Bentley*. Chapel Hill: University of North Carolina Press, 2002.

Oshinsky, David M. *A Conspiracy So Immense: The World of Joe McCarthy*. New York: Free Press, 1983.

Packer, Herbert L. *Ex-Communist Witnesses: Four Studies in Fact Finding*. Stanford, Calif.: Stanford University Press, 1962.

Philbrick, Herbert A. *I Led 3 Lives*. New York: McGraw-Hill, 1952.

Sabin, Arthur J. *In Calmer Times: The Supreme Court and Red Monday*. Philadelphia: University of Pennsylvania Press, 1999.

Schrecker, Ellen. *The Age of McCarthyism: A Brief History with Documents*. Boston: Bedford Books, 1994.

———. *Many Are the Crimes: McCarthyism in America*. Boston: Little, Brown, 1998.

Schultz, Bud, and Ruth Schultz, eds. *It Did Happen Here: Recollections of Political Repression in America*. Berkeley: University of California Press, 1989.

Simon, James F. *The Antagonists: Hugo Black, Felix Frankfurter, and Civil Liberties in Modern America*. New York: Simon and Schuster, 1989.

Stone, Geoffrey R. *Perilous Times: Free Speech in Wartime from the Sedition Act of 1798 to the War on Terrorism*. New York: W. W. Norton, 2004.

Swearingen, M. Wesley. *FBI Secrets: An Agent's Exposé*. Boston: South End Press, 1995.

Urofsky, Melvin I. *The Warren Court: Justices, Rulings, and Legacy*. Santa Barbara, Calif.: ABC-CLIO, 2001.

Weinstein, Allen, and Alexander Vassiliev. *The Haunted Wood: Soviet Espionage in America—The Stalin Era*. New York: Random House, 1999.

Wills, Garry. *Bomb Power: The Modern Presidency and the National Security State*. New York: Penguin Press, 2010.

PAMPHLETS

Cannon, James P. "Socialism on Trial: The Official Court Record of James P. Cannon's Testimony in the Famous Minneapolis 'Sedition' Trial." New York: Pioneer Publishers, 1942.

Dennis, Eugene. "Dangerous Thoughts: The Case of the Indicted Twelve." New York: New Century Publishers, October 1948.

National Non-Partisan Committee to Defend the 12 Communist Leaders. "Due Process in a Political Trial: The Record vs. The Press in the Foley Square Trial of the 12 Communist Leaders." New York: undated.

INDEX

ABOUT THE AUTHOR

Scott Martelle, a former staff writer for the *Los Angeles Times*, is a veteran journalist and author of the critically acclaimed *Blood Passion: The Ludlow Massacre and Class War in the American West* (Rutgers University Press, 2007). A native of Maine, he grew up in Wellsville, New York, and now lives with his wife, Margaret, and their two sons in Irvine, California, where he teaches and works as a freelance journalist.